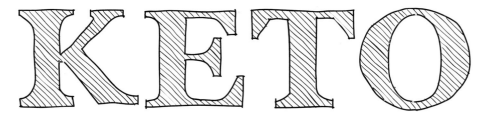

GROWING UP KETO

A PRACTICAL GUIDE FOR KIDS AND PARENTS WITH
OVER 110 RECIPES THE WHOLE FAMILY WILL LOVE

KRISTIE H. SULLIVAN, PHD

WITH GRACE SULLIVAN AND JONATHAN SULLIVAN

VICTORY BELT PUBLISHING

Las Vegas

THIS BOOK IS DEDICATED TO ALL OF THE CHILDREN GROWING UP BATTLING OBESITY, AND TO THE FAMILIES STRUGGLING ALONG WITH THEM. MAY THIS BOOK HELP YOU UNDERSTAND THAT IT ISN'T YOUR FAULT AND THAT FOOD CAN BE BOTH NUTRITIOUS AND DELICIOUS. YOU DON'T HAVE TO FEEL DEPRIVED AT THE TABLE OR ON THE PLAYGROUND.

First published in 2021 by Victory Belt Publishing Inc.

Copyright © 2021 Kristie H. Sullivan, PhD

ISBN-13: 978-1-628603-96-5

Cover design by Kat Lannom

Front and back cover food styling by Marcella Capasso

Front and back cover photos by Kat Lannom and Justin-Aaron Velasco

Interior design and illustrations by Yordan Terziev and Boryana Yordanova

Printed in Canada

TC 0121

MY STORY

When I was three years old, I began to have an insatiable appetite. Then clothing in stores became too tight for me. My kindergarten classmates called attention to my big belly and big arms. Loudly.

By elementary school, I knew that I ran funny (because folks laughed), that I was easily out of breath, and that I was terrible at sports. My classmates told me so.

One day, the entire fourth grade class watched as two kickball team captains exchanged blows and then wrestled each other into the dirt before being pulled apart by teachers, each of them yelling, "No, you take her!" and "I had her last time and we lost! You take her!" They had chosen teammates one by one. Not only was I the last to be chosen, but I was designated the teammate most likely to cause a loss. No one wanted me.

The only times I was chosen for teams were at the field day tug-of-war, where my team made me be the weight at the end of the rope, and when we chose teams for the softball spelling bee—an inside academic "sport" where I was the team captain and mine was finally the winning team.

I was lucky to grow up obese in a small town at a time when most kids were polite to my face because they knew their mamas knew my mama and we all knew each other's families and preachers. To make fun of another classmate would bring shame upon the one who was rude, so the snickers and name-calling went on mainly behind my back.

As a high school junior, I once found bright yellow cardboard signs taped to the bumper of my car. "WIDE LOAD," they said. I had worked late on the school paper that day, so nearly everyone in the school had seen the signs by the time I left campus. During my senior year, the high school quarterback, who was one of the most popular boys in school, of course, wrote in my yearbook that I had "more personality" than any other girl in the senior class.

Fortunately, I was smart and ambitious. Graduating high school and moving on to college was one of the best things that ever happened to me. While I was teased and called names in college, too, I excelled in my classes, and I found people who were interested in similar academic endeavors. Dating, or not dating, wasn't a big deal like it was in my hometown, where there were only 133 kids in my graduating class and most of the popular kids took turns dating each other.

Professional work environments were better; however, I know that I was overlooked for opportunities because of my appearance. I watched more attractive and less capable women giggle their way into opportunities, often using my ideas and my work to help them succeed.

I suppose I've spent much of my life being rejected not because of who I was, but because of how I looked, and for what I now understand wasn't my fault.

I was obese because of the incorrect information given to me by doctors, nutritionists, and public health organizations. Had I known, and had my parents known, we most certainly would have restricted carbohydrates early on.

But we didn't know. Instead, we ate low-fat foods, counted calories, and tried to exercise. We could restrict food for only so long, and then we were off our diets and typically gaining weight once again. Those struggles made me stronger in many ways, but they were painful. When I finally learned about keto and why it works, and when I lived through the transformation firsthand, I knew I had to share my experience with others.

I started with my family. My husband, David, who grew up wearing "husky" pants, trimmed down to his lowest adult weight. His high school ring is forever too big for him. He also lost (and found) his wedding ring twice before conceding to get a new one. Our daughter, Grace, whose story you will read more about in Chapter 1, finally heard encouraging words from her pediatrician about her weight. Like me, she will always struggle with her weight, but unlike me, she isn't a morbidly obese teen and can easily find clothing that fits and looks great on her. Our son, Jonathan, has never known what it's like to be obese, but he lost over 30 pounds while growing 3 inches and no longer worries that his thighs are "too big." He has more sustained energy, and we rarely encounter a hangry Jonathan now.

As our lives changed, I became sensitive to those I saw all around me facing the same struggles. Adults and children wanted to lose weight. They felt the same pain and shame I'd known too well.

I've described it like finding my way out of a burning building. Once I discovered a route to safety by eating low-carb, I looked back and saw others screaming from the windows. The fresh air that filled my lungs felt so good that I had to run back inside and guide others out. If I could show them the path, then we could crawl out together to safety.

Medical professionals, who should be like firefighters helping to douse the flames, aren't always fully on board. There are a few who support ketogenic or low-carb diets, and their numbers are growing, but we need more with hoses of knowledge to help snuff out the damage caused by insulin resistance and metabolic disorders.

Until then, those of us who have escaped can continue offering safety nets and oxygen masks to those still struggling to find their way out of obesity. It is my deepest hope that this book provides the support your family needs to follow a low-carb or keto diet for better health, and that sharing our family's experience might help empower yours.

CHAPTER 1:
GROWING UP KETO

Sharing some of our family's favorite dishes makes me feel a little vulnerable. A few of the recipes in this book are just a little fussy. They take a bit more care and attention. But most of them are barefoot, hair pulled back, makeup off, casual meals that aren't fancy but are filling and tasty.

I created many of these recipes as I was watching the clock, knowing that we needed to eat quickly and get on the road to somewhere else. All of them are tasty enough to share with you in the hopes that your family will find a few new favorites that make mealtime easier.

This book is highly personal to me. I was a chubby toddler, fat kid, overweight teen, and morbidly obese young adult. In between, I lost and gained weight, trying every possible diet imaginable. I prayed for miracles, ate grapefruit, and even tried acupuncture. At age twenty-nine, I had weight-loss surgery. I went from 313 pounds to 178 pounds and then began steadily gaining weight all over again. Until I discovered keto in 2013.

This is the guide I wish I'd had as a child and as a mother to young children.

IS KETO OR LOW-CARB SAFE FOR CHILDREN?

I'm not medically qualified to answer whether any diet is safe for either children or adults. Instead, I'll list what my children eat now compared to what they used to eat—which is what many of their friends still eat.

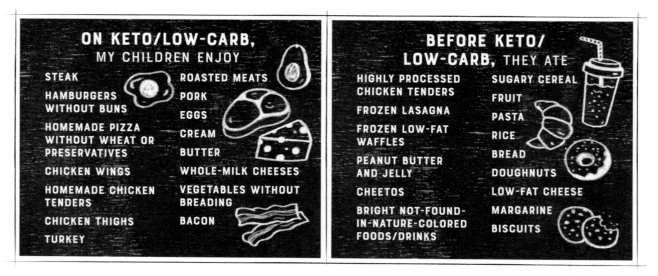

ON KETO/LOW-CARB, MY CHILDREN ENJOY

- STEAK
- HAMBURGERS WITHOUT BUNS
- HOMEMADE PIZZA WITHOUT WHEAT OR PRESERVATIVES
- CHICKEN WINGS
- HOMEMADE CHICKEN TENDERS
- CHICKEN THIGHS
- TURKEY
- ROASTED MEATS
- PORK
- EGGS
- CREAM
- BUTTER
- WHOLE-MILK CHEESES
- VEGETABLES WITHOUT BREADING
- BACON

BEFORE KETO/LOW-CARB, THEY ATE

- HIGHLY PROCESSED CHICKEN TENDERS
- FROZEN LASAGNA
- FROZEN LOW-FAT WAFFLES
- PEANUT BUTTER AND JELLY
- CHEETOS
- BRIGHT NOT-FOUND-IN-NATURE-COLORED FOODS/DRINKS
- SUGARY CEREAL
- FRUIT
- PASTA
- RICE
- BREAD
- DOUGHNUTS
- LOW-FAT CHEESE
- MARGARINE
- BISCUITS

When you compare these two lists, it's pretty clear that most of our food comes from farms rather than food scientists. (There are a few exceptions, like cheese powder, which we find irresistible; see it used in the Better Than the Box Mac 'n' Cheese recipe, page 190, and in the Nacho Chips recipe, page 206.) Grace and Jonathan primarily eat foods that their great-great-grandparents would have enjoyed. Even the breads and desserts that we make are created mostly from ingredients previous generations would recognize.

As for processed foods, my kids still enjoy minimally processed deli meats, cheeses, pepperoni, and sausage. Much of the highly processed and ultra-refined stuff that they previously ate is now homemade, and even they will tell you that the homemade versions (mostly) taste better.

Arguably, the more nutritionally complete whole foods that my family enjoys now are far healthier than the foodlike products they used to consume. The evidence is in their overall health, which results in perfect labs; very little, if any, missed school for sick days; healthy weight; and more overall energy. In addition, the medical professionals who treat my children are not only aware of their diets but fully support the way we eat, and that includes the specialists they have seen for various reasons.

Do I believe keto or low-carb is safe and healthy for kids? Absolutely! I've seen the changes in my children's lives, and I believe that meats, veggies, and full-fat dairy are a winning combination for people of all ages.

LOW-CARB OR KETO?

What's the difference, and which should your family follow?

Like much of life, there are variations in the approach to low-carb or keto and especially among definitions of low-carb, where there are nuances like "liberal low-carb" and "moderate low-carb." "Very low-carb" is generally considered keto.

Keto is short for *ketogenic.* It refers to the body being in a state of ketosis, in which it primarily burns fat for fuel rather than glucose. This happens when the body is starved of carbohydrates, which are metabolized as glucose. Given little energy from carbohydrate sources, the body burns fat for fuel. That fat can come from your body or from the foods you eat. When the body burns fat, it produces ketones.

A keto diet is one that keeps the body in ketosis. In general, the easiest way to stay in ketosis is to restrict your carb intake to fewer than 20 grams per day or to roughly 7 grams per meal, especially for those who have metabolic dysfunction. Healthier, leaner, more active people with a healthy metabolism may be able to eat as much as 50 grams of carbs per day and still remain in ketosis. That isn't common, however, and may be more applicable to athletes than to the general population.

A healthy child might thrive on a moderate or even a liberal low-carb diet. A moderate low-carb diet is typically considered to include 20 to 50 grams of carbs per day, while a liberal low-carb diet is over 50 grams of carbs per day and could go as high as 100 grams per day. Healthy growing children can thrive at those levels, and so can many adults.

Determining which level of carbohydrate is right for you or your child can be important for long-term success. Grace, David, and I keep our carb intake below 20 grams per day to feel our best. If I eat closer to 30 grams, even in the form of veggies, then my food cravings increase, and I find it harder to control my appetite. Grace also finds that her hunger increases if she doesn't eat enough fat and protein. Learning to listen to your body and especially your hunger cues is very important.

Jonathan also follows his hunger cues and finds his cravings and hunger controlled even when he eats higher levels of carbs. Most of his meals are keto, but he can enjoy a small apple with peanut butter, his favorite bedtime snack, or a wrap made with low-carb bread. His goal is no more than 25 grams of carbs per meal, and he probably eats an average of 30 to 40 grams of carbs per day. He often eats only two meals per day—an unusual routine for a teenage boy.

Often, the most important change anyone can make is to avoid ultra-processed and highly refined foods that are nutritionally void. You know the ones: they often come in brightly colored packages, are shelf stable for six months or more, contain little to no protein, and are generally comprised of sugar (carbs). Even foods that many people consider healthy, like cereal, oatmeal, and pasta, offer no nutritional value other than carbs.

Don't ever believe that your brain must have carbs to function. Yes, the brain uses glucose, but if you're not consuming glucose, your liver can make it. Gluconeogenesis is an amazing process by which the body makes all of the glucose it needs when it needs it. There are essential amino acids and essential fatty acids, but you won't find an essential carbohydrate.

Lastly, ketosis is not the same as ketoacidosis, which is a serious medical condition. People who have type 1 diabetes are most at risk for ketoacidosis, so talk with a medical professional and understand your risks. Healthy people, however, have no reason to fear being in a state of ketosis. In fact, when the body uses fat for fuel, people report having more sustained energy without peaks and valleys of hunger or "hanger." This sustained energy means that you can go longer periods without food without feeling ill effects. People also report having more mental clarity when they're in ketosis. As long as your body runs on fat, you carry all of the food you need with you every single day.

GETTING KIDS ON BOARD

Depending on the ages of your children, transitioning them to keto or low-carb can be as simple as getting them to agree to it—which isn't always easy. With my kids, I provided information but never forced them to forgo carbs. When they decided to follow keto, I supported them in every way I could.

The three steps I'd offer to those of you with children who are old enough to decide for themselves are to

1) Help them decide whether to eat low-carb or keto

2) Provide ample opportunities for them to enjoy food and not feel deprived

3) Support them along the way with positive feedback and rewards

HELP THEM DECIDE

For children who are old enough to understand the concept of macronutrients (fat, protein, and carbohydrates), it may be helpful to share general information about how important it is to control blood glucose. Younger children can understand that protein makes us stronger and eating fat can help us avoid hunger. On keto, carbohydrates are restricted because they raise blood glucose, which spikes insulin and can lead to increased hunger and fat storage. Older children might enjoy reading about insulin resistance and how to avoid or manage diseases associated with metabolic dysfunction. My own kids remarked early on that they are less hungry when they avoid carbs. In fact, by middle school, Grace learned to use her hunger as a gauge for whether a meal contained enough protein and fat to keep her full for four to six hours.

> Remember that kids develop independently of age, so use these suggestions as a general guide. Only you know for certain what is developmentally appropriate for your children.

If your child is using keto or low-carb to manage a medical condition such as epilepsy, diabetes, PCOS, fatty liver, or gut issues, then it is important for them to understand the relationship between the foods they eat and the management of their health. In this situation, there may not be a "day off" from carbohydrate restriction because even the smallest missteps could impact their health.

If your children are too young to understand nutrition, then helping them make the transition to keto can be as simple as providing ample choices of low-carb foods that they enjoy along with some substitutions for the higher-carb foods they like. Very young children often eat what they see others eating, so setting an example yourself is an opportunity to help them develop good eating habits while helping their taste buds adapt.

My children were nine and twelve, respectively, when they changed their eating habits. My daughter, Grace, was first. My husband, David, and I had been keto for a few months at the time. Grace saw us losing weight and enjoyed many of the same meals we ate, so she decided to give it a try. Here are Grace's and Jonathan's stories.

Grace's story

Like me as a child, Grace began to gain weight before she started preschool. Because I knew firsthand how hard it was, I tried to provide "healthy" foods for her. Her pediatrician became increasingly alarmed about Grace's weight gain. She directed: "Give her skim milk!" I did. "Don't allow sugary soft drinks!" I didn't. "Feed her more fruits and veggies!" I did. "Keep her active!" I tried.

Following the doctor's directives, I bought low-fat cheese and other low-fat products. We had "five a day" fruits and veggies, including watermelon and canned peaches (both high in carbs). We used low-fat salad dressings and sauces and primarily drank water. In fact, at the end-of-year kindergarten celebration, it pained me to see that my daughter was the only child who chose water from the coolers. The other kids were enjoying sugary soft drinks, yet my sweet G was among the few who were overweight. It seemed so unfair that she was struggling just as I had with a voracious appetite in spite of doing everything "right."

In an effort to keep her active, I enrolled her in dance, recreational basketball, soccer, and swimming. She even went to a "fitness for youth" program at a local fitness center. The added activity only seemed to fuel her hunger.

At the time, I was too obese to engage in recreational activities with her. I tended to sit at the park while she played. And I was far too embarrassed to play in the pool with others around. These are among my biggest regrets as a parent.

By the time Grace was nine, she understood the struggle all too well. She also had seen my mother wrestle with diabetes, and she told me that she wanted to avoid it. I had given her a book about eliminating sugar and starches to read to help her understand. She is fiercely independent (so much like me!), and I knew that one of the keys to her success on keto would be her own determination, not mine.

Grace has since told me that she never read the book, but I felt better knowing she had it as a resource. She has told me that the first years of eating low-carb were difficult for her, especially after school when her brother, who was full carbivore (that is, a carb lover who consumed little else), ate popcorn and other high-carb foods. In hindsight, I wish we had set different boundaries for him to make her choices easier. But now, she generally doesn't struggle when others eat high-carb foods around her. If there is something she craves, like Milano cookies, she calls for Mom to remake them into a low-carb version; see my recipe for Sullivanos on page 258.

Jonathan's story

Like Grace, Jonathan needed to be empowered to make his own food choices. I wanted to avoid food battles with him. Unlike Grace, who took to keto quickly, it took him far longer to come around to the high-fat side.

Jonathan had always been close to normal weight. Even though he enjoyed high-carb foods and was only moderately active, his metabolism was clearly different from Grace's. He met any mention of avoiding pasta, potatoes, or rice with firm disapproval. We gave him latitude in his food choices to avoid control issues and because he was already a picky eater. We knew that he struggled with hanger, so we encouraged higher-protein foods and discouraged sugar, a position that he did not embrace.

It wasn't until August 2019, six years after David, Grace, and I changed our diet, that Jonathan finally agreed to give keto a try. The impetus? A recommendation from his pediatrician. The same doctor who had once told me that he was Italian and that I could "never convince him that pasta was bad" suggested that Jonathan might want to restrict carbohydrates. During a well visit, the doctor expressed concern that Jonathan's percentile in height was disproportionate to his percentile in weight. He noted that keto had worked for the other members of our family and that perhaps it could be helpful for Jonathan, too.

Initially, my son resisted dietary changes. Once I suggested that Jonathan simply track how many carbs he ate that day, as I suspected he was heavy on carbs and low on protein. Before dinner, he had consumed nearly 300 grams of carbs! Even he was surprised.

I gently suggested that he could try eating lower-carb without being as strict about it as the rest of the family. We settled on a target of 25 to 30 grams of carbs per meal, which allowed Jonathan to enjoy the fast-food chicken tenders that he loves as well as a small apple with peanut butter, a favorite snack. Today, he naturally eats two meals a day with very little snacking in between. He rarely gets hangry and knows to build meals around protein. He still has a sweet tooth, but we can satisfy it with chocolate chip cookies (page 238) or scones (page 242).

The transition to keto for both of my children was easier because they made the decision for themselves, and because they were mature enough to do so.

If your kids are too young to understand nutrition or make their own decisions about what they eat, then helping them make the transition to low-carb can be as simple as providing ample choices of low-carb foods that they like with some substitutions for the higher-carb foods they enjoy. Sometimes a gradual transition with treats only weekly and then only monthly gives them time to develop an appreciation for low-carb foods without an abrupt loss of foods they like.

If you have a younger child who is accustomed to a high-sugar, high-carb diet, then the transition can be trickier, especially if extended family and caregivers are not supportive. (More about those unhelpful adults later.) Slowly phasing out those foods can be easier than going cold turkey for those who are too young to understand.

You might start by eliminating the highest-carb offenders, such as doughnuts and other pastries, and introducing lower-carb options. Over time, their taste buds are likely to change, and as treats become less frequent and are replaced with other foods, eating low-carb will become more natural and automatic for them.

AVOID DEPRIVATION

The second step after the decision to try low-carb or keto is made is to help your children enjoy the new foods. Kids should not feel deprived. Heck, no one should feel deprived! At the end of Jonathan's first week of eating low-carb, he said, with not a little surprise, "Mom, I'm not missing a thing!" My heart leaped! Not feeling deprived is the key to sustaining this way of eating and is the foundation for long-term success.

In fact, avoiding feelings of deprivation has been the impetus for 75 percent of my recipes. Much of that work was done for my daughter. Sweet G loved macaroni and cheese. Boxed or baked, it was among her favorite foods. As a result, I've made cauliflower mac and cheese, cabbage noodle mac and cheese, and the Better Than the Box Mac 'n' Cheese that appears on page 190, which uses shirataki noodles. She has enjoyed them all. We also make chicken tenders that rival her favorite drive-through version (page 136), and she even developed a signature dipping sauce for them (page 120).

Nearly every cake, muffin, pie, ice cream, and cookie in this book was inspired by Grace's tastes. When she missed Milano cookies, I created Sullivanos (page 258). When she wanted a banana split ice cream cake, I created an epic dessert layered with banana-flavored cake and three flavors of ice cream—strawberry, chocolate, and vanilla. We topped each slice with low-carb chocolate sauce and chopped peanuts. (You can find that recipe in my previous book, *Keto Gatherings*.) I double-dog-dare you to claim that my children have been deprived. My goal has been to not deprive them of joy from food, and especially from sharing food with others, while also helping them avoid the struggles associated with obesity and related metabolic dysfunction.

Jonathan is often less receptive to my culinary creations, so keeping him satisfied required a different approach. Because he's a picky eater, we sat down and made a list of low-carb foods that he likes. That list was pretty limited—meats, cheddar cheese, eggs, and green beans. He eats more moderately low-carb than the rest of us, so he also enjoys apples, an occasional small banana, peanut butter, fast-food chicken tenders, and low-carb wraps.

In addition to listing foods he liked, we went shopping together, which gave us a chance to consider low-carb options that he might enjoy but weren't staples in our house. Like most people, he's more likely to try foods that he selects and more likely to sample meals that he helps create. Involving kids in meal planning and shopping is a great way to ensure you have foods they will look forward to eating.

Talk to your children about what they like. If they're missing a favorite food, or if their friends are enjoying a high-carb food, chances are there's a good low-carb substitute. After all, in the first few months of my cooking keto, David kept asking, "Are you sure we can eat this?" The food was so delicious that it didn't remotely resemble the diet food he'd eaten in the past.

Take one look at the recipes in this book, and you'll see that we've packed it with low-carb versions of kid favorites, including treats. These days, I make sweets mainly for special occasions, and after seven years of keto, we're more likely to forgo dessert than to indulge. We've also paid careful attention to foods that travel well, whether you're packing a lunch or planning for an overnight trip. Kids need familiar foods that don't make them feel different from their peers. That's why trail mix (see page 204) and pizza (see page 134) are great options. These recipes taste like "regular" foods and are loved by carbivores and low-carb eaters alike, so you can easily make ample portions for your kids to share with friends.

Encourage your children by giving them a stack of sticky notes and asking them to flag recipes in this book that they would like to try. You can use the Kids in the Kitchen information to figure out ways to get them involved in food prep. Creating meals that everyone can enjoy is a surefire way to prevent feelings of deprivation.

PROVIDE ONGOING SUPPORT

The third and final step is to provide ongoing support for your children, especially for those who eat outside the home and/or who struggle to eat low-carb or keto. One of the biggest challenges in helping them not feel deprived is to extend that feeling beyond the home.

Supporting them through social challenges with their peers

Eating is often social, so when kids are dining with others—friends, classmates, clubs, church groups, scout troops, and so on—eating differently can be hard. In fact, it's the biggest challenge my children say they faced. One of the most important things you can do is to support them through these social challenges.

As Grace points out, friends connect over food, so eating different foods than their peers eat can make kids feel singled out or left out. We have a few tips for making this easier, but there will be times when friends eat high-carb foods. This is why it's important for children to understand why they eat this way and to feel empowered to choose.

To help my kids avoid feeling different and feeling deprived, I always try to make sure that they have access to keto options they enjoy. I have never sent "special" foods just for them, but I've prepared dishes that they can share with others. Grace and Jonathan aren't sharing "keto" foods; they're just foods they like. Their friends have enjoyed low-carb snacks like pepperoni and cheese sticks, nuts, Marinated Roasted Cheese (page 196), and trail mix (page 204). I've made mini cakes (page 224), egg cups (page 84), and cauli mash (page 208). In fact, several times other parents have asked me for the recipes for foods I've sent for sleepovers or parties. If you really want to win cool points, be the parent who makes homemade marshmallows (page 232), caramel sauce (page 250), and chocolate syrup (pages 252 to 255)!

Another technique I've used as a parent, especially when the kids were younger, is to explain to the adults who are providing food that we avoid sugar and carbs. By doing that, I'm enlisting their aid, not to keep my children on a "diet" but to support their food choices. In fact, I make it clear that the kids can choose to eat whatever they want, but I want them to have choices that I know won't make them feel bad.

If your child is following keto for a medical condition like epilepsy or diabetes, then you might want to explain that eating keto is a medical necessity, not a food preference. We would never apologize for a child having a nut allergy, nor should we apologize for or feel embarrassment about a child having insulin resistance or another medical condition. Framing eating keto as a medical imperative should help ensure that other adults are on board. Giving your children an adult ally when you aren't present is a powerful way to extend support to them and to help them feel better about making food choices that differ from their friends' choices.

It's also important to empower kids to understand and articulate why they avoid carbs. My kids are often asked, "Don't you want ice cream/cupcakes/etc.?" when they really don't. Grace typically has more confidence than Jonathan in explaining that she doesn't want those high-carb foods because they make her feel bad. Knowing that she doesn't want them, others can consume them around her without feeling too guilty. There have been times, though, when both kids accepted a treat after getting some pressure from a well-meaning friend or adult.

Unlike food allergies, many adults may not understand keto or low-carb, so you may have to offer specific examples of what your child enjoys, especially if the social activity is overnight or longer. For a sleepover or weekend trip, I might ask whether the group will be eating out and whether I might send food for meals. For example, I might offer to provide snacks that I know my kids can rely on for meals if needed. We've included an icon for recipes we've prepared for social events to give you some ideas; see page 48 for more on that icon.

In addition to social activities outside of school, kids often attend school parties and extracurricular activities that involve snacks and treats. These shorter events are sometimes easier for them to handle. Kids who are fat adapted (that is, who primarily burn fat for fuel instead of relying on carbs [glucose]) can simply skip eating and enjoy the camaraderie and activities. At these kinds of events, skipping sugary treats may go unnoticed.

Again, touch base with the adults who are responsible for providing the treats. As a parent, you might be able to suggest nonfood rewards or provide low-carb foods as part of the celebration. David and I still giggle when we remember robotics meets where the other parents brought chips, cookies, and candy, while we packed precooked bacon, pepperoni, and string cheese. Guess whose cooler got raided most frequently? And we were happy to share.

Eating out

If I know that the kids will be eating at a restaurant with others, I often explain to the parents serving as chaperones or hosting the meal that a bunless burger or fajitas without beans and rice is a good option. If they're going to a pizza place, I suggest chicken wings. Any restaurant that offers grilled meats is typically a safe option for keto kids.

If you can't find out the menu in advance, or if your kids are older, help them order with confidence by reviewing typical options with them. Most menus are made available online, so you can spend some time chatting with them about good options at different types of restaurants. Eventually, kids will gain confidence in ordering on their own, especially when they see you model it or when you take the time to role-play with them.

More than once, Grace has texted me the link to a restaurant's online menu asking for suggestions. Every time, I stop what I'm doing and offer suggestions that I think she might enjoy. Only once in over seven years has a menu seemed impossible to navigate. My dear Sweet G was at a vegan restaurant where every dish had very little protein but quite a few carbs and moderate fat at best. I felt helpless trying to make suggestions, especially because I knew she had eaten only a package of almonds earlier that day. While the others ordered, she was able to locate a keto-friendly option half a block away. She explained to her

friends that there really weren't any good options for her at the vegan place, so she ordered takeout from the other restaurant, sat with them while they enjoyed their meal, and then picked up her food after they finished. She was able to eat on the drive home without inconveniencing anyone.

Had she been younger, I would have communicated with the other parents in advance or even placed the order myself once I had communicated with the adults in charge. We make sure to give our children prepaid debit cards or enough cash to pay for their own food when needed.

Packing school lunches

School cafeterias rarely offer good keto or low-carb foods, so we've always packed lunches. We've marked the recipes in this book that travel well with an icon (see page 48). One of our best investments for packed lunches has been hot food storage containers that are shaped like bowls. They keep foods warm enough to enjoy hours later and make it super easy to send leftovers for meals.

Grace's lunches were sometimes the envy of her friends, especially in middle school. She began to ask me to pack extra food so she could share. One day she came home and announced that she'd promised food to several friends and two teachers and asked me to make a double recipe for her lunch the following day. Of course, I ran to the grocery store that night and had it all hot and packed the next morning.

In addition to leftovers, we frequently pack deli meat with string cheese and some berries, veggies with ranch, nuts, and cold chicken salad. Remember, the most important foods to include in a lunch box are foods your kids will enjoy.

Even if you follow all of these tips for eating away from home, be prepared for your children to feel left out at times. They may resent that their bodies are different, especially they eat keto or low-carb for medical reasons. This is when it's especially important that they know you're in their corner and they can count on you.

Holidays and special occasions

Whether it's a celebration with friends and classmates or with extended family, children are likely to need support on holidays and special occasions, especially if the occasion is food or candy centric, like Halloween or Thanksgiving. Here are some of the ways we've learned to delight in all things festive while enjoying a ketogenic lifestyle.

First, prepare for celebrations in advance by making sure that your children have delicious options. One of the reasons we've included more than twenty dessert recipes in this book is to provide families with tasty options. You'll find birthday cake (page 224), marshmallows (page 232), ice cream sandwiches (page 266), and even party beverages (pages 274 to 283).

We think it's unrealistic not to have special foods for celebrations. Having options can help your family develop new food traditions, especially if you select recipes that bring the kids into the kitchen. Grace and Jonathan still enjoy hot chocolate when the winter turns chilly, and they can enjoy ice cream in summer. We have Easter food traditions and favorite Christmas cookies—all keto!

Second, be intentional about creating nonfood traditions. This was harder than expected because it didn't happen naturally for us. Food had become central to our celebrations, so David and I actually brainstormed what we could *do* with our children outside of the kitchen. Christmas was one of the more challenging holidays, but we found ourselves enjoying nights out riding around local neighborhoods to view the lights. We also began to spend more time decorating and wrapping gifts as a family. We even started simplifying our Christmas menus because we realized that the fridge was overstuffed—and so were we with all of the gatherings we shared with extended family.

Third, we began to give gifts of activities—new bikes, concert tickets, family trips, and so on. Those gifts brought more fun memories as we spent time enjoying them not just at the holidays but into the future.

Fourth, brainstorm nonfood items for filling Christmas stockings, Easter baskets, and the like. At Christmas, our kids get a piece or two of low-carb chocolate, but they also get things they want, like gadgets, earrings, and playing cards. Our Easter baskets often have a summer theme. When the children were younger, they got new bathing suits, swim goggles, flip-flops, or kites. They might get books, bubbles, or sunglasses as well.

Finally, navigate holidays with relatives and others by initiating new traditions that do not revolve around food. Set the stage in advance by asking grandparents or other family members to avoid making high-carb treats for the kids. You can also suggest nonfood gifts if they like to spoil your children on Valentine's Day or Halloween. To set firm boundaries while also supporting their relationship with your children, you can say something like, "I know you like to get the kids treats for Valentine's Day, and they always love it. But since we aren't eating sugar, maybe this year you could get them *[insert something your children would enjoy, like small toys, stickers, colorful pens, balls, or games]* instead." Suggesting nonfood treats that the children will appreciate allows the giver to connect and indulge without providing sweets that you have to police. The most important thing you can do is to have the conversation with other adults ahead of time, without the children around. And, as always, give your kids the freedom to choose.

Dealing with well-intentioned but unsupportive others

On occasion, other well-intentioned adults will offer snacks or treats that aren't part of the plan. This challenge becomes particularly difficult when the child wants the "forbidden" food and/or the adult equates the food with love, and even trickier when the adult doesn't understand the nutritional need for eating low-carb or keto. With other adults in our children's lives, we often have to be very direct, especially if a low-carb lifestyle is warranted for medical conditions. Rather than debating what's best for your child, be clear that *you* have determined what's best.

If pressed, you might explain why your family eats this way, focusing on the health benefits. Even if your child needs to lose weight, focus on health aspects, not weight. Adults tend to see weight-loss diets as punitive when low-carb or keto really isn't. Help them understand that your child feels better, has better moods, has more energy, has less hunger, and more. List any improvements you've seen to help other adults connect what they might see as restriction to positive effects.

If adults are responsible for making or providing meals or snacks for your children, encourage them by listing what your kids *can* eat. Provide examples or prepare meals and send them with the children. I always prepared plenty of food to send with my kids so that the grandparents could enjoy the food, too. This makes it easier for the children *and* the caregivers. Most often, the grandparents were grateful to have food on hand that saved them time in the kitchen and allowed them more time for play. And who doesn't love tasty food?

If your children are old enough, empower them to explain to others why they want to avoid high-carb foods. A simple statement such as, "I don't care for that because it makes me feel bad," will have a much bigger impact on an adult than anything a parent can say. As long as your child is making and articulating that decision, your job is far easier.

Also empower your child to make choices. You don't want them to think that "if I eat that, Mom and Dad will be mad." Explain the consequences, such as, "You might feel a little sick," or, "The sugar might make you feel hungrier," but give them the latitude to decide. Most of the time, they will make good choices.

TALKING WITH YOUR CHILDREN ABOUT LOW-CARB OR KETO

I was the kid who heard, "You have such a pretty face!" over and over again. I was coerced, chided, and begged to lose weight. The adults in my life didn't know any more than I did that the solution was as simple as restricting carbs and increasing protein and fat. Still, the words we use when we talk about food and weight can be construed as blaming. Without intending to, we can communicate that kids aren't good enough because of their weight or appearance.

With that in mind, I strongly encourage you to talk to your children about health, not weight. Even on a strict keto diet, some may never be at an "ideal" weight. Who among us is tall enough, thin enough, or attractive enough? Most of us feel inadequate in terms of our appearance, so emphasizing good foods for strong bodies is important.

Offer ongoing and supportive feedback without commenting on physical appearance. You can say, "Your skin looks much healthier!" or ask, "How do you feel?" but avoid comments about size or weight that might make kids self-conscious. For girls especially, shifting the focus away from appearance is critical, although both males and females are at risk for disordered eating and body dysmorphia. I encourage you to seek professional help for any child who exhibits warning signs of disordered eating. Two good online resources in the United States are the National Eating Disorders Association (NEDA) and the Eating Disorders Coalition. You might also find support at the International Association of Eating Disorder Professionals (IAEDP).

What do children need to understand about keto? Do they need to understand macronutrients?

TOTAL VERSUS NET CARBS

Total carbs is the amount of carbohydrate in a food or recipe without subtracting fiber. When you subtract fiber from the total carb count, you get what is referred to as net carbs. Which should you count? The answer often depends on whom you ask, what you're eating, and who is eating. Counting net carbs is probably safe for healthy children who are primarily eating meats, eggs, dairy, and vegetables. But if your family consumes a lot of packaged foods, especially those labeled low-carb or keto, then counting net carbs may not be as healthy as you think. For anyone using keto or low-carb to treat a medical condition like diabetes, epilepsy, or PCOS, counting total carbs is generally much safer and is likely to yield better results.

Should children be counting carbs, protein, or fat? Probably not unless the child has a significant medical condition that requires them to stay in ketosis or carefully manage blood glucose, as is the case for a child with type 1 diabetes. In that situation, please follow the guidance of your family's healthcare providers. Most children, especially when food is prepared by adults, simply need to understand what their most nutritious options are—meat, eggs, dairy, and veggies. If kids are old enough to select foods on their own or are eating away from home, then it might be good to teach them some basic label-reading skills and advise them to keep their carbs below a certain threshold per meal.

For example, Grace is aware of the carbs in most vegetables and understands that limiting her consumption of higher-carb vegetables is a goal at each meal. She also understands that she needs adequate protein and fat to feel satiated. She has learned this through trial and error and from listening to her hunger cues. Grace can read labels and counts total carbs. Her goal is typically no more than 20 grams of total carbs per day with a minimum of 20 grams of protein per meal and an equal or greater amount of fat. She doesn't stress about it, nor does she track, but she makes food choices around those general parameters.

Jonathan eats more moderately low-carb, with a goal of no more than 25 grams of total carbs per meal. Ninety percent of his meals have less than 10 grams of carbs, but being able to go up to 25 grams gives him the flexibility to enjoy some favorite fast foods, low-carb wraps, and higher-carb vegetables. Keep in mind that Jonathan is metabolically healthy and has the flexibility to eat more carbs at some meals.

When he first started eating keto, we never discussed grams of protein or fat; we simply focused on minimizing carbs. Within the first few months, he went on a trip with friends. While the friends selected convenience store snacks (in this case, candy bars), Jonathan read every nutrition label on every candy. When he returned home, he happily told me that he had selected a chocolate bar because it had only 23 grams of carbs! He reasoned that it was under his threshold of 25 grams of carbs per meal, so it was a perfectly acceptable choice.

That experience prompted me to remind him to check ingredients, prioritize protein, and eat enough fat to feel satiated. It was a good learning experience for both of us because I realized that he needed a bit more detail and support than I had given him. Nonetheless, as a metabolically healthy teen, he was fine to eat the chocolate and didn't experience blood glucose swings or cravings as a result. Moreover, for the kid who used to eat 300-plus grams of carbs in the first six hours of the day, that candy bar was not a terrible choice.

How strict do kids need to be?

That depends. Grace needs to be pretty strict with limiting carbs in order to avoid cravings and hunger and for health reasons. The few times she's been unable to be consistent with her limit of 20 grams per day, she's noticed the effects. Any child who has a metabolic disorder or other health condition probably needs to focus on being 100 percent consistent. The body will burn glucose if it is available. Starving the body of glucose and forcing it to use fat (ketosis) is what provides health advantages.

But some children are metabolically healthier than others. Jonathan started eating keto because he was beginning to gain weight. With his hanger, I suspect that he was having some blood glucose swings as well, but he was never diagnosed as having a metabolic disorder. Because he is healthy, he seems to have some flexibility. He can enjoy a higher-carb meal from time to time, but he doesn't seem to miss most high-carb foods. The few times he eats higher-carb foods, he does so with friends and in very limited portions, like that one chocolate bar.

The most important answer to this question is to consider the health and circumstances of your children. If a metabolically healthy child has a higher-carb meal once a month or so, then it isn't likely to matter too much. If a child has a medical condition, however, then even occasional higher-carb meals can be a bad idea. Not only can such a meal throw their body for a loop, but it can take the child as long as two weeks to recover from the impact. Moreover, a high-carb meal can cause cravings to return with a vengeance. Some kids, like many adults, benefit from being strictly on-plan and will say that being 100 percent keto is easier than being 90 percent keto. Just as with adults, kids need to know which category they fall into for long-term success.

CHAPTER 2:
KITCHEN BASICS

If your children have little experience in the kitchen but want to be hands-on with food preparation, they will probably benefit from a review of kitchen basics, including food safety and sanitation, proper knife use, measuring techniques, and common cooking methods.

In this chapter, we've provided a brief introduction to each of these topics, but your family might want to spend more time talking and reading about kitchen basics. Cooperative extension agencies often have excellent free resources, and some even offer free classes. You can also find videos demonstrating knife skills, safe food handling procedures, and various cooking methods on YouTube.

If you aim to get your children in the kitchen helping, there are a lot of ways to do so. Even if they aren't yet hands-on with the preparation, you can start by having them help round up bowls, pans, utensils, and ingredients. They can also read the recipe to you; you can even put them in charge of making sure that steps or ingredients are not missed. Lastly, involve them in cleanup. Whether that includes putting away ingredients, washing dishes, or just clearing all of the dirty workspaces, having them participate in cleanup will help them appreciate the work that goes into food preparation. Look to our Kids in the Kitchen feature for specific ideas for getting kids involved with each recipe.

Even if the kids are just sitting close by while I'm cooking, I cherish that time together. When they're close by, they tend to talk with me. I learn what's on their minds, what's happening at school, and what their friends are up to. Not only do we create memories, but we also share a connection that goes far deeper than our tummies. Time together in the kitchen provides an opportunity to connect in an informal, nonthreatening, and rewarding way.

FOOD SAFETY AND SANITATION

Basic food safety and sanitation can help keep all members of the family safe. Most of these guidelines are simple enough that even young children can understand them. The four primary guidelines are

- Maintain a clean workspace, including clean hands
- Handle raw foods separately, especially raw meat
- Cook foods to safe temperatures
- Store foods at safe temperatures

Using these four guidelines for food safety and sanitation can help your family stay healthy while cooking nutritious and tasty meals together at home.

Keep it clean

Always wash hands, countertops, and cooking tools before starting to cook.

Warm soapy water is sufficient for cleaning hands and most surfaces. When washing hands, be sure to lather up the backs of your hands, between the fingers, and under the nails. Use the twenty-second rule to ensure that hands get more than a quick rinse. Hands should also be washed after food preparation and immediately after handling raw meat.

Make hand-washing fun for younger kids by singing a silly song while they scrub or playfully scrubbing their hands and your hands together. Be careful not to proceed with a recipe while they wash their hands so they don't rush or feel left out.

Countertops, cutting boards, dishes, and utensils should be cleaned with hot soapy water. Be sure to clean them as soon as possible after handling raw meat and before prepping other ingredients.

Clean vegetables and fruits by running them under cold water. Some vegetables, especially leafy greens, are best cleaned by rinsing them in a bowl of cold water. Prep veggies by cutting away any areas that look damaged or bruised. Precut or bagged produce may be labeled as washed and ready to eat, which means that it should be safe to consume. Still, we tend to err on the side of caution and rinse those vegetables and fruits as well.

If using canned goods, you might want to use soapy water to wipe the lids before opening the cans.

We keep a stash of clean towels by the kitchen sink and replace them if they become too damp. We use the towels mainly for drying our hands but also designate some towels for wiping down cabinets, drying dishes, or patting dry produce.

Keep raw foods separate, especially meats

Bacteria and germs can spread from one food to another. Raw meat, poultry, seafood, and eggs should be stored away from other foods. Practice this from the shopping cart to grocery bags and in the refrigerator. It's good to have one shelf for raw meat and a separate shelf or drawer for raw veggies and fruit. We also store dairy (butter, cream, cheese) in a separate area of the fridge. This not only keeps food safe but also helps us know when we are out of staples.

If you use a cutting board, utensils, a bowl, and/or a plate to prepare raw meat, be sure to wash them, and do not reuse those items for prepping other foods until they have been cleaned. Do not place cooked foods on surfaces that have held raw meat without cleaning those surfaces first.

Using separate cutting boards for meats and vegetables is a good practice. Glass or acrylic cutting boards are nonporous and generally thought to be easier to clean than wood cutting boards, which can harbor bacteria. Plastic, acrylic, or glass can also be cycled through the dishwasher to help kill germs.

Cook foods to safe temperatures

While vegetables can be enjoyed raw or cooked, meat, poultry, and seafood need to be cooked to safe temperatures and then kept warm until serving. Remember that heat kills bacteria that can cause illness.

Using a food thermometer to make sure that food is cooked to safe temperatures is a good practice. The recommended temperatures are listed below. Carefully insert the thermometer into the thickest part of the food. Use your best judgment as to whether your child can safely use a food thermometer.

While you can't always tell whether meat is done just by looking at it, a visual cue for poultry is that the juices run clear when it's cut and the meat is no longer pink in the center.

Keep foods at safe temperatures

Whether shopping, preparing, serving, or storing, an important part of food safety is keeping foods at proper temperatures.

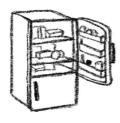

STORING

After shopping for groceries, be sure to refrigerate or freeze cold items within two hours of leaving the store. If food has been sitting at room temperature for more than two hours, it's best to throw it out. Store meat, poultry, seafood, dairy, and produce in the refrigerator at 40°F or colder. Refrigerating most fruits and veggies not only keeps them safe from bacteria but also ensures quality. The exceptions are tomatoes, spaghetti squash, and onions, which often are not refrigerated.

Most cooked foods should be consumed within four days or discarded. When reheated, leftovers should reach a temperature of at least 165°F.

Lastly, be sure to marinate foods in the refrigerator, not at room temperature, if they are to marinate for longer than thirty minutes.

SERVING

Just-cooked foods should be kept at 140°F or above if you plan to leave them out for more than an hour. Cold foods should be kept at 40°F or below until ready to serve.

In temperatures above 90°F, such as an outdoor picnic, prepared food should not be left out for more than an hour.

FREEZING

If you plan to freeze fresh meat, poultry, or seafood, it's best to do so within three days of purchasing it. Wrap it in aluminum foil, plastic wrap, or freezer paper and then place it in a freezer bag or other freezer-safe container.

Leftovers can be frozen for future meals. The foods that freeze best are soups, stews, casseroles, and foods cooked in sauces. Dishes containing a lot of dairy don't always freeze well because the dairy can separate when reheated.

We've included an icon for recipes that freeze well (see page 48). We especially appreciate freezer options when we're all eating at different times or looking for lunch options or when Mom, who is the primary cook in our house, is traveling and Dad is doing double duty as cook and dishwasher.

THAWING

Successfully using frozen ingredients or having tasty freezer meals depends on proper thawing. Gradual thawing in the refrigerator is slow but is generally safest and yields the best results. We set thawing meat, poultry, and seafood in bowls to make sure that the juices do not contaminate other foods in the fridge.

If you don't have the time or patience to thaw foods in the fridge, you can speed up the process by placing the food in a watertight bag and submerging the bag in a bowl of cold water. Change the water every thirty minutes to thaw the food more quickly. Shrimp and scallops can be safely thawed in a colander under cold running water. Cook the foods immediately after thawing.

Lastly, although it isn't always ideal, you can thaw foods in the microwave using the defrost setting (or reduced power). A microwave tends to work best for defrosting cooked foods; raw meat may cook a bit on the edges.

METHODS FOR PREPARING INGREDIENTS

Some recipes call for grated cheese, while others use shredded cheese. You'll also see vegetables like onions listed as minced in one recipe but sliced in another. There's a reason that food is prepared in different cuts and sizes, and the difference can impact the final product, so it's worth taking the time to become familiar with various techniques for prepping ingredients. Also use the recipe instructions and photos to guide you.

CHOP—Chopped ingredients can be any size and may not be uniform in shape. Peppers, onions, tomatoes, and zucchini are commonly chopped for use in recipes.

CUBE—Most recipes that call for cubed ingredients indicate the size of the cube, such as 1 inch. Meats and poultry are often cut into cubes to help them cook uniformly. Vegetables can also be cubed.

DICE—Diced ingredients, typically vegetables, are cut into small enough pieces to cook quickly but also add some texture and taste to the dish. Ingredients might be diced for a sauce or soup.

GRATE—When a recipe calls for an ingredient to be grated, it generally indicates a result that is smaller and finer or thinner than shredding. For example, Parmesan cheese is often grated but can also be shredded. Onions and other vegetables might be grated when you don't want large pieces in a dish. When an ingredient is grated, it can cook into the final product and add flavor without impacting the texture.

MINCE—Foods that are minced are cut finely enough to blend into a dish without yielding a distinctive bite. Ingredients with strong flavors, like garlic, ginger, and onions, are often minced so that they flavor a dish without overpowering it.

SHRED—Shredded foods are slightly larger than grated. Shredding can be used to help a food cook more quickly or to blend in more easily, which is the case with melting cheese. Shredded raw veggies can also add texture and flavor to a dish.

SLICE—Slices can be vertical or horizontal and are generally thin. Consider vegetables like cucumber and zucchini. Some recipes might have you slice them into rounds (vertical cuts), while others call for long (horizontal) slices. Quartering vegetables is a form of slicing them. After being quartered, vegetables can be more thinly sliced as needed.

METHODS FOR COMBINING FOODS

Whether you are cooking or baking, the methods you use to combine ingredients can have a big impact on the outcome. Stirring too frequently can cause vegetables to become too soft, just as overmixing a batter can cause muffins to sink when baked.

BLEND—Blending can be done with a blender, a food processor, or sometimes a hand mixer or an immersion blender. Blending ingredients often breaks them down into a homogeneous product, like the Cheesy Cauli Mash on page 208. Recipe instructions often tell you how well blended, how thick, or how creamy the end result should be, so look for those clues.

CREAM—Ingredients like butter, cream cheese, and melted cheese are sometimes combined with ingredients like sweeteners or eggs using a method called creaming. A handheld mixer or stand mixer is helpful for getting a smooth consistency when creaming ingredients.

MIX—Mixing generally involves combining ingredients, but it can take different forms. For the Orange Blossom Trail Mix (page 204), you're combining mostly dry ingredients using a spoon or spatula. For baking, mixing ingredients can refer to combining dry ingredients with a whisk or using a hand mixer to create a batter or dough. Be sure to read the entire recipe carefully to determine which tools you should use for mixing.

WHIP—To make frostings (like the Chocolate Buttercream Frosting on page 226) or homemade marshmallows (page 232), you will need to whip ingredients. Whipping incorporates air into the mixture, making whipped cream, frostings, and marshmallows light and airy. You can whip ingredients with a hand mixer or with a whisk attachment on an immersion blender or a stand mixer. With a strong arm and a lot of patience, you can use a whisk to whip some ingredients, like heavy cream, by hand.

COOKING METHODS

Use this section to introduce yourself and your kids to various cooking methods. You can even experiment by cooking the same foods in different ways. For example, try boiling a few pieces of broccoli while you roast a few others. The end results will vary in ways that may surprise you. Boiled broccoli tastes a bit fresher and more neutral and can have a more tender texture depending on how long it's boiled. Roasted broccoli tends to be more flavorful and has a hardier texture.

You may be surprised to find a food that you don't care for cooked one way is delicious when prepared by a different method. For what it's worth, I'll confess that I much prefer most vegetables roasted over boiled. The same is true for meats. I tend to reserve boiling for soups and stews, but each method has its own merits, and it's good to learn the differences. Learning about different methods will also help you follow the instructions when making a new recipe.

Boiling and simmering

Boiling involves cooking a food such as a chicken, a roast, or even vegetables like broccoli, cauliflower, or radishes in a pot of water or other liquid. Boiling requires enough heat to make the water bubble vigorously. You can boil foods with or without a lid. Using a lid traps the steam, allowing the food to cook more quickly and preventing the pot from boiling dry. If you boil without a lid, you should keep a closer eye on the food and be prepared to add more liquid if needed. In addition to boiling foods in water, broths and tomato-based sauces can be used for boiling.

If boiling, take care not to get burned from the steam. Also, when adding ingredients to a pot of boiling liquid, use tongs or a slotted spoon to gently lower them into the pot and avoid splattering hot liquid. You need to keep a careful watch to make sure that the pot doesn't boil dry. If it does, the food will scorch. Not only will your dish be ruined, but you can also ruin the pot, so don't venture too far from the stove while something is boiling.

Simmering is similar to boiling, but at a lower heat. When a recipe calls for simmering, the liquid in the pot should be just hot enough to see a few tiny bubbles popping up. I use simmering to thicken sauces and to make meat more tender. Simmering is like a whisper, while boiling is more like a shout. Keep an eye on a pot that is simmering. If simmering a sauce, be sure to stir it occasionally to keep it from becoming too thick on the bottom. Dishes with dried herbs especially seem to benefit from a slow simmer.

Baking and roasting

Baking and roasting are similar. I tend to think of casseroles, cakes, brownies, and cookies as baked and meats or veggies as roasted, but there are exceptions. Chicken, bacon, and other meats can also be baked. Baking generally calls for temperatures below 375°F—not always, but mostly. Roasting tends to happen at temperatures greater than 375°F.

The goal of baking is to generally cook an entire dish like a casserole or cake to doneness from edge to edge. Roasting tends to brown the tops of meats or veggies, creating a crust or caramelization that adds a rich depth of flavor.

Sautéing, pan-frying, and stir-frying

While similar, there are subtle differences between and uses for these three methods. Many of the recipes in this book call for sautéing meats or veggies. To sauté, use medium-high heat and add a fat like ghee, bacon fat, coconut oil, or olive oil. When the pan is hot, add the meat or vegetables. Ingredients for sautéing are generally cut into uniform bite-sized pieces and given time to brown before being stirred.

Stir-frying is similar but typically involves higher heat and more oil (although I tend to use a lot of oil when sautéing as well). Technically, a wok is used for stir-frying, but you can use a large skillet. As in sautéing, foods are generally cut into small pieces. Because of the higher heat, stir-fried foods are kept in constant motion.

Pan-frying is also similar but uses lower heat and requires a good layer of oil in the skillet. You might pan-fry burgers, chicken thighs or breasts, or pork chops. (The Chicken Mud recipe on page 164 uses pan-frying to cook the chicken.) The lower heat allows the outside of the meat to brown with a nice crust while the inside cooks through. When pan-frying, you generally turn meats only once or twice. Pan-fried vegetables are similarly left to cook through and turned as few times as possible.

Slow cooking, pressure cooking, and air frying

Each of these methods requires a special appliance, and each has different advantages. There are popular multi-cookers that can perform all of these techniques and more and might be worth the investment if these cooking methods appeal to you. You can use the Orange-Braised Pork recipe on page 146 to test the differences between slow cooking and pressure cooking.

Slow cooking is a popular way of cooking roasts, soups, stews, and even egg dishes. The low heat requires a longer cooking time, but the advantage is that the cooking time is completely hands-off. Most slow cooker recipes involve placing all of the ingredients in the slow cooker, setting the time and temperature, and going on your way. On the low setting, some larger meats and roasts require eight to ten hours of cooking. I've used the low setting to slow cook a whole chicken overnight or while I've been away at work. The high setting often cooks meals within four to six hours. In addition to hands-free cooking, slow cookers allow you to make complete meals, which minimizes cleanup and ensures that the entire meal is ready at the same time.

Pressure cooking was incredibly popular with my great-grandparents' generation, but their manual pressure pots were a lot different from the popular pressure cookers used today, such as the Instant Pot. Pressure cooking combines high heat and high pressure to cook foods quickly. Electric pressure cookers are thought to be safer than manual pressure cookers because of their built-in safety features that manage the release of pressure. With a pressure cooker, meat can go from frozen to completely cooked in less than thirty minutes. As with a slow cooker, the cooking time is completely hands-free; unlike a slow cooker, an entire meal can be prepared quickly. Personally, I don't care for plain pressure cooked meats, but I have enjoyed stews and cheesecakes made in a pressure cooker. In fact, the pressure cooking method yields a richer, more tender cheesecake texture unrivaled by careful oven water baths.

Air frying combines high heat and circulating air to cook foods fast. An air fryer works well for frying foods like chicken wings, burgers, and jalapeño poppers and for warming foods like leftover Deep Dish Supreme Pizza (page 134). An air fryer yields a fried cooking texture without requiring additional oil. It leaves foods crisp and browned and cooks foods more quickly than an oven or cooktop.

GENERAL TIPS FOR SUCCESSFUL COOKING OR BAKING

When it comes to cooking, practice may not always make for perfect results, but it sure doesn't hurt. Most of what you need to know can be learned through trial and error, but taking the time to read these tips *before* heading into the kitchen can make a big difference in your confidence and your success.

- **Read the recipe from start to finish** before beginning and look at the accompanying photo to see how the end result should look. Reading the recipe in advance tells you which tools and equipment you need, how much time it might take to prepare, and how much space you need to work.

- **Gather all of the ingredients before starting.** Grabbing the ingredients ahead of time helps ensure not only that you have the correct amounts of the right ingredients, but also that you won't forget to add an ingredient.

- **Pay attention to the exact ingredients listed.** If a recipe calls for large eggs, using extra-large or small eggs may yield a different result, especially when baking. Use unsalted butter unless salted butter is specifically listed. If fresh herbs or veggies are called for, don't substitute dried herbs or frozen veggies without making adjustments. Some of the recipes in this book call for part-skim (reduced-fat) mozzarella cheese for making bread dough. Be sure to use the right kind; using higher-fat mozzarella will affect your results.

- **Measure carefully.** All recipes require you to measure the ingredients. It's important to measure accurately for your dish to turn out right, especially if you're baking.

HALVING RECIPES

There may be times when you want to reduce the number of servings for a recipe. In general, it's safe to do so for most recipes. Be careful when baking because not all baked goods will turn out perfectly when halved. When reducing recipes, you will likely have to reduce the cooking times and use smaller pots, pans, or baking dishes.

There is a difference between wet and dry measures. Dry ingredients can be measured in cups, ounces, or grams. For most dry ingredients, you can scoop and then level the top for a reasonable measure. For example, when measuring baking powder, scoop the measuring spoon into the can of powder and then use the edge of the container or a straightedge like a knife to scrape away the excess. Liquid ingredients are measured in cups, fluid ounces, or milliliters, usually using in a cylindrical glass.

Remember that measuring volume is different from weight. A cup or tablespoon measures volume, while weight is measured in ounces or grams. Measuring dry ingredients by weight is the more accurate method. A food scale generally costs less than $12 and can be a smart investment.

It's worthwhile to spend time learning about measurements and their equivalents. See the conversion chart, opposite.

You can memorize it or make a handy cheat sheet to tape on the inside of a cabinet door. Conversion charts are helpful not only for scaling recipes but also for understanding how amounts relate. For example, when you know that ¼ cup equals 4 tablespoons, you can use a tablespoon to measure if needed. Also, when you know that there are 16 tablespoons in a cup, it's easier to calculate carbs if the serving size is given in tablespoons. And knowing that 3 teaspoons make 1 tablespoon can save you from dirtying multiple measuring spoons, which is important to me when I'm measuring a lot of spices.

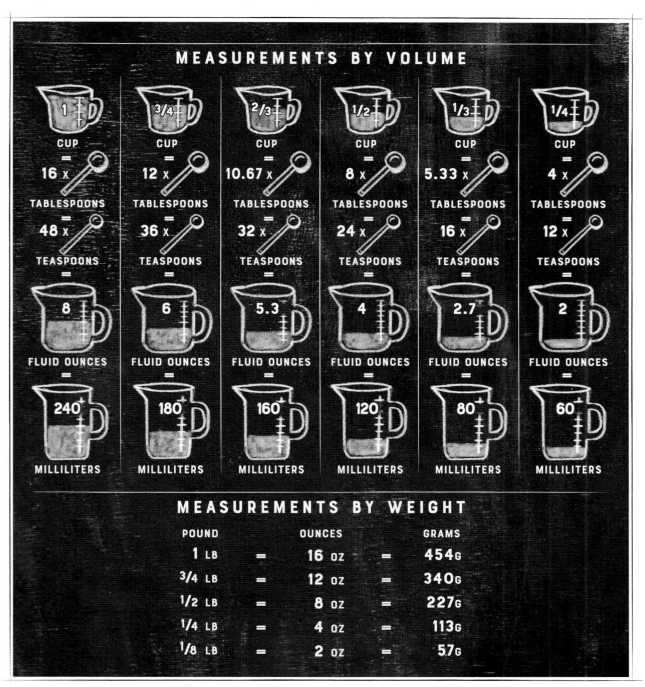

MEASUREMENTS BY VOLUME

1 CUP	3/4 CUP	2/3 CUP	1/2 CUP	1/3 CUP	1/4 CUP
=	=	=	=	=	=
16 x TABLESPOONS	12 x TABLESPOONS	10.67 x TABLESPOONS	8 x TABLESPOONS	5.33 x TABLESPOONS	4 x TABLESPOONS
=	=	=	=	=	=
48 x TEASPOONS	36 x TEASPOONS	32 x TEASPOONS	24 x TEASPOONS	16 x TEASPOONS	12 x TEASPOONS
=	=	=	=	=	=
8 FLUID OUNCES	6 FLUID OUNCES	5.3 FLUID OUNCES	4 FLUID OUNCES	2.7 FLUID OUNCES	2 FLUID OUNCES
=	=	=	=	=	=
240 MILLILITERS	180 MILLILITERS	160 MILLILITERS	120 MILLILITERS	80 MILLILITERS	60 MILLILITERS

MEASUREMENTS BY WEIGHT

POUND		OUNCES		GRAMS
1 LB	=	16 OZ	=	454 G
3/4 LB	=	12 OZ	=	340 G
1/2 LB	=	8 OZ	=	227 G
1/4 LB	=	4 OZ	=	113 G
1/8 LB	=	2 OZ	=	57 G

NOTES ABOUT SWEETENERS

There are many options for ketogenic sweeteners, and many opinions about which ones are best. As a general rule, I prefer to use the natural sweeteners erythritol, monkfruit, and stevia. I have also used, and like, xylitol and allulose. (Allulose is not a natural sweetener but appears to be safe.)

Artificial sweeteners such as aspartame, phenylalanine, and acesulfame potassium (Ace K) often raise blood glucose and keep cravings high, so I avoid them. In addition, some sugar alcohols that are ubiquitous in sugar-free products, including maltitol, sorbitol, and mannitol, not only raise blood glucose but also can cause intestinal distress.

Sucralose is an artificial sweetener that I use from time to time; however, pure sucralose, which is 600 times sweeter than sugar, is not the same as Splenda. To make Splenda, maltodextrin is added to sucralose to provide bulk so that Splenda measures cup for cup like sugar. The problem is that maltodextrin is a food starch and has a higher glycemic index than pure sugar! I do not recommend Splenda for that reason.

To help you determine which sweetener to choose, I'll describe their uses by texture, form (liquid, granulated, or powdered), and intensity. Regardless of which, if any, sweetener you choose to use, please be mindful that each of us is impacted differently. If you have diabetes or are managing a health condition like epilepsy, please use a meter to monitor your blood glucose and see whether a certain sweetener affects you adversely.

- **LIQUID SWEETENERS.** Most liquid sweeteners are very intense, with just a few drops providing the equivalent sweetness of ¼ to ½ cup of sugar. The liquid sweeteners with which I am most familiar are liquid sucralose and liquid stevia. The intensity of liquid stevia seems greater than that of liquid sucralose, although it varies widely by brand. Start with just a drop or two of either and add only a drop at a time until the taste is sweet enough for you.

- **GRANULATED SWEETENERS.** In addition to sweetness, granulated sweeteners add bulk, which can be important in baked goods. Granulated erythritol and xylitol are examples of bulk sweeteners. Pure sucralose and powdered stevia are other non-liquid options, but they do not provide the bulk that the other types do. When I need bulk, I often use erythritol or xylitol and then add some powdered pure sucralose or stevia to achieve the desired sweetness. If you're using stevia, look for brands with 90 percent or higher stevioside to avoid the bitter aftertaste that is common in stevia products.

  In several of the recipes in this book, I recommend xylitol and/or allulose instead of erythritol or an erythritol blend. These include the marshmallows (page 232), the ice creams (pages 244 to 249), the Caramel Sauce (page 250), and the chocolate syrups (pages 252 to 255). You *can* use erythritol in these recipes, but because erythritol doesn't caramelize well, tends to crystallize when cooled, and yields a very hard texture when frozen, I recommend avoiding it in these cases.

- **POWDERED SWEETENERS.** Some recipes call for powdered sweetener. Using the powdered form can be important when you need a smooth texture, as in a ganache, a buttercream frosting, or a creamy chilled dessert. If a recipe calls for powdered sweetener, you don't have to buy a separate product; you can simply run your preferred granulated sweetener through a blender or clean coffee grinder until it is powdery.

WHY? WHY, WHY, WHY, WHY, WHY?

My children abused the word *why* from the time they could speak by overusing it daily. And I vowed never to tell them, "Because I said so!" Some days it took more control than others to avoid telling them that, but most of the time I summoned the patience to explain why, feeling that if they understood my reasoning, they would be better enabled to use their own logic for independent problem-solving when they needed it. Doing so also gave them permission to question the world they are growing up in, and I believe that's a good thing.

Admittedly, there were times when I had to say, "I can't explain right now, but I will later," and other times when I had to confess, "I'm not entirely sure, but I bet we can find out. Let's look that up." Sometimes their questions came up during car rides, so we began keeping a small notepad in the car so that we could write things down to look up later.

So, when putting this book together, we made note of potential "why" questions. Why do you use oat fiber? Why is this oil better than that oil? Why do you bake instead of fry this dish? Why should you use a rimmed baking sheet? And so on. I'm sure we missed a few, so you might want to jot down your own questions and see if you can discover the answers. Have fun and remember, "Because I said so!" is rarely the best answer.

INGREDIENT-RELATED QUESTIONS

Why do low-carb or keto baked goods use so many eggs/so much cheese?

For the protein! And not just because it's good for you. The bread recipes in this book do not contain gluten, which is a protein found in wheat. Gluten is what gives traditional bread its texture and rise. In the absence of gluten, baked goods would be more like crackers.

Adding eggs, cheese, and whey protein isolate or egg white protein powder is a low-carb way to give baked goods structure. These ingredients also provide some lift, especially when combined with baking powder.

Bacon fat and ghee have a higher smoke point than other fats, which means that you can use them to cook foods at higher heat (up to 375°F for bacon fat or over 450°F for ghee) without them burning.

Why do you fry foods in bacon fat or ghee? What about other fats?

Butter tends to burn more easily than bacon fat or ghee, so it isn't ideal for frying, but it's perfect for a quick sauté. It is also used in baking because it helps baked goods brown nicely.

Most sautéed or stir-fried dishes are cooked over medium-high heat (around 340°F). Safe fats to use at that temperature include ghee, coconut oil, lard, and tallow. Light sesame oil and olive oil are also good options.

For cold applications, such as salad dressings or the dipping sauce on page 189, I'm most likely to use avocado oil, which has a very mild flavor, but olive oil also works well.

Oat fiber is the pure insoluble fiber from the outside of the oat. It is naturally gluten-free and gives baked goods a fantastic wheatlike mouthfeel without adding carbs.

Why do you use oat fiber?

A word of caution: LifeSource is the only brand of oat fiber I use. Other brands tend to have a very strong taste and really aren't palatable. Also, oat fiber is not available in stores (at least not in my area). I order it from Netrition, but you can find it on Amazon as well.

When possible, I've listed coconut flour as an alternative to oat fiber. If coconut flour is not suggested as an alternative, then either I haven't tried using it in that recipe or I used it and did not get good results.

Coconut aminos is an excellent substitute for soy sauce for people who avoid soy, but there are differences between the two ingredients. Coconut aminos is slightly sweet and not salty like soy sauce. The flavor is also less intense. If using soy sauce, opt for lite soy sauce to reduce the amount of sodium in the dish, and use about half as much.

Why do some recipes call for coconut aminos or a lesser amount of soy sauce?

Many people prefer tamari, which is not wheat-based like soy sauce. If using tamari, reduce the amount of salt in the recipe just as you would if using soy sauce.

Why do you use pork rind dust in recipes, and where can I find it?

Pork rind dust is made by grinding up pork rinds. For the best results, use the fluffier types of pork rinds that have less fat than the more dense and hard cracklin's. Even stale pork rinds can be ground into dust and stored in the pantry until needed. I use a small blender to pulverize them.

You can also buy pork rinds already crushed; these are often labeled as pork rind crumbs or pork panko. These products are a bit more expensive than buying whole pork rinds and crushing them yourself, but some people appreciate the convenience.

Even those who don't like to eat pork rinds alone often don't mind them used in recipes. Because they are high in protein and fat and have some collagen in them, they act as a binder. I use them instead of flour or as a breading to avoid gluten. The bonus is that unflavored pork rinds have zero carbs!

Why do you use whole-milk mozzarella in some recipes and part-skim in other recipes?

When I'm cooking rather than baking, I use full-fat mozzarella cheese for the flavor and fat. In most baked goods, however, I use part-skim mozzarella. Although keto is a high-fat diet, the fat in the cheese can inhibit rise and make the dough too wet. Using reduced-fat cheese increases the ratio of protein to fat for better results. Remember that we want the *protein* from the cheese in most baked goods.

Why do you use unsalted butter in most recipes?

Using unsalted butter allows you to control the amount of salt in a recipe. This is especially important in baked goods, where too much salt can affect the rise, and the salt can't be easily adjusted after baking.

Also, the amount of salt in salted butter varies widely by brand, which means a dish can easily taste too salty depending on which brand of butter you buy. Using unsalted butter is always safer so that you can adjust the salt level according to your preference. That said, a few recipes in this book do use salted butter. In those cases, the additional salt is welcomed for flavor, but you can use unsalted butter and adjust the salt to your liking.

Granulated sweetener is the more common form in my recipes. If a recipe calls for powdered sweetener, it's typically for making a frosting or a chilled dessert like the filling in the Pumpkin Spice Roll (page 264).

Why do you sometimes use both granulated or powdered sweetener and liquid sweetener?

Liquid sweetener comes in handy when you want to take advantage of the synergy created when different sweeteners are combined. For example, using erythritol and stevia often helps mitigate the cooling effect of erythritol while avoiding the bitterness associated with using too much stevia. Liquid sweetener also enhances the sweet flavor while allowing you to avoid any grittiness associated with adding more granulated sweetener.

For all of its wonderful properties, erythritol tends to crystallize when cooled. If made with erythritol, sauces like the chocolate syrups on pages 252 to 255 can become gritty when cooled or refrigerated. Allulose and xylitol do not crystallize. Allulose also yields a softer texture, even in baked goods such as cheesecake.

Why do you sometimes recommend allulose or xylitol instead of erythritol?

Xylitol caramelizes as well, which is why I use it in the caramel sauce on page 250. If you use it in baked goods, such as the Vanilla Pound Cake (page 236) or the Chocolate Chip Cookies (page 238), you will notice that your treats have a more traditional golden color like baked goods made with sugar. Do take care when using xylitol, as it is toxic to pets.

Lastly, erythritol freezes hard as a rock when used in ice cream. You can let the ice cream thaw for five to ten minutes before eating it, or you can use allulose or erythritol for creamy, scoopable ice cream right out of the freezer.

In many cases, you *can* use frozen vegetables; just be sure to thaw them completely before using them in a recipe. Also, frozen vegetables tend to have a higher moisture content than fresh ones. Let them drain in a colander or use a clean kitchen towel to remove as much moisture as possible before adding them to a recipe.

Why can't I use frozen vegetables instead of fresh?

Because they taste better! Homemade condiments and sauces are also less expensive, and you can control the sweeteners used.

Why do you make your own ketchup and BBQ sauce?

Many commercial brands of ketchup and BBQ sauce are sweetened with questionable ingredients or have food starches added to them. If you're metabolically healthy and are able to eat higher levels of carbs, these products may be fine for you to consume. If you have to be very careful with ingredients, however, then making your own condiments and sauces is easy, inexpensive, and delicious.

COOKING- AND BAKING-RELATED QUESTIONS

Why do you mix the dry ingredients together first in most baking recipes?

Giving the dry ingredients a quick mix with a whisk or rubber spatula helps keep them from clumping when the wet ingredients are added. It also ensures that the baking powder is thoroughly distributed and allows batters and doughs to come together more quickly since everything is measured and combined before mixing.

Why did my egg whites not form stiff peaks?

Egg whites can be finicky. If they fail to whip up to perfection, there could be a few culprits. First, any trace of oil in the bowl or on the beaters will keep egg whites from whipping. You can also overheat egg whites, causing them to weep. For best results, always let egg whites come to room temperature before whipping them. Make sure to use a clean, dry bowl, and add a pinch of cream of tartar after they begin to whip.

Why does the pan size and type matter?

When baking, the size of the pan or dish matters as much as the type. If you use a larger dish than the recipe calls for, the contents will be spread over a larger area, so they will be thinner. That means the baked good will cook faster and may burn. The cheesecake on page 256 is made in an 8-inch springform pan. If you used a 9-inch pan, the cake would be very thin and would cook more quickly. A 7-inch pan would yield a thicker cheesecake that would take longer to bake.

When the size of the baking dish matters, I indicate the exact size that I used to develop and test the recipe. If you need to use a different-sized dish, try to use an equivalently sized one. For example, a 9-inch square baking pan can be replaced by a 9 by 2-inch round cake pan. Websites like Joy of Baking and What's Cooking America can help you find similar-sized pans to use in the event that you don't have the exact size of dish called for in a recipe.

Keep in mind that baked goods generally cook faster in a dark metal pan than in a glass or ceramic pan. Lightweight aluminum pans conduct heat poorly and may require longer baking times. I tend to use metal pans when baking breads or cookies but glass or ceramic for casseroles. When I use a skillet, it's typically made of cast iron.

Why do I need to preheat the oven?

In most cases, you want the oven preheated and ready to go before you slide in your masterpiece. If the oven isn't fully preheated, you run the risk of the food drying out as the oven heats, and it can cook unevenly as the top or bottom heating element kicks in to bring the oven to the correct temperature. The cooking times for all of the recipes in this book assume that the oven is fully preheated.

Because many factors can affect baking times, these times can seem more like suggestions than hard-and-fast rules.

First, oven temperatures may vary. Unless your oven is professionally calibrated, it is likely to be off by as much as 20°F to 25°F.

Altitude can affect baking times, too. The higher the altitude, the harder it is to adhere to the baking times in a recipe. If you live at a high altitude, try raising the oven temperature by 10°F to 15°F and adding another tablespoon or two of liquid so that your baked goods do not dry out.

As noted earlier, using a different size pan than the one called for can impact the baking time, as can the type of pan you use (glass, ceramic, or light or dark metal).

My favorite baking instruction is "bake until done," which is what my grandmother wrote on all of her recipes. It's one of the reasons why I provide guidance in each recipe suggesting how the finished product should look or feel, like "golden brown" or "just firm to the touch."

Why do my baked goods often take more/less time than the recipe says?

Crumbly baked goods were probably overcooked. Reduce the baking time the next time you make the recipe. For now, embrace the crumble by scooping the dessert into a bowl and topping it with a dollop of freshly whipped cream.

Chocolate baked goods are notorious for overbaking, which yields a dry or crumbly texture. Be sure to remove them from the oven as soon as they're set and do not overbake. Pressing gently on the top of a chocolate baked good can help you determine whether it's done. If you feel a slight resistance, then it's ready to be removed from the oven. If your finger leaves even a slight indentation, then it needs to bake a bit longer.

Why are my baked goods crumbly?

Low-carb baked goods use ingredients such as almond flour, coconut flour, and oat fiber. The texture of foods made from these ingredients tends to change a bit as they cool.

In most cases, baked goods become softer unless you give them time dry out and crisp up, like the chocolate chip cookies on page 238. Cakes become more moist and brownies more dense over time, reinforcing the adage that patience really is a virtue.

Why do you suggest letting most baked goods cool before eating them?

Unless you're going to consume them quickly, most keto baked goods should be refrigerated because they contain no preservatives. You can safely leave most items at room temperature for up to two or three days, but most will keep for at least a week when refrigerated.

Warm leftover baked goods in the microwave on reduced power, wrap them in aluminum foil and reheat them in the oven, or use an air fryer.

Why do you store most keto baked goods in the refrigerator?

HOW TO USE THE RECIPES

As you scan the recipes, please take note of a few special features we've included to help guide your use of the recipes.

Recipe icons

First, there are icons to quickly guide you as to whether a recipe contains potential allergens or is a great option for freezing, packing, or sharing.

 DAIRY-FREE: If you or someone in your family avoids dairy, these recipe marked with this icon are either dairy-free or are equally delicious when made with the dairy-free substitutes or omissions noted.

 EGG-FREE: For those with allergies, these recipes are either egg-free or can be made egg-free.

 NUT-FREE: For those with allergies, these recipes are either nut-free or can be made nut-free. Although peanuts are technically legumes, not nuts, they are included in this category for the sake of convenience.

 FREEZES WELL: If your family likes to have ready-to-eat meals on hand, these recipes are great for keeping your freezer well stocked. Each one has been tested by freezing and reheating and has gotten approval from family or friends.

 GOOD FOR TRAVEL/PACKED LUNCHES: Recipes marked with this icon travel well and are ideal for meals eaten on the go, whether packed in a Thermos or tossed into a backpack.

 SUITABLE FOR SOCIAL EVENTS: These recipes are for sharing at parties, potlucks, and sleepovers. No one will think of these as keto foods; they are simply delicious foods.

Kids in the Kitchen

Not only have we packed this book with recipes that kids of all ages can enjoy, but we've also included mostly simple recipes that kids can help create. Bringing the kids into the kitchen is a great way to get them involved and to help them become more independent when making their own food decisions. Kids are more likely to try new foods and enjoy meals when they've had a hand in making them.

In each recipe, you'll see a feature called Kids in the Kitchen. Here, you'll find suggestions for how kids can be involved. Small hands might enjoy sprinkling ingredients like cheese over a dish or giving dry ingredients a stir, while older kids can tackle more challenging tasks.

Using measuring spoons and cups is a fantastic way to introduce various math skills that are developmentally appropriate. You can even let kids use a kitchen scale for more precise measurements.

If your children are old enough to handle raw eggs or meat, it's important to teach them the basic food safety techniques discussed on page 31.

Tweens and teens can also learn knife skills as well as practice various cooking techniques, such as using higher heat to sauté ingredients or lower heat to create a creamy cheese sauce (see page 128). Let them practice whipping egg whites to stiff peaks and then folding the egg whites into a batter to create Rolls Without Rolls (page 60).

Whether they're learning how to crack eggs or to practice food safety, bringing kids into the kitchen allows them to develop practical life skills while you create precious memories as a family.

Serving sizes and nutrition information

Since this book was written for kids of all ages, determining a serving size for each recipe wasn't easy. Clearly, the amount a younger child might eat is different from a teen's appetite, which creates an obvious dilemma in establishing serving sizes and providing nutrition information. In most cases, we erred on the side of smaller portions with the intention that those with larger appetites might consume two servings and then could easily double the nutrition numbers. Where possible, we have indicated the nutrition per piece, such as per breadstick or per candy, so that each individual can decide how much to eat according to hunger and/or carbohydrate restrictions.

With the nutrition information, you will see erythritol (sugar alcohol) listed separately from carbs. We did this because sugar alcohols are generally safe to deduct from total carbs; however, they are included in case you need to count them. Oat fiber carbs are listed separately as well. Oat fiber is insoluble fiber. Because it isn't absorbed, it does not impact blood glucose and is generally considered safe to consume without counting the carbs. If you have type 1 or 2 diabetes, please use your glucometer to monitor your body's reaction to oat fiber.

CHAPTER 3:
BREADS

In our first six months or so of eating keto, we missed bread. In fact, it was daunting when we realized how much bread we typically ate—biscuits, bagels, pita, and so on. We ate breakfast sandwiches, had wraps for lunch, and generally ate some type of bread with dinner. I even made homemade sourdough bread!

It was only natural to begin experimenting with bread replacement recipes. My first attempts were biscuits, and I have a few options on my website, cookingketowithkristie.com, that are actually pretty good. I also developed a wrap bread recipe through trial and error that makes a nice substitute for pita bread and is great for lunches. As I continued to experiment and learned more about various alternative flours, I also began to realize that there is very little flavor in bread.

Consider that for a moment. Whenever I ate traditional high-carb bread, it was never plain. I nearly always smeared it with butter, cream cheese, peanut butter, mayonnaise—in other words, fat! Fat adds flavor! On keto, it's easy to have flavor with all of the high-fat foods that we enjoy. We also realized that even lower-carb breads add carbs to a meal. We began to limit carbs in bread form so that we could enjoy carbs from flavorful foods like tomatoes and other veggies. As our tastes changed, we eventually realized that bread is convenient when used for a sandwich or as a vehicle for a handheld burger or hot dog.

Even as we began to eat less bread, I continued to experiment with recipes—not as much for my own family, who sometimes asked why I was even bothering to try to create substitutes, but for others, because I know that the transition to life without bread isn't always easy. That's why this chapter includes bagels, biscuits, and even a baguette recipe! I've also included a recipe for "rolls" that can be used to make hamburger or hot dog buns or hoagie rolls.

I invite you to use the recipes included here to learn and experiment. These recipes intentionally use a variety of ingredients such as psyllium husk powder, almond flour, oat fiber, whey protein isolate, and cheese. Not only did I want to offer families dairy-free and/or nut-free options, but I also wanted you to learn how different ingredients yield different results. Once you get a feel for the textures, tastes, and techniques for making low-carb breads, you might just want to experiment on your own!

ANYTHING DOUGH

MAKES
enough dough
for 6 bagels

This dough can be anything! My Sesame Bagels (page 64), Sausage and Cheese Pinwheels (page 74), Open-Faced Calzones (page 144), and Wrapped Piggies (page 176) all use this dough, or a variation of it, as a base. It's similar to crescent roll dough, but not as flaky. You can even use it as a topping for pot pie. This recipe is especially great because it exemplifies a basic tenet of cooking: if you use a little imagination, you can create anything!

½ cup blanched almond flour

¼ cup oat fiber, or 2 tablespoons coconut flour (see Note)

2 teaspoons baking powder

¼ teaspoon salt

1½ cups shredded part-skim mozzarella cheese (about 6 ounces)

2 ounces (¼ cup) cream cheese

3 tablespoons boiling water

1. In a small bowl, whisk together the almond flour, oat fiber, baking powder, and salt and set aside.

2. Melt the mozzarella and cream cheese in a 2-quart saucepan over low heat. As the cheeses melt, stir with a spatula to combine them. Add the dry ingredients and continue to mix, still over low heat. Stir in the boiling water and remove from the heat.

3. Transfer the dough to a large bowl and use your hands to knead it gently for 15 to 20 seconds. Let the dough rest for 15 to 20 minutes before using, or chill it for at least 1 hour if using it to make bagels. If making the dough ahead, wrap it in plastic wrap, place in an airtight container, and refrigerate for up to 3 days.

NOTE: *If you use oat fiber, the only brand I recommend is LifeSource. If you opt for coconut flour, the texture of the bread will be a bit softer.*

 This dough is easy to make and fun to work with. Although heating the cheese and working with the boiling water requires some caution, younger hands can enjoy shaping the dough into bagels, wrapping the piggies, or other simple projects.

CALORIES: 174 | **FAT:** 13.9g | **PROTEIN:** 9.3g | **CARBS:** 3.5g | **FIBER:** 1g | **OAT FIBER:** 2g

EASY CHEESY BISCUITS

MAKES
9 biscuits

Nine biscuits? Shouldn't it be six or twelve? Those are the standards when buying rolls or making muffins, but did you ever wonder why? I did, and I went on a bit of a rabbit trail trying to figure it out. It doesn't appear that there's any good reason, so I'm breaking tradition with a yield of nine biscuits for this recipe. If you're preparing a meal for a family of four, everyone gets two, and the dishwasher earns the bonus! These biscuits are soft and cheesy with a wonderful breadlike texture. It is truly one of my favorite biscuit recipes to make since it's quick and easy.

½ cup blanched almond flour

¼ cup oat fiber, or 2 tablespoons coconut flour (see Note, page 52)

2 teaspoons psyllium husk powder

2 teaspoons baking powder

½ teaspoon salt

½ teaspoon garlic powder (optional)

3 tablespoons hot (but not boiling) water

1 tablespoon melted unsalted butter

2 large eggs

1½ cups shredded cheddar cheese (about 6 ounces)

1. Preheat the oven to 375°F. Line a large cookie sheet with parchment paper.

2. In a large bowl, whisk together the almond flour, oat fiber, psyllium, baking powder, salt, and garlic powder, if using. Pour in the hot water, melted butter, and eggs and stir until a dough begins to form. Add the cheese and mix to combine.

3. Drop the dough by the spoonful onto the lined cookie sheet, making a total of 9 biscuits, about 2 inches in diameter. A medium-sized cookie scoop works well for this task. Be sure to leave at least 1 inch of space between biscuits.

4. Bake for 25 to 30 minutes, until lightly browned and firm to the touch. Let cool on the pan for at least 10 minutes before serving.

5. Refrigerate leftovers for up to a week, or freeze for up to 2 months.

TIPS! *To make this simple recipe even faster, mix the dry ingredients ahead of time and store in a freezer-safe container in the freezer. When you want to make a batch of biscuits, preheat the oven, toss the water, butter, eggs, and cheese into the dry mix, and bake as directed.*

Try baking half of the dough as biscuits and combine the other half with breakfast sausage to make a delicious sausage ball.

Drop biscuits are great for getting kids involved because the dough is less fussy and more forgiving than a yeast dough. Depending on their age and skill level, kids can help gather ingredients, measure, and stir. They can also crack the eggs and use a large spoon or cookie scoop to drop the biscuits onto the cookie sheet. You can remind them to set the timer before they help with the cleanup, which is essentially washing the measuring spoons and mixing bowl and putting away the ingredients.

CALORIES: 144 | FAT: 11.9g | PROTEIN: 7.5g | CARBS: 2.9g | FIBER: 1.3g | OAT FIBER: 1.3g

CHEESY BREADSTICKS

MAKES
12 breadsticks

These cheesy breadsticks are everything cheesy breadsticks should be—warm, gooey, and healthy! Be sure to use a good-quality Parmesan cheese; you can also substitute a nice Romano or Asiago cheese or use a blend of all three. My family enjoys these breadsticks with pizza sauce, which makes them taste very much like cheese pizza, but you can leave it off for a more traditional breadstick.

⅓ cup blanched almond flour

½ teaspoon baking powder

4 ounces (½ cup) cream cheese, softened

1½ cups shredded mozzarella cheese (about 6 ounces), divided

2 large egg whites, or 1 large egg

1 teaspoon Italian seasoning, divided

¼ teaspoon garlic powder

⅛ teaspoon salt

1 batch No-Cook Pizza Sauce (page 124) (optional)

½ cup shredded Parmesan cheese

Chopped fresh basil leaves, for garnish (optional)

1. Preheat the oven to 350˚F. Line a cookie sheet with parchment paper and lightly grease the paper.

2. In a medium bowl, whisk together the almond flour and baking powder. Add the cream cheese, ¾ cup of the mozzarella, and the egg whites and use a spatula or wooden spoon to thoroughly mix into a thick dough. Sprinkle in ½ teaspoon of the Italian seasoning, the garlic powder, and salt and stir to combine.

3. Put the dough on the prepared cookie sheet and spread it into a 5 by 9-inch rectangle, about ½ inch thick. Bake until just browned and cooked through, 6 to 8 minutes.

4. Remove from the oven and top the bread with the pizza sauce (if using), the remaining ¾ cup of mozzarella, and the Parmesan. Sprinkle the remaining ½ teaspoon of Italian seasoning over the top.

5. Return the pan to the oven and bake until the cheeses are melted and lightly browned, another 14 to 18 minutes. Remove from the oven and use a pizza cutter or sharp knife to cut the bread into 12 sticks about 1½ inches wide and 3 inches long. Serve warm, garnished with fresh basil if desired.

6. Refrigerate leftovers for up to 5 days. Reheat in a preheated 300˚F oven or in a skillet over low heat.

Younger hands can help sprinkle the cheeses on the dough at the end, but otherwise, this one might be a bit difficult for small children to help with. Older kids can probably make this recipe on their own; they might have fun adding various toppings after the initial baking time.

CALORIES: 116 | **FAT:** 9g | **PROTEIN:** 6.5g | **CARBS:** 2.5g | **FIBER:** 0.3g

CRUSTY BAGUETTES

MAKES
2 baguettes
(12 slices)

Every person who has sampled this bread has enjoyed it, but it isn't easy to bake. It's easy to *make*, but knowing exactly when it's done can be tricky. I've found that I have to bake it at least 10 minutes beyond the time I think it is done. Telltale signs are a dark, crusty exterior and a hollow sound when you tap the bottoms of the loaves. If the loaves shrink as they cool, they were underbaked or overmixed. No need for alarm if they turn purple or dusky gray after baking, though—that's just the psyllium. I like to use slices of these baguettes to make French toast (see page 78).

½ cup oat fiber, plus more for dusting if desired (see Note, page 52)

¼ cup psyllium husk powder

1 tablespoon baking powder

½ teaspoon salt

2 large eggs

6 ounces (¾ cup) cream cheese, softened

¼ cup boiling water

2 teaspoons white vinegar

TIPS! *For best results, bake the baguettes on a baguette pan, which is perforated. This yields a much crustier exterior and tends to cook the bread more evenly.*

You can also shape the dough into rolls instead of baguettes. You may need to adjust the baking time.

1. Preheat the oven to 350°F and line a baguette pan or cookie sheet with parchment paper (see Tips).

2. In a small bowl, whisk together the oat fiber, psyllium, baking powder, and salt. Set aside.

3. Use a stand mixer to whip the eggs until frothy. Add the cream cheese and mix until blended with the eggs. Be sure to scrape down the sides of the bowl with a spatula as needed.

4. Add the dry ingredients ¼ cup at a time, mixing lightly until incorporated. Pour in the boiling water and vinegar and stir by hand to make a thick batter. Do not overmix.

5. Let the dough rest for 10 to 15 minutes, then divide it in half. Shape each portion into a baguette about 6 inches long and 2½ inches in diameter. Place on the lined baguette pan or cookie sheet. Use a sharp knife to cut slits across the top of each baguette. Dust the tops with oat fiber, if desired.

6. Bake until the outsides are crusty and dark brown and the baguettes are cooked through, 80 to 90 minutes. They should feel solid, not soft.

7. Let cool on a wire rack for at least 5 minutes before slicing with a serrated knife.

8. Store leftover bread at room temperature for up to a week, or freeze for up to 2 months.

Younger kids will enjoy mixing the dough and shaping it into baguettes. An older child will be able to score the tops of the loaves with a sharp knife.

CALORIES: 79 | FAT: 5.8g | PROTEIN: 1.9g | CARBS: 4.4g | FIBER: 3.2g | OAT FIBER: 2g

ROLLS WITHOUT ROLLS

MAKES
4 hot dog or hamburger buns or 8 hoagie rolls

This recipe was a huge hit when I shared it in an interactive online cooking class. It is a bit of a chameleon, meaning that you can use the dough to make many different shapes of bread. For example, you can use a muffin top pan or make your own round molds to form hamburger buns, or you can use a cylindrical mold for hot dog buns. My favorite way to enjoy this bread is as hoagie rolls, which are even easier to make if you have a brownie pan with individual wells. The instructions included here are for making hot dog buns, since my family was excited to be able to hold hot dogs again. The buns take a little extra effort if you have to create aluminum foil molds for them, but the batter is simple to prepare. If you have a hot dog bun pan, then the task is easy. Keep in mind that different baking vessels will yield varying numbers of rolls and may require adjustments to the baking time. Use the baking time range here as a guide.

I tend to double this recipe and make a batch of hot dog buns and a batch of hamburger buns at the same time. If I have helpers, I'll double the double batch.

---

4 large eggs

¼ teaspoon cream of tartar

¾ cup shredded part-skim mozzarella cheese (about 3 ounces)

¼ cup whole-milk cottage cheese or full-fat ricotta

2 tablespoons oat fiber (see Note, page 52)

2 tablespoons whey protein isolate

1 tablespoon psyllium husk powder

2 teaspoons baking powder

¼ teaspoon salt

1. Preheat the oven to 350°F. Grease a hot dog bun mold, or create 4 molds using aluminum foil and a tall, slender bottle such as a spice bottle or caper jar. (You can also use a drinking glass or any ovenproof cylinder that is roughly 5 inches long and 1½ to 2 inches in diameter.) Don't forget to grease those molds, too.

2. Set 3 mixing bowls side by side. Separate the eggs, placing the whites in the first bowl and the yolks in the second bowl. Whip the egg whites with a hand mixer until they have just begun to stiffen. Add the cream of tartar and continue whipping until stiff peaks form. Set the whipped whites aside.

3. Add the mozzarella and cottage cheese to the bowl with the egg yolks. Use the hand mixer to beat just until the yolks lighten in color and the cheeses are blended. Do not overmix.

4. In the third bowl, whisk together the oat fiber, whey protein isolate, psyllium, baking powder, and salt. Add the dry mixture to the yolk and cheese mixture a little at a time, beating with the mixer as you go.

This recipe is made in distinct stages in three mixing bowls. The tasks of creating and greasing the molds, separating the eggs, whipping the whites (see my tips on page 46), and folding all of the ingredients together require different skills and techniques, making this a great recipe for tweens and teens to learn a lot about baking. Let the kids get creative with using different pans to make hot dog buns, hamburger buns, or other different-shaped breads.

CALORIES: 179 | FAT: 10.1g | PROTEIN: 18.9g | CARBS: 2.8g | FIBER: 0g | OAT FIBER: 2.5g

VARIATIONS:

HAMBURGER BUNS. This dough can be used to make hamburger buns; simply use a muffin top pan instead of a hot dog bun mold. Sprinkle sesame seeds on top, if desired.

HOAGIE ROLLS. You can cut the hot dog buns in half to make 8 hoagie rolls, which are perfect for small sandwiches (see page 174). When making hoagie rolls, I like to bake the dough in a brownie pan with individual wells or in mini loaf pans instead of a hot dog bun mold. Sprinkle everything bagel seasoning on top for more flavor.

5. Use a spatula to gently fold one-third of the whipped egg whites into the yolk mixture. Add another third of the whites and gently fold into the dough, then repeat with the final third of the whites.

6. Divide the dough evenly among 4 wells of the greased hot dog bun mold or among the greased foil molds. Bake until golden brown, 25 to 30 minutes. Let cool for 5 to 7 minutes before removing the buns from the mold(s), then transfer to a cooling rack until ready to use. Slice the buns lengthwise with a serrated knife just before serving.

7. Refrigerate leftover buns for up to 10 days, or freeze for up to 2 months.

YEASTY LOW-CARB ROLLS

MAKES
12 rolls

This is one of the few low-carb yeast breads in which you can actually taste the yeast. It's a perfect roll for mini breakfast sandwiches made with chicken tenders (see page 136) or bacon and eggs, or as an herb-topped roll with a slice of ham. Be sure to allow time for the dough to rise, which gives the bread a really nice texture. Also, don't be afraid to bake these rolls longer than you think they need. The tops will brown a little faster than many low-carb breads. You can lay a piece of foil over the pan during the last 10 to 15 minutes of baking if the rolls are browning too rapidly.

½ teaspoon granulated sugar

1 (¼-ounce) packet active dry yeast

1 tablespoon hot (but not boiling) water

½ cup blanched almond flour

⅓ cup oat fiber (see Note, page 52)

2 tablespoons baking powder

¼ teaspoon salt

2 cups shredded part-skim mozzarella cheese (about 8 ounces)

4 ounces (½ cup) cream cheese

2 large eggs

1 tablespoon ghee or unsalted butter, for rolling

1. In a small bowl, stir together the sugar, yeast, and hot water and set aside to activate the yeast.

2. In another bowl, whisk together the almond flour, oat fiber, baking powder, and salt and set aside.

3. Melt the mozzarella and cream cheese in a 3-quart saucepan over low heat. When the cheeses are completely melted and mixed, remove from the heat and stir in the flour mixture. You may find that the dough comes together more easily if you use your hands.

4. Add the eggs and the activated yeast mixture. Use a wooden spoon or your hands to mix the dough until smooth. Cover the pan with a clean kitchen towel and set aside in a warm place to rise for 25 to 30 minutes.

5. Preheat the oven to 375°F. Grease an 8-inch round baking pan.

6. Coat your fingers liberally with the ghee and roll the dough into balls about 1½ inches in diameter. You should get 12 balls. Place the dough balls in the greased pan.

7. Bake until the tops are browned and the rolls are firm to the touch, 25 to 30 minutes. If the tops begin to brown too much, cover loosely with foil for the remaining baking time.

8. Refrigerate leftover rolls for up to 5 days, or freeze for up to 2 months.

Tweens and teens might enjoy helping with this recipe, but younger kids may not be able to make the dough. Some younger kids might enjoy rolling the dough balls with supervision. Feeding and activating the yeast can also be entertaining to kids. Explain that the hot water and sugar help wake and feed the live organisms that have been dormant in the yeast. Take care that the water isn't too hot for the yeast.

CALORIES: 115 | FAT: 9.5g | PROTEIN: 5.1g | CARBS: 2.2g | FIBER: 0.7g

SESAME BAGELS

MAKES
6 bagels (1 per serving)

I've developed three different types of bagel recipes. This one is simple to make and can be flavored in various ways, which is why I have included it in this book. These low-carb sesame bagels make great sandwiches for breakfast or lunch. They are handy for travel and for those times when everyone else seems to be enjoying a bagel, such as at a sleepover. This recipe gives kids the best of both worlds: eating like their peers and staying on plan. Schmear these bagels with Veggie Bacon Cream Cheese Spread (page 100) or Cinnamon Walnut Cream Cheese Spread (page 76).

1 batch Anything Dough (page 52), chilled

1 tablespoon sesame seeds

1. Preheat the oven to 350°F. Line a cookie sheet with parchment paper.

2. Divide the dough into 6 equal portions. Shape each portion into a ball and then use your fingers to poke a hole in the middle to create a bagel shape. Place on the lined cookie sheet, leaving at least 1 inch of space between bagels.

3. Sprinkle the sesame seeds over the bagels.

4. Bake until golden brown, 16 to 18 minutes. Let cool completely before serving.

5. Refrigerate leftovers for up to a week, or freeze for up to 2 months.

TIPS! *Be sure to use part-skim, not full-fat, mozzarella in the dough to help the bagels hold their shape.*

If the dough is too warm, it will spread into a thin mess as it bakes. Be sure to refrigerate it for at least 1 hour before baking.

You can also use a doughnut pan to yield a bagel shape.

VARIATIONS:

CINNAMON BAGELS. Add 2 tablespoons of granulated sweetener and ½ teaspoon of ground cinnamon to the dough and omit the sesame seeds.

EVERYTHING BAGELS. Add a dash of garlic powder and a dash of onion powder to the dough and sprinkle the tops of the bagels with everything bagel seasoning instead of sesame seeds.

Kids who are just learning to use the stove can practice with very low temperatures to melt the cheeses and make the dough. Once the dough is made, kids of all ages can form the bagels. Let them roll the dough into "snakes" and then shape them into circles, or follow the instructions I've provided for making a ball of dough and then punching a hole in the middle.

CALORIES: 182 | FAT: 14.5g | PROTEIN: 9.5g | CARBS: 3.7g | FIBER: 1.2g | OAT FIBER: 2g

TORTILLAS

MAKES
12 tortillas
(2 per serving)

My husband and kids have been doing keto and low-carb long enough that they generally prefer to skip tortillas altogether, but their eyes lit up when I used these low-carb tortillas to make Simple Cheese Quesadillas (page 172). These can tag along in lunch boxes and are especially convenient for younger children who thrive on finger foods. I have served these tortillas with the Sheet Pan Fajitas (page 184) as well.

⅓ cup coconut flour

⅓ cup oat fiber (see Note, page 52)

2 tablespoons psyllium husk powder

½ teaspoon salt

½ teaspoon garlic powder

½ teaspoon onion powder

¼ teaspoon ground cumin

½ cup refined coconut oil, melted, or avocado oil

2 cups boiling water

1. Preheat the oven to 350°F. Line two large cookie sheets with parchment paper.

2. Put the dry ingredients in a mixing bowl and whisk to combine. Add the oil, then stir in the boiling water ⅓ cup at a time, mixing well after each addition. Use a spatula to mix until all of the water is incorporated and a soft dough has formed.

3. Roll the dough into twelve 1-inch balls. Place each ball on a piece of parchment paper. Cover with a second piece of parchment and use a small rolling pin or your hands to flatten the balls into 6-inch round tortillas about ¹⁄₁₆ inch thick.

4. Transfer the tortillas to the lined cookie sheets using the parchment paper. Bake until lightly browned, 8 to 10 minutes. Flip the tortillas to brown the other side, if needed. Do not overbake.

5. Remove from the oven and use immediately or let cool for 8 to 10 minutes before storing in an airtight container with pieces of parchment paper between them. They will keep for up to 5 days in the refrigerator or up to 2 months in the freezer.

TIPS! *If the tortillas are overbaked, they will become crisp and not pliable. The crisp tortillas can be used for chips but do not work well for quesadillas, soft tacos, or fajitas.*

The baking time may vary based on the thickness of your tortillas. Roll the dough as thinly as you can while keeping it sturdy enough to transfer without breaking.

This recipe gives us all an excuse to play with our food! Once the dough has cooled a bit, kids can help create the dough balls and flatten and roll them into tortillas. Skilled hands are needed to transfer the tortillas from the parchment paper to the lined cookie sheets, but if someone has an oopsie, just reroll the dough and learn from the mistake.

CALORIES: 199 | FAT: 18.9g | PROTEIN: 0.9g | CARBS: 5.4g | FIBER: 4.2g | OAT FIBER: 2.7g

OPTION

90-SECOND TOAST

MAKES
2 or 3 pieces

Okay, you've seen 90-second bread, but hear me out. This is 90-second *toast* because it's pretty awesome toasted but kind of "meh" straight out of the microwave. This is the closest I've come to something like a toasted English muffin. It's great with Mom's Eggs (page 99), smeared with flavored cream cheese spread (see pages 76 and 100), transformed into French toast (see page 78), or made into a sandwich.

My goal in creating this recipe was to keep the carbs as low as possible by minimizing the amount of almond flour and to create a texture that wasn't eggy. That's why I stretched one egg over two or three pieces. My preference is to divide the batter among three 3½-inch-diameter ramekins, but for thicker bread (such as for making French toast), you can use only two ramekins. You can also use an 8 by 4-inch loaf pan for a more traditional "square" bread. If you don't have ramekins, any small, flat-bottomed bowl or coffee cup will work; just make sure it's microwave-safe.

3 tablespoons blanched almond flour

2 tablespoons oat fiber, or 2 teaspoons coconut flour (see Note, page 52)

1 teaspoon psyllium husk powder

1 teaspoon baking powder

¼ teaspoon salt

2 tablespoons hot (but not boiling) water

1 tablespoon melted unsalted butter or coconut oil

1 large egg, beaten

1. Put the almond flour, oat fiber, psyllium, baking powder, and salt in a mixing bowl and use a spatula to combine. Add the hot water, melted butter, and beaten egg and stir into a thick batter.

2. Grease 3 ramekins, about 3½ inches in diameter, with butter. Divide the batter evenly among the ramekins and smooth it to the edges. Microwave all 3 ramekins together for 90 seconds. Use an oven mitt or kitchen towel to remove the ramekins from the microwave; they will be hot.

3. Use a spatula to loosen the edges of the bread and invert the bread onto a cooling rack. Let cool for about 5 minutes before slicing with a serrated knife. Toast in a toaster, in a hot skillet, or under the oven broiler until just browned.

4. Refrigerate leftover untoasted bread for up to a week, or freeze for up to 2 months.

TIP! *Make several batches ahead of time and store in the refrigerator until ready to be toasted.*

Tweens and teens can easily make this recipe. Younger children will enjoy mixing the batter and cracking the egg but might struggle to divide the batter among the ramekins. Children of all ages should take care when removing the hot ramekins from the microwave.

(BASED ON 3 PIECES) **CALORIES:** 151 | **FAT:** 13.2g | **PROTEIN:** 5.2g | **CARBS:** 3.1g | **FIBER:** 2.3g | **OAT FIBER:** 2g

BREAKFAST

My kids are spoiled—or maybe I am! Either way, neither they nor I expect breakfast to consist of traditional breakfast foods. Grace is just as likely to eat leftover fajitas or deli meat, cheese, and mayo as she is to have eggs since she doesn't care for them. From time to time she makes a smoothie with whey protein isolate or egg white protein powder and a little MCT oil to add fat. We prefer to get our nutrition from fresh foods rather than the highly processed and refined protein powder and oil, but a smoothie is a nice treat once in a while, especially during strawberry season, when she makes her strawberry protein smoothie.

Jonathan's palate is much more mundane. Most days he enjoys a simple plate of bacon and eggs, which he often cooks himself. He likes his eggs well-done, or what many would consider overcooked. While I prefer scrambled eggs shiny and soft, he likes them completely dry, lightly browned, and rubbery. He prefers a texture similar to an omelet, but without fillings. When we were working on the breakfast recipes, it was his idea to include both styles. Jonathan also wanted to include recipes for eggs because he enjoys making them himself. He reasoned that if he can make eggs, other kids can, too. And I agree! If learning how to scramble eggs to their idea of perfection increases the chance that they'll eat eggs and gives them a sense of pride, then let's get cracking!

Jonathan enjoys peanut butter waffles with chocolate chips. They are simple enough that I can whip them up on a school day. He also enjoys boiled eggs, which is why I included that recipe. If only I could get him to make those! He prefers them fresh but will eat cold deviled eggs.

My two kids rarely eat the same meals, but they agree that Chocolate Hazelnut Muffins are favorites. Of course, J. likes them warm from the oven, and G. prefers them chilled. They also argue about who eats more of them, but I suspect some misplaced blame, as the adults in the house like these muffins as well!

David and I tend to skip breakfast but enjoy a cup of coffee or two each morning. Some weekdays we enjoy bacon with our coffee since the protein helps us feel full longer. Weekends, vacations, and holidays are different: that's when I'm most likely to make crepes with bacon gravy, bagels with flavored cream cheese, French toast, or sausage-crusted quiche, which is not only one of David's favorites but also a perfect potluck or brunch dish. I've yet to meet anyone who doesn't enjoy it.

The "best" breakfast is one that keeps hunger at bay for at least four hours, one the kids will actually eat, and one I can make quickly so that I have time to find a missing shoe or homework paper or to sign the permission form that was due yesterday!

EGG WRAPS

MAKES
2 wraps
(1 serving)

These wraps can be filled with a variety of yumminess, such as cream cheese, feta cheese, shredded cheese, bacon, ham, spinach, scrambled eggs, avocado, or bell peppers, making it an ideal breakfast option for families with diverse food preferences. (That's mom-speak for a crew of picky eaters who rarely like the same foods.) Older kids can choose their own fillings and make the wraps for themselves. The wraps can also be eaten by littles as they are chauffeured through the car line at school.

1 large egg

½ cup shredded mozzarella cheese (about 2 ounces)

⅛ teaspoon salt

Ghee, for the pan

1. Put the egg, cheese, and salt in a small blender and blend to combine.

2. Heat an 8-inch skillet over medium heat and add just enough ghee to lightly coat the pan. Spread half of the egg mixture in the pan and smooth it over the entire surface, creating a thin coating of egg. Cook until lightly browned, about 2 minutes, then flip it over and cook until the other side is lightly browned.

3. Remove the egg wrap from the skillet, add more ghee to the pan, if needed, and make a second wrap using the remaining egg mixture. Serve warm with your choice of fillings.

4. Egg wraps can be made in advance and refrigerated until needed. Place pieces of parchment paper between the wraps and store in an airtight container so that they remain pliable. Refrigerate for up to 10 days, or freeze for up to a month.

Younger kids might not be ready to cook the egg wraps in a skillet, but they might enjoy putting the ingredients in the blender and giving it a whirl. Since more help can also take more time, these would be perfect to make ahead on a weekend and get the kids involved with food prep so that weekday mornings run more smoothly.

CALORIES: 282 | FAT: 20.7g | PROTEIN: 19.7g | CARBS: 2.4g | FIBER: 0g

SAUSAGE AND CHEESE PINWHEELS

MAKES
6 servings

While they take too long for weekday mornings at our house, these rolls can be made ahead and warmed in the microwave, a skillet, or the oven for a quick breakfast. They're good served with the Veggie Bacon Cream Cheese Spread on page 100.

1 batch Anything Dough (page 52), chilled

8 ounces breakfast sausage, cooked and crumbled (remove any casings)

½ cup shredded cheddar cheese (about 2 ounces)

2 teaspoons water

Fresh thyme leaves, for garnish (optional)

1. Preheat the oven to 400°F. Line a large rimmed baking sheet with parchment paper.

2. Place the dough on a piece of parchment paper and roll or press it into a rectangle measuring about 10 by 12 inches. It should be about ⅛ inch thick.

3. Top the dough with a layer of sausage, sprinkling it over the top of the dough from edge to edge. Sprinkle the cheese over the sausage.

4. Starting at the long edge closest to you, begin rolling the dough to create a log. Use the parchment paper to help keep the roll even.

5. Place the log on the lined baking sheet. Bake until the dough is golden brown and firm to the touch, 35 to 40 minutes. Slice and serve warm, garnished with fresh thyme if desired.

6. Refrigerate leftovers for up to 5 days, or freeze for up to 2 months. To reheat, wrap in foil and place in a preheated 300°F oven or in a skillet over low heat. If frozen, let thaw in the refrigerator and then reheat.

TIP! *If you're having trouble rolling out the dough, place it in the refrigerator to chill for 30 minutes or so.*

Younger children might enjoy rolling out the dough or measuring the rectangle to oversee quality control. They could also sprinkle the sausage or cheese over the top of the dough. Older children will enjoy making these as much as eating them and can get creative by adding ingredients or changing up the sausage and cheddar cheese filling to favorites like ham and Swiss or pepperoni and mozzarella.

CALORIES: 213 | FAT: 18.5g | PROTEIN: 10g | CARBS: 2.1g | FIBER: 0.2g | OAT FIBER: 1.3g

CINNAMON WALNUT CREAM CHEESE SPREAD

MAKES
1¼ cups
(2 tablespoons
per serving)

Before keto, we used to love the sweet version of this cream cheese spread made by a popular bagel chain. Now we love it on Plain Bagels (page 64), 90-Second Toast (page 68), waffles, pancakes, muffins, and the back of a spoon! It's great to provide this option to kids, and fun to see the ways in which they enjoy it. The walnut oil is optional but adds a rich, nutty flavor.

3 tablespoons finely chopped raw walnuts

1 (8-ounce) package cream cheese, softened

¼ cup powdered sweetener

2 tablespoons heavy cream

1 teaspoon maple extract

½ teaspoon vanilla extract

½ teaspoon walnut oil or walnut extract (optional)

½ teaspoon ground cinnamon

1. Toast the walnuts in a small saucepan over low heat for 2 to 3 minutes, watching carefully and stirring frequently so that they don't burn. Set aside to cool.

2. Use a spatula or a hand mixer to mix the cream cheese and sweetener until smooth. Add the heavy cream, extracts, walnut oil (if using), and cinnamon and mix to incorporate. Stir in the toasted walnuts and refrigerate for at least 1 hour before serving.

3. Refrigerate the spread for up to a week.

TIP! *Bagels with cream cheese spread are handy for those days when breakfast has to be eaten on the way to school. This spread is also great alongside any of the other breads in Chapter 3.*

This is a great recipe to get younger children helping in the kitchen. An adult or older child will need to toast the walnuts, but a younger child can help measure ingredients or use a spatula to combine everything. Imagine the conversations you can have about measurements while you work together!

CALORIES: 118 | **FAT:** 11.7g | **PROTEIN:** 2.2g | **CARBS:** 2g | **FIBER:** 0.4g | **ERYTHRITOL:** 6.2g

CLASSIC FRENCH TOAST

MAKES
8 pieces
(2 pieces per
serving)

Who doesn't love French toast? Especially when it's topped with warm melted butter, warm low-carb maple syrup, some Cinnamon Walnut Cream Cheese Spread (page 76), a dollop of peanut butter, or some fresh berries and a dusting of powdered sweetener, as shown here. While we like to make ours with 90-Second Toast, you can also use slices of Crusty Baguette (page 58).

2 large eggs

⅓ cup heavy cream

1 teaspoon vanilla extract

⅓ cup powdered sweetener, plus more for dusting if desired

½ teaspoon ground cinnamon

⅛ teaspoon salt

Ghee or coconut oil, for the pan

2 batches 90-Second Toast (page 68), sliced in half (see Note)

1. Put the eggs, cream, vanilla extract, sweetener, cinnamon, and salt in a blender and blend until smooth. Pour the mixture into a shallow dish wide enough to accommodate a slice of toast.

2. Heat a large nonstick skillet over medium heat. Add just enough ghee to lightly coat the pan.

3. Dip a piece of toast in the egg mixture, then use a spatula to quickly flip it and coat the other side. Do not let the bread soak; remove it from the egg mixture immediately and place it in the hot skillet. Cook for 2 to 3 minutes on each side, until the egg mixture is set and firm.

4. Repeat with the remaining pieces of toast and egg mixture. Serve warm, dusted with powdered sweetener if desired.

5. Refrigerate leftovers for up to 5 days, or freeze for up to a month. If refrigerated, reheat in the toaster or in a skillet over low heat. If frozen, let thaw in the refrigerator before reheating.

NOTE: *When making the 90-Second Toast for this recipe, divide the batter between two rather than three ramekins per batch so that you get four thick pieces that you then cut in half horizontally.*

TIP! *If you don't have time to dip and cook each piece of toast individually, double the recipe, cube the toast, and toss it into a greased 8-inch square baking pan, then pour the egg mixture over the top and bake at 350°F for 35 to 45 minutes, until set.*

This recipe can become a family affair. One person can make the egg mixture while another prepares the bread slices. Then you'll need someone to dunk the bread and someone to cook the French toast. Designate someone else to prepare the toppings, and it will be all elbows to the table to enjoy it! Don't forget to assign someone to do the dishes.

CALORIES: 234 | FAT: 21.5g | PROTEIN: 7.2g | CARBS: 3.1g | FIBER: 1.7g | ERYTHRITOL: 6g | OAT FIBER: 2.1g

CREAMY BACON GRAVY

MAKES
6 servings
(about ¼ cup
per serving)

Bacon gravy is one of the best things I've ever made, and it doesn't have to be for breakfast! Try it over any roasted meat. It's also good over Easy Cheesy Biscuits (page 54), 90-Second Toast (page 68), or scrambled eggs (see pages 98 and 99). My kids have even used it to smother steamed or roasted veggies.

1 cup beef broth

½ cup heavy cream

1 teaspoon garlic powder

1 teaspoon onion powder

¼ teaspoon salt

4 ounces (½ cup) cream cheese, cut into small chunks

1 tablespoon bacon fat

1 pound thick-cut bacon, cooked and crumbled

Fresh thyme leaves, for garnish (optional)

1. Simmer the broth and heavy cream in a 2-quart saucepan over medium heat for 15 to 18 minutes, until thickened.

2. Stir in the garlic powder, onion powder, and salt. Lower the heat, add the cream cheese, and stir until the cream cheese is melted. Add the bacon fat and cooked bacon and stir to combine. Serve immediately, garnished with fresh thyme if desired.

3. Refrigerate leftovers for up to 5 days. Reheat in a skillet over low heat. You may need to add a tablespoon or two of beef broth if the gravy is too thick when reheated.

TIP! *Bacon can be baked in a single layer in the oven at 350°F for about 30 minutes. You can also purchase precooked bacon to make this recipe more quickly.*

Older kids can easily make this gravy on their own. Kids who aren't quite old enough to manage the stovetop can help gather ingredients. You might also have them measure ingredients into a bowl so that they avoid the risk of burns from adding ingredients directly to the simmering broth mixture.

CALORIES: 540 | **FAT:** 47.3g | **PROTEIN:** 22.4g | **CARBS:** 2.3g | **FIBER:** 0.1g

EASY BOILED EGGS WITH BUTTER

MAKES
2 servings

Jonathan insisted on providing a recipe for boiled eggs—first, because he often enjoys them, but mostly because he thinks that kids will enjoy making them on their own. In fact, he enjoyed setting the timer with me and deciding how many minutes the eggs should cook to have a firm, solid yolk. Don't skip adding the butter to the boiled eggs. If you haven't tried it, it's fantastic!

2 cups water

6 large eggs

Dash of salt

2 tablespoons unsalted butter, softened

1. Bring the water to a boil in a 1-quart saucepan over medium heat. As soon as it begins to boil, use a slotted spoon to lower the eggs into the water.

2. When the water begins to boil again, set a timer for 10 minutes for eggs with a firm, solid yolk. (If you like your yolks more runny, cook the eggs for less time.)

3. When the timer goes off, immediately remove the pan from the heat and use a slotted spoon to remove the eggs from the water. Place the eggs in a bowl of cold water and let cool for at least 15 minutes.

4. When the eggs are cool enough to handle, peel them. Slice the eggs in half, sprinkle with salt, and serve warm topped with the butter.

5. Refrigerate leftover boiled eggs for up to 5 days.

Older kids can manage this recipe alone as long as they know how to use the stovetop and are careful with the boiling water. Younger children might be able to use a slotted spoon to remove the eggs from the water or might enjoy peeling the cooled eggs.

CALORIES: 334 | **FAT:** 27.4g | **PROTEIN:** 19g | **CARBS:** 1.7g | **FIBER:** 0g

EGGS IN A BASKET

MAKES
6 pieces (1 piece per serving)

Like all moms, I love both of my children equally, but when it comes to recipes, I have a few favorites. This is one of them! Maybe it's the smoked Gouda, but I think it's the cream that makes this an amazing dish. The eggs are so creamy, especially if you use the shorter cook time. These are easy to make and are perfect for weekend meal prep, especially if you have capable helpers. Feel free to use whatever cheeses you or your kids prefer. I like these with a little avocado and a grape tomato or two.

12 thin slices deli ham

6 large eggs

¾ cup shredded smoked Gouda cheese (about 3 ounces)

½ teaspoon dried thyme leaves

Dash of salt

Dash of ground black pepper

6 tablespoons heavy cream, divided

Fresh thyme leaves, for garnish (optional)

1. Preheat the oven to 350°F. Lightly grease 6 wells of a standard-size muffin tin.

2. Press two slices of ham into each greased muffin well, forming a cup with the bottom and sides of the muffin tin covered by ham. Be careful not to tear the ham.

3. Crack an egg into each of the ham cups. Do not stir. Top each egg with 2 tablespoons of shredded cheese.

4. Divide the thyme evenly among the ham cups and sprinkle each with salt and pepper. Pour 1 tablespoon of cream into each cup.

5. Bake for 14 to 16 minutes for eggs with soft yolks, or 17 to 20 minutes for fully cooked yolks. Garnish the egg cups with fresh thyme leaves, if desired, and serve.

VARIATION:

HAM AND CHEESE QUICHES. You can beat the eggs, cream, thyme, salt, and pepper together and pour it over the ham and cheese like a quiche, if you prefer. Bake until set and lightly browned, 18 to 22 minutes.

Since the ham slices need to line the muffin tin without tearing, younger kids might need some help or supervision in the beginning. After that, kids can enjoy cracking the eggs into the ham cups. If you're worried about eggshells, your helper can break an egg into a cup or small bowl and then pour the egg into the muffin tin, or an adult can crack the egg and let a younger helper pour it into the tin. Kids can also add the cheese, seasonings, and cream to prepare the dish for the oven. You can allow children to customize this dish by choosing their own cheese and seasonings or adding other ingredients, such as a little chopped bacon.

CALORIES: 300 | **FAT:** 24.5g | **PROTEIN:** 17.2g | **CARBS:** 2.4g | **FIBER:** 0g

OPTION

GRACE'S GOOD MORNING STRAWBERRY PROTEIN SMOOTHIE

MAKES
1 serving

Grace came up with this recipe on her own when she was in middle school. My only question to her was whether it kept her from feeling hungry before lunchtime. When she assured me that it did, I reasoned it wasn't a bad breakfast option, particularly if she was able to make it herself! Using powdered freeze-dried strawberries means that this smoothie can be enjoyed year-round as well.

¾ cup crushed ice

¼ cup heavy cream

¼ cup cold water

1 teaspoon MCT oil or avocado oil

¼ teaspoon strawberry extract (optional)

⅛ teaspoon vanilla extract

2 to 3 drops liquid sweetener (to taste)

2 tablespoons whey protein isolate or egg white protein powder (see Notes)

2 teaspoons unsweetened freeze-dried strawberry powder (see Notes)

2 to 3 strawberries, hulled (optional)

Measure all of the ingredients into a blender. Blend on high for 30 to 40 seconds, until the smoothie is thick and creamy. Serve immediately.

NOTES: *Whey protein isolate has the lactose and casein removed and is generally a better option for blood glucose and insulin. If you're sensitive to whey, egg white protein powder is a nice substitute. In both cases, look for brands that have no added sweeteners and zero carbs. Isopure and Jay Robb are two brands I trust.*

Freeze-dried strawberries are often sold in the baking aisle but can also be shelved with the snacks. Read the ingredient list to make sure that no sugar or sweetener has been added. Trader Joe's brand has no sugar added, but manufacturers sometimes change their products, so always check. To powder the freeze-dried berries, I use a small blender. Store leftover strawberry powder with the desiccant included in the original package. You might surprise your favorite kids of any age with some Strawberry Milk (page 280).

Kids will enjoy powdering the strawberries, but make sure they remove any desiccant from the package before turning on the blender. (Yes, I've made that mistake twice!) Older kids will easily be able to make this smoothie on their own, while younger kids might need a little help measuring the ingredients.

CALORIES: 365 | FAT: 26.2g | PROTEIN: 26.5g | CARBS: 7.5g | FIBER: 1g

CHOCOLATE HAZELNUT MUFFINS

MAKES
12 muffins
(1 per serving)

Chocolate plus hazelnut equals one of my husband's favorite flavor combinations. That big kid used to claim he was buying Nutella for the children, and then one day I found his private stash in the garage. On a high shelf. Those days are over with keto, but I see his grin when he knows that a batch of these muffins is going into the oven. Hazelnut flour not only brings the wonderful flavor of hazelnuts but is lower in total carbs than almond flour—another great reason to bake with it! The coffee powder serves to enhance the chocolate taste but can be omitted.

1⅔ cups hazelnut flour or blanched almond flour

½ cup unsweetened cocoa powder

⅓ cup oat fiber (see Note, page 52)

1½ teaspoons baking powder

1 teaspoon instant coffee powder (optional)

½ teaspoon salt

½ cup (1 stick) unsalted butter, softened

2 ounces (¼ cup) cream cheese, softened

¾ cup granulated sweetener

3 large eggs

⅓ cup hazelnut oil or melted coconut oil

8 drops liquid sweetener

1 teaspoon hazelnut extract

½ teaspoon vanilla extract

¼ cup heavy cream

1. Preheat the oven to 350°F. Line a standard-size muffin tin with paper liners or thoroughly grease the pan.

2. Put the flour, cocoa powder, oat fiber, baking powder, coffee powder (if using), and salt in a medium bowl and whisk until thoroughly combined.

3. In another mixing bowl, cream the butter, cream cheese, and granulated sweetener with a hand mixer. Beat in the eggs, oil, liquid sweetener, and extracts.

4. Add the dry ingredients and the cream to the wet ingredients and mix well by hand. Divide the batter among the prepared wells of the muffin tin, filling them about three-quarters full.

5. Bake for 12 to 16 minutes, until the muffins are firm to a light touch and a toothpick inserted in the center of a muffin comes out clean.

6. Refrigerate leftover muffins for up to a week, or freeze for up to 3 months.

TIP! *Use parchment paper muffin liners for the best results. Little is more frustrating than losing half of your muffin to the paper liner!*

I can envision older kids making this recipe entirely on their own; it would be perfect for those who want to begin baking alone. Younger kids might be pleased with the tasks of mixing the dry ingredients and scooping the batter into the muffin tin. A small ladle or large cookie scoop works well for this purpose, and most kids love the chance to use gadgets! If you're comfortable with raw eggs, save the task of licking the beaters for the child who's been the best listener.

CALORIES: 280 | FAT: 28g | PROTEIN: 14g | CARBS: 5.5g | FIBER: 2.9g | ERYTHRITOL: 14.2g | OAT FIBER: 1.3g

PEANUT BUTTER WAFFLES

MAKES
6 regular waffles or 12 mini waffles (1 regular waffle or 2 mini waffles per serving)

"Peanut, peanut butter! And jelly! Peanut, peanut butter!" There's no jelly in these waffles, but they are great with fresh berries. My kids also like to smear a little peanut butter on top. These are among my favorite waffles, keto or not. Picky J. likes them too, especially when I toss a few low-carb chocolate chips into the batter. Ideally, the waffles should cool just a bit on a cooling rack, but good luck with that. In my house, these usually go straight from the waffle maker to the plate with the kids arguing over who gets the next waffle.

⅓ cup creamy peanut butter

2 ounces (¼ cup) cream cheese, softened

⅓ cup granulated sweetener

4 large eggs

⅓ cup blanched almond flour

¼ cup oat fiber, or 1 tablespoon coconut flour (see Note, page 52)

1 teaspoon baking powder

2 teaspoons vanilla extract

SPECIAL EQUIPMENT:

Regular-size or mini waffle maker

1. Preheat a waffle maker per the manufacturer's instructions.

2. Use a hand mixer to whip the peanut butter and cream cheese until fully combined and smooth. Add the sweetener and blend until dissolved. Add the eggs, one at a time, beating well after each addition. Stir in the remaining ingredients to form a thick batter.

3. Pour about ¼ cup of the batter into the waffle maker (or 2 heaping tablespoons if using a mini waffle maker) and cook until the waffle is golden brown and slightly crisp. Repeat with the remaining batter, making a total of 6 regular or 12 mini waffles. Serve warm.

4. Refrigerate leftovers for up to a week, or freeze for up to 3 months.

TIP! *Make a double batch on the weekend and store them in packs of four. Refrigerate what you think your family will eat for the week and put the rest in the freezer. Your future self will thank you!*

Younger kids will get a kick out of measuring the ingredients, mixing up the batter, and using the waffle maker. Be sure to supervise so that no one gets burned. We use a pair of silicone-tipped tongs to remove the waffles from the waffle maker when they are done.

CALORIES: 264 | **FAT:** 22.3g | **PROTEIN:** 11.6g | **CARBS:** 5.7g | **FIBER:** 2.9g | **ERYTHRITOL:** 7.4g | **OAT FIBER:** 2g

SAUSAGE-CRUSTED MEAT LOVER'S QUICHE

MAKES
8 servings

Perfect for brunch or a potluck, this quiche has been well loved by everyone who has tasted it. The sausage crust is a nice alternative to soggy low-carb alternatives and adds heft to a dish often thought of as "light." The ratio of eggs to cream yields a tender, almost silky filling that allows the bacon and ham to take center stage. I once called this the Barnyard Quiche since it features the best of the barnyard! While there are no veggies in it, feel free to toss in some steamed broccoli, chopped green onions or spinach, or whatever favorites your own little critters will enjoy.

1 pound breakfast sausage, room temperature (remove any casings)

⅓ cup blanched almond flour or crushed pork rinds

⅓ cup grated Parmesan cheese

1 pound bacon (about 14 slices), cooked and chopped, divided

8 ounces ham, cubed

2 cups shredded cheddar cheese (about 8 ounces)

7 large eggs

1½ cups heavy cream

⅛ teaspoon salt (omit if the bacon and ham are salty)

TIP! *To make this quiche in a 9 by 13-inch baking dish, increase the number of eggs to nine and bake the quiche for 45 to 55 minutes, until set.*

1. Preheat the oven to 350°F. Line the bottom of a 9-inch springform pan with parchment paper.

2. Use your hands or a hand mixer to combine the sausage, almond flour, and Parmesan. Press the sausage mixture firmly across the bottom and up the sides of the lined springform pan, making sure the sausage crust reaches to just below the rim of the dish; it will shrink and pull away from the sides as it cooks.

3. Sprinkle the bacon, ham, and cheddar cheese evenly over the crust, reserving 2 tablespoons of bacon to sprinkle over the egg mixture just before placing the pan in the oven.

4. Use a blender or whisk to beat the eggs, cream, and salt until frothy. Pour the egg mixture over the bacon, ham, and cheese. Top with the remaining bacon.

5. Bake for 60 to 75 minutes, until the eggs are set in the center and the sausage is fully cooked. If the top begins to brown too quickly, cover the pan loosely with aluminum foil and continue baking.

6. Remove from the oven and let the quiche sit for at least 10 minutes before removing the outer ring of the springform pan. Slice and serve.

7. Refrigerate leftovers for up to 6 days, or freeze individual portions for up to 3 months. Reheat in the microwave on low power or enjoy chilled.

This is the perfect teen or tween recipe. From mixing the sausage crust to pressing it into the pan, this dish is fun to make! Multiple hands can help with the pressing, sprinkling, and mixing. Depending on their ages, children can make the crust, crack the eggs, beat the egg mixture, or sprinkle in the bacon, ham, and cheese.

CALORIES: 886 | **FAT:** 73.6g | **PROTEIN:** 48.1g | **CARBS:** 6.4g | **FIBER:** 0g

GRACE'S GOOD MORNING CHOCOLATE PEANUT BUTTER SMOOTHIE

MAKES
1 serving

Chocolate and peanut butter seems like a perfect start to any morning, especially if it's a school day. Except for the noise of the blender, this is a peaceful, quick breakfast. I hear that it's even better alongside a slice or two of bacon!

2 teaspoons unsweetened cocoa powder, plus more for garnish if desired

1 tablespoon warm water

¾ cup crushed ice

2 tablespoons whey protein isolate or egg white protein powder (see Notes, page 86)

1 tablespoon creamy peanut butter

¼ cup cool water (omit if using almond milk)

¼ cup heavy cream or unsweetened almond milk

1 teaspoon MCT oil, or 2 teaspoons avocado oil

¼ teaspoon vanilla extract

¼ teaspoon salt

4 drops liquid sweetener, or to taste

1. Make a chocolate syrup by mixing the cocoa powder and warm water in a small bowl until the powder dissolves.

2. Put the ice, whey protein isolate, peanut butter, chocolate syrup, water (if using), cream, oil, vanilla extract, salt, and sweetener in a small blender and blend well.

3. Adjust the sweetener to taste, pour into a tall glass, and serve immediately. Dust the top with more cocoa powder, if desired.

TIP! *For an even quicker breakfast, you can blend all of the ingredients except the ice in advance and store the mixture in the blender cup. When you're ready to enjoy your smoothie, add the ice, blend, and you're off!*

Like the strawberry smoothie on page 86, older kids can definitely make this recipe on their own. If you're making it with a younger child, it can be fun to point out that mixing the cocoa powder with water rather than cream or oil helps it dissolve more easily. You could even experiment with each and talk about why the cocoa powder mixes most easily with water.

CALORIES: 440 | **FAT:** 34.6g | **PROTEIN:** 30.7g | **CARBS:** 7.2g | **FIBER:** 2.7g

SAVORY BREAKFAST CREPES

MAKES
9 crepes (3 per serving)

Grace was about eight years old when she discovered "creeps." We had been out shopping, and as we took a break for dinner, she spied a restaurant named "Coffee and Crepes." She squealed when she read the sign as "coffee and creeps"! This was before our keto reformation, and I was happy to introduce her to the world of sweet and savory crepes. We thought those days were over until I figured out how to make a low-carb version. Now, once again, the possibilities are endless!

SAVORY CREPES:

4 large eggs

2 ounces (¼ cup) cream cheese, softened

2 tablespoons heavy cream

¼ cup blanched almond flour

2 tablespoons oat fiber, or 2 teaspoons coconut flour (see Note, page 52)

⅛ teaspoon baking powder

Ghee, for the pan

FILLING:

4 ounces (½ cup) cream cheese, softened

9 slices bacon, cooked

4 large eggs, softly scrambled

¾ cup shredded cheddar cheese (about 3 ounces)

1 batch Creamy Bacon Gravy (page 80)

Sliced green onion tops, for garnish

1. Make the crepes: Put all of the crepe ingredients except the ghee in a blender and blend until smooth.

2. Heat a 7-inch nonstick skillet over medium heat and add just enough ghee to coat the bottom of the pan. Pour a thin layer of batter over the melted ghee and tilt the pan to completely cover the bottom with the batter. Cook the crepe until lightly browned, 4 to 6 minutes, then flip it over and cook until lightly browned on the other side, 2 to 3 minutes.

3. Remove the crepe from the pan and place on a cooling rack to cool. Repeat with the remaining batter to make a total of 9 crepes, layering parchment paper between the finished crepes.

4. Fill the crepes: Schmear 2 teaspoons of cream cheese down the center of each crepe. Top the cream cheese with a slice of bacon. Divide the scrambled eggs evenly among the crepes, placing the eggs on top of the bacon. Sprinkle 1 tablespoon of the cheddar cheese over the eggs in each crepe. Beginning at one edge, roll each crepe into a cylinder, rolling parallel to the filling.

5. Place 3 crepes on each plate and top with ½ cup of the gravy just before serving. Garnish with the green onions.

6. If there are leftovers, it's best to store the crepes separately from the filling and gravy. Refrigerate the components for up to 4 days.

TIP! *The crepes can be made in advance and stored unfilled in the refrigerator for up to 2 weeks or in the freezer for up to a month. Be sure to place sheets of parchment paper or wax paper between the crepes when storing them.*

CALORIES: 731 | FAT: 61g | PROTEIN: 37.7g | CARBS: 6g | FIBER: 1g | OAT FIBER: 2g

Younger children might have a difficult time frying the crepes, but they can crack the eggs and press the buttons on the blender. Tweens and teens can practice their skills cooking the crepes and learning how to adjust the cooktop heat. As for the filling, it's probably too complicated for younger children, but they might be able to add the bacon or sprinkle the cheese on top of the eggs. Again, older kids can learn a lot from stuffing the crepes and making the Creamy Bacon Gravy. Knowing how to make crepes is a fun party trick they can show off at sleepovers or use to impress their future college friends. In fact, once they know how to make crepes, they can explore lots of filling options, allowing for different dietary restrictions and flavor preferences.

SCRAMBLED EGGS TWO WAYS

MAKES
1 serving

Eggs and bacon is a classic breakfast and a terrific option for a low-carb diet. In our house, there's a bit of a debate about how the eggs should be cooked. Here, we present two options for you to try: firmly cooked and softly scrambled. See which one is your favorite! We use precooked bacon because it's faster and easier, but you can begin with raw bacon; just be sure to cook it until it's done.

J'S EGGS AND BACON

Jonathan makes this breakfast four out of seven days per week. He never seems to tire of it, and it keeps his thirteen-year-old body full longer than any other meal! If you don't like your eggs quite so firm, check out my version, opposite, for the way scrambled eggs *should* be prepared. Of course, J. will tell you that his version is better!

4 large eggs

4 slices bacon, cooked

Salt and pepper

1. Crack the eggs into a tall glass. Use a fork to beat them until uniformly yellow.

2. Heat the bacon in a 9-inch skillet over high heat. When the bacon sizzles and becomes crisp, remove it from the pan, using a pair of tongs to coat the skillet with bacon fat.

3. Pour the beaten eggs into the hot skillet. They will sizzle when they hit the pan. Let the eggs cook for 20 to 30 seconds before stirring. Move the spatula from one side of the pan to the other to sweep the eggs into a curtain-like texture. When the eggs become firm and lightly browned on one side, flip them over and cook until just browned on the other side.

4. Remove the eggs from the pan, sprinkle with salt and pepper, and serve with the bacon.

Tweens and teens can easily make this recipe on their own as long as you're comfortable with them using the stovetop.

CALORIES: 460 | **FAT:** 32.4g | **PROTEIN:** 36g | **CARBS:** 2.8g | **FIBER:** 0g

MOM'S EGGS

I like to think of this version of scrambled eggs as being for people with a refined palate. These eggs are soft and buttery—a perfect way to ease into the day. You can serve them with bacon or sausage or enjoy them plain. A sprinkle of your favorite cheese is also a perfect accompaniment.

1 teaspoon unsalted butter

2 large eggs, beaten

Salt and pepper

1. Melt the butter in a 7-inch skillet over low heat. Pour the eggs into the skillet. Use a spatula to scramble the eggs, stirring frequently.

2. When the eggs begin to form soft curds, 2 to 3 minutes, turn off the heat. Continue stirring until the eggs are just set and still slightly shiny.

3. Remove the eggs from the pan and place on a plate. Sprinkle with salt and pepper and serve.

Armed with a spatula and some supervision, even younger kids can try their hand at these softly scrambled eggs, although adults will need to supervise the stovetop heat setting. Teens and tweens can prepare this recipe with confidence.

CALORIES: 225 | **FAT:** 18.3g | **PROTEIN:** 12.6g | **CARBS:** 1.2g | **FIBER:** 0g

VEGGIE BACON CREAM CHEESE SPREAD

MAKES
1¼ cups
(2 tablespoons per serving)

Oh yeah, this spread is a favorite savory option. It is a treat not only on Sesame Bagels (page 64), but also on bagel sandwiches or served with keto crackers or simple grilled meats for a bump in fat and flavor. If you like, you can thin it with a little heavy cream and broth to give it more of a diplike consistency. The dip is great with bacon chips, cheese chips, or crudités.

1 (8-ounce) package cream cheese, softened

½ teaspoon salt

½ teaspoon garlic powder

¼ teaspoon onion powder

3 tablespoons cooked and finely chopped bacon

3 tablespoons finely diced carrots

3 tablespoons finely diced red bell peppers

2 tablespoons finely diced celery

2 tablespoons finely diced red onions

1. Use a spatula or hand mixer to thoroughly combine the cream cheese, salt, garlic powder, and onion powder. Stir in the bacon, carrots, bell peppers, celery, and red onions by hand until the ingredients are evenly distributed. Refrigerate for at least 2 hours before serving.

2. Refrigerate the spread for up to a week.

TIP! *If you don't want to buy large quantities of the veggies, head to your grocery store salad bar. You can easily pick up only what you need for this recipe for a couple of dollars.*

 This is the perfect opportunity for older children to practice those knife skills! Once mastered, this recipe is a breeze to put together.

CALORIES: 89 | **FAT:** 8.4g | **PROTEIN:** 2g | **CARBS:** 1.9g | **FIBER:** 0.2g

CINNAMON MAPLE CREPES

MAKES
9 crepes (3 per serving)

If you enjoy the Savory Breakfast Crepes on page 96, you can easily switch out the filling for something sweet. My biggest kid, David, adores these even though he will tell you that he doesn't like sweets so much anymore. These remind him of a breakfast dish from his childhood, so I always put an extra crepe or two on his plate.

SWEET CREPES:

4 large eggs

2 ounces (¼ cup) cream cheese, softened

¼ cup blanched almond flour

2 tablespoons oat fiber, or 2 teaspoons coconut flour (see Note, page 52)

2 tablespoons heavy cream

2 tablespoons granulated or powdered sweetener

½ teaspoon vanilla extract

⅛ teaspoon baking powder

Dash of ground cinnamon

Ghee, for the pan

CINNAMON MAPLE FILLING:

4 ounces (½ cup) cream cheese, softened

¼ cup powdered sweetener

3 drops liquid sweetener

½ teaspoon ground cinnamon, plus more for sprinkling

¼ teaspoon maple extract

⅛ teaspoon vanilla extract

¼ cup heavy cream

¼ cup freshly whipped cream, for garnish (optional)

Fresh berries of choice, for serving (optional)

1. Make the crepes: Put all of the crepe ingredients except the ghee in a blender and blend until smooth.

2. Heat a 7-inch nonstick skillet over medium heat and add just enough ghee to coat the bottom of the pan. Pour a thin layer of batter over the melted ghee and tilt the pan to completely cover the bottom with the batter. Cook the crepe until lightly browned, 4 to 6 minutes, then flip it over and cook until lightly browned on the other side, 2 to 3 minutes.

3. Remove the crepe from the pan and place on a cooling rack to cool. Repeat with the remaining batter to make a total of 9 crepes, layering parchment paper between the finished crepes.

4. Make the filling: Put the cream cheese, sweeteners, cinnamon, and extracts in a bowl. Use a hand mixer to mix until well blended. Add the cream and mix until light and fluffy.

5. Fill the crepes: Place a heaping tablespoon of the filling down the center of a crepe. Begin at one edge and roll the crepe into a cylinder, rolling parallel to the filling. Repeat with the remaining filling and crepes.

6. Place 3 crepes on each plate and sprinkle with cinnamon. Garnish with whipped cream and serve with fresh berries, if desired.

7. Refrigerate leftovers for up to 2 days, or freeze for up to a month.

TIP! *The crepes can be made in advance and stored unfilled in the refrigerator for up to 2 weeks or in the freezer for up to a month. Be sure to place sheets of parchment paper or wax paper between the crepes when storing them.*

CALORIES: 474 | FAT: 43.9g | PROTEIN: 14.7g | CARBS: 6.4g | FIBER: 1g | ERYTHRITOL: 24.6g | OAT FIBER: 2g

Younger kids can help blend the batter, but cooking the crepes is better left to older kids or adults. Young ones might enjoy mixing up the filling and rolling the crepes. You could save the special job of sprinkling on the cinnamon for the younger set as well. Tweens and teens can have fun making these with friends and varying the fillings, such as by omitting the cinnamon and adding 2 tablespoons of peanut butter.

SHEET PAN BLUEBERRY PANCAKES

MAKES
6 servings

If you've ever been the sentinel at the stove flipping pancakes, then you know the dilemma: do people begin eating as the pancakes come off the skillet, waiting their turn, or do you call everyone to the table at once when the entire batch is cooked, but no longer fresh and hot? Using a quarter sheet pan to bake all of the batter at once eliminates that problem. Pull the pan from the oven, cut the pancake into squares, and everyone can sit down to a hot breakfast together.

---

1 tablespoon white vinegar

¾ cup heavy cream

1 cup blanched almond flour

½ cup oat fiber, or 3 tablespoons coconut flour (see Note, page 52)

¼ teaspoon salt

½ teaspoon baking powder

⅓ cup granulated sweetener

3 large eggs, beaten

2 tablespoons unsalted butter, melted

1 teaspoon vanilla extract

4 drops liquid sweetener

½ cup fresh blueberries

Low-carb maple syrup, for serving

1. Preheat the oven to 350°F. Line a 9 by 13-inch rimmed baking sheet with parchment paper.

2. Mix the vinegar into the cream and set aside.

3. Put the dry ingredients in a large bowl and mix together. Add the beaten eggs, melted butter, vanilla extract, liquid sweetener, and cream and vinegar mixture and stir with a spatula until just combined; do not overmix. Gently fold in the blueberries.

4. Pour the batter onto the lined baking sheet. Bake until set and just golden, 24 to 28 minutes. Cut into squares and serve with maple syrup.

5. Refrigerate leftovers for up to 5 days, or freeze for up to a month.

TIP! *For thinner pancakes, you can use a 10 by 14-inch jelly roll pan and shorten the baking time to 20 to 24 minutes.*

The ease of this recipe gives you a lot of opportunities to involve older children. From mixing the vinegar into the cream to make "buttermilk" to folding the berries into the batter, this is a perfect first recipe for them to make on their own. And it's a great way for them to impress their friends at sleepovers.

CALORIES: 291 | FAT: 26.8g | PROTEIN: 8.1g | CARBS: 5.6g | FIBER: 2.3g | ERYTHRITOL: 12.3g | OAT FIBER: 4g

BACON, EGG, AND CHEESE BREAKFAST TACOS

MAKES
4 tacos
(2 servings)

Feed me this breakfast every morning for 365 days, and I'd still look forward to having it on day 366! Simple, cheap, fast, filling, and tasty—that's a perfect start to any day. This recipe makes a breakfast taco that can be eaten on the go. We fill ours with a schmear of cream cheese, softly scrambled eggs, shredded cheddar cheese, and green onions, but there's really no wrong way to fill it. You can try ham, sausage, boiled eggs, bell peppers, spinach, or any combination you like. Prepare the shells and fillings ahead of time so that the family can DIY breakfast whenever they want.

TACO SHELLS:

4 thick slices cheddar cheese

8 slices cooked bacon, halved

FILLINGS:

2 tablespoons cream cheese, softened

2 eggs, lightly scrambled

½ cup shredded cheddar cheese (about 2 ounces)

1 green onion top, chopped

TIP! *We typically use cheddar cheese for the taco shells, but provolone, Havarti, Gouda, and Swiss work well, too. The key is to use thick slices. If the cheese is too thin, the shells will be too delicate. You can omit the bacon, but it is more than a tasty token; it helps hold the crispy cheese shell together as you eat the taco!*

1. Make the taco shells: Lay a piece of parchment paper that is at least 5 inches square on a plate. Place a slice of cheese on the paper. Place 4 half-slices of bacon on top of the cheese, leaving at least a ½-inch gap in the center of the cheese.

2. Microwave on full power for 50 to 65 seconds, until the cheese is lightly browned around the edges. If it is not beginning to firm up, microwave in additional 20-second bursts.

3. The cheese should remain pliable for 15 to 20 seconds after you remove it from the microwave. Fold the cheese over the side of a baking dish or the handle of a wooden spoon to create a taco shell shape. As the cheese cools, it will harden.

4. Repeat with the remaining cheese and bacon, making a total of 4 taco shells.

5. Assemble the tacos: Spread one-quarter of the cream cheese on the inside of each taco shell. Divide the scrambled eggs among the shells and top each with 2 tablespoons of shredded cheese. Sprinkle the green onions evenly over the tacos just before serving.

6. Refrigerate leftover shells and fillings separately for up to 3 days. Fill the shells just before serving.

If a child can use scissors, they can cut the parchment paper to size. To avoid burns, removing the cheese from the microwave is a task that should fall to an older child or adult. Brainstorm with the kids what toppings they might like. If possible, have them help prep the fillings by scrambling the eggs, shredding the cheese, or chopping the green onion. A light hand is needed to schmear the cream cheese without breaking the shell.

CALORIES: 488 | FAT: 38.5g | PROTEIN: 30g | CARBS: 3.2g | FIBER: 0g

CREAMY BAKED EGGS

MAKES
2 servings

This dish is warm, rich, and creamy and an easy way to have a hot breakfast without watching over the stove. I also enjoy making this recipe for guests because it can easily be doubled or tripled. Serve it with bacon or 90-Second Toast (page 68) to dip in the runny yolks. It is extra yummy served over Easy Cheesy Biscuits (page 54). If you don't have fresh thyme, you can use ¼ teaspoon of dried, but if you've ever considered growing thyme, this dish will make it worth your while.

4 large eggs

⅓ cup heavy cream

2 tablespoons unsalted butter, cut into 6 pieces

¼ cup shredded cheddar cheese (about 1 ounce)

1 teaspoon fresh thyme leaves

1. Preheat the oven to 300°F. Lightly grease a small, shallow baking dish such as a gratin dish.

2. Break the eggs into the dish one at a time, spacing them so that the yolks are about 1 inch apart.

3. Pour the cream over the eggs. The yolks should be just visible above the cream.

4. Scatter the pieces of butter over the eggs and cream. Sprinkle the cheese and thyme over the top.

5. Bake until just set, 12 to 15 minutes. Let cool for 8 to 10 minutes before serving.

6. Refrigerate leftovers for up to 3 days.

TIPS! *If your family isn't a fan of runny egg yolks, then baking the dish longer will fully cook the yolks.*

Add 3 pieces of cooked, chopped bacon before pouring in the cream to make this an extra hearty meal.

This recipe is fun for younger kids who can break eggs into the baking dish or slowly pour the cream over the top. You can also solicit help sprinkling in the cheese and thyme. Children who are just learning to cook might want to tackle this recipe on their own.

CALORIES: 468 | **FAT:** 42.5g | **PROTEIN:** 20.3g | **CARBS:** 2.8g | **FIBER:** 0g

CHAPTER 5:
SAVORY SAUCES AND SEASONINGS

We've included a chapter on sauces and seasonings to provide kid-friendly options and to provide basic flavors that can be mixed and matched to please a variety of palates. These simple recipes are a great way to involve kids in the kitchen. If they can measure and stir, they can make most of these recipes. The exceptions might be the three that need to be heated or simmered, but most middle school and older kids can probably handle those, too.

Grace and Jonathan love dipping sauces. In fact, they treat them like sides. Their top three tend to be universal favorites—ketchup, BBQ sauce, and ranch. We've included recipes for all of those, plus a few other classics, like Sweet Mustard Sauce and a chicken tender sauce styled after a fast-food favorite.

We make our own sauces because commercial brands tend to be packed with sugar and starches. Not only is it super easy to make sauces from scratch, but the homemade versions are less expensive and taste better, especially when you can adjust the seasonings to your preference. All of these sauces taste great with burgers, grilled chicken, Drive-Thru Chicken Tenders (page 136), and Cheesy Corn Dog Nuggets (page 182). The Simple Cheese Sauce is a favorite over eggs and any type of vegetable, cooked or raw.

The taco seasoning and its nacho cheese variation are used to create tasty favorites. We have given you ideas for using these mixes to season meats, make Nacho Chips (page 206), and make flavorful dips. For easy meal prep, pick a lazy day and make up a batch of each! You will likely devise your own ways to use these seasonings. You might even be inspired to create your own dry seasoning mixes.

Have fun sprinkling, coating, squirting, dipping, and dunking! Life can be as flavorful as you make it.

TACO SEASONING

MAKES
about ¾ cup
(1½ teaspoons
per serving)

A great taco seasoning is like a great backpack: it can take you anywhere you want to go, as long as you're going southwest. These basic taco spices can be used to season ground beef, chicken, or pork, which can then be used to make tacos, nachos, or even soup. Use your imagination one tablespoon of flavor at a time. We've found that two tablespoons will season one pound of meat nicely. Also, please try the Nacho Cheese Seasoning variation. Your family will love it on pork rinds, cheese chips, or even pepperoni chips.

¼ cup chili powder

2 tablespoons ground cumin

2 tablespoons paprika

2 teaspoons garlic powder

2 teaspoons onion powder

½ teaspoon salt

Put all of the ingredients in an airtight jar and mix to combine, or seal the lid and shake to combine. Store in the pantry or in the refrigerator. Use within 3 months for the best flavor.

VARIATION:

NACHO CHEESE SEASONING. To the ingredients listed, add ⅓ cup cheddar cheese powder (or ¼ cup if you'll be using the seasoning on cheese chips). Note that some commercial cheese powders are better than others. Anthony's is the brand I prefer because it does not contain maltodextrin or other food starches. Please read the ingredients and the nutritional information before purchasing.

NOTE: *Over time, this seasoning mix might get a little clumpy. Using a food-safe desiccant packet (which you can order online) can help reduce moisture and keep the spices from sticking together.*

 There are lots of ways to teach kids about using measuring spoons here. Use this as an opportunity to discuss ratios and proportions and to multiply or divide fractions by making a larger or smaller batch of seasoning.

CALORIES: 12 | FAT: 0.5g | PROTEIN: 0.6g | CARBS: 2g | FIBER: 1.1g

OPTION

BBQ SAUCE

MAKES
about 1½ cups
(2 tablespoons
per serving)

This is the fourth BBQ sauce recipe I've made and the first that both kids have truly loved. It's likely because the flavors are subtle, the sauce is thick and a bit sweet, and it tastes like the commercial brands they once loved.

1 (8-ounce) can tomato sauce

3 tablespoons tomato paste

2 tablespoons apple cider vinegar

1 tablespoon bacon fat or unsalted butter

1 tablespoon Worcestershire sauce

¼ cup granulated sweetener

½ teaspoon garlic powder

½ teaspoon onion powder

½ teaspoon smoked paprika

½ teaspoon salt

½ teaspoon maple extract

⅛ teaspoon cayenne pepper (optional)

1. Put the tomato sauce, tomato paste, vinegar, and bacon fat in a small saucepan and whisk to combine.

2. Bring to a simmer over low heat. Simmer for 4 to 6 minutes, stirring occasionally. The sauce should thicken as it simmers. Once thickened, add the Worcestershire sauce, sweetener, garlic powder, onion powder, smoked paprika, and salt.

3. Remove from the heat and stir in the maple extract and cayenne pepper, if using. Use immediately, or refrigerate for up to 10 days.

TIP! *After making this sauce, I portion it into 4-ounce canning jars. Those jars can be frozen for up to 6 months so that fresh BBQ sauce is ready whenever you need it.*

Like most of the recipes in this chapter, kids can enjoy getting involved measuring and mixing, doubling or halving. Because the sauce simmers, kids will need to be able to use the stovetop with or without supervision. Discuss with them how simmering the sauce helps it thicken and gives the final product more flavor.

CALORIES: 20 | **FAT:** 1.3g | **PROTEIN:** 0.4g | **CARBS:** 2.1g | **FIBER:** 0.5g | **ERYTHRITOL:** 4.7g

SWEET MUSTARD SAUCE

MAKES
about ½ cup
(2 tablespoons
per serving)

Sweet, tangy, and easy to love, this sauce is perfect with the Drive-Thru Chicken Tenders (page 136), but it also makes a great spread for Homemade Hoagies (page 174). It can be used as a dip for raw veggies as well.

¼ cup avocado oil or light olive oil

3 tablespoons prepared yellow mustard

1 tablespoon apple cider vinegar

1 tablespoon mayonnaise

¼ teaspoon garlic powder

¼ teaspoon salt

¼ teaspoon cayenne pepper, plus more for sprinkling (optional)

4 to 6 drops liquid sweetener (to taste)

Put all of the ingredients in a small bowl and whisk to combine. Sprinkle more cayenne on top, if desired. Use immediately, or refrigerate for up to 10 days.

TIP! *For a creamier, milder sauce, add a bit more mayonnaise 1 teaspoon at a time.*

Let kids mix this up for themselves and package it for lunches if they want. Younger kids might enjoy using a whisk to incorporate the oil into the sauce. You can also let kids adjust the amount of mayonnaise to make the sauce more or less creamy.

SAVORY SAUCES AND SEASONINGS

CALORIES: 152 | **FAT:** 17g | **PROTEIN:** 0.4g | **CARBS:** 0.4g | **FIBER:** 0.3g

RANCH DIPPING SAUCE

MAKES
about 1½ cups
(2 tablespoons
per serving)

I've toned down the seasonings a bit in this recipe, with less garlic and onion powder to please younger palates. Feel free to kick up the volume if you prefer a zestier flavor. I've listed the dill weed as optional because Grace isn't fond of dill, but I love it. Some recipes are made for compromise!

1 cup mayonnaise

½ cup sour cream

½ teaspoon white vinegar

1 teaspoon dried parsley

½ teaspoon dried chives

½ teaspoon dried dill weed (optional)

½ teaspoon garlic powder

½ teaspoon onion powder

¼ teaspoon ground black pepper

⅛ teaspoon salt

Put all of the ingredients in a small bowl and stir until smooth and creamy. Refrigerate for at least 30 minutes before serving. The sauce will keep in the refrigerator for up to a week.

Younger children can help measure and mix, while older kids can easily make this recipe on their own. Encourage them to play with the spices, especially adding more or less dill and/or garlic powder. They can also mix up the spices and store them for an even quicker ranch dipping sauce when needed.

CALORIES: 154 | **FAT:** 18.1g | **PROTEIN:** 0.3g | **CARBS:** 0.3g | **FIBER:** 0g

KETCHUP

MAKES
about 1½ cups
(2 tablespoons
per serving)

Like the homemade BBQ sauce on page 114, I have simplified this ketchup recipe to make it more kid-friendly. The end result is worth the work because it can actually be passed off as the real deal. In fact, I like this better than any commercial ketchup I've tried. And it's cheap! Most 8-ounce cans of tomato sauce cost less than 30 cents, which is certainly budget-friendly.

1 (8-ounce) can tomato sauce

3 tablespoons tomato paste

2 tablespoons apple cider vinegar

1 tablespoon bacon fat or unsalted butter

¼ cup granulated sweetener

2 drops liquid sweetener (optional)

½ teaspoon salt

Put the tomato sauce, tomato paste, vinegar, and bacon fat in a small saucepan and whisk to combine. Bring to a simmer over low heat, then continue to simmer until slightly thickened, 4 to 5 minutes. Stir in the sweetener(s) and salt. Use immediately, or refrigerate for up to 10 days.

TIP! *Like the BBQ sauce, this ketchup can be portioned into 4-ounce canning jars and frozen for up to 6 months.*

Definitely let your children help make this sauce. Not only is it simple, but they will be more likely to enjoy it if they participate in making it. Helping make it also gives them bragging rights to their friends, many of whom might never have realized that ketchup can be homemade.

CALORIES: 19 | **FAT:** 1.3g | **PROTEIN:** 0.4g | **CARBS:** 1.6g | **FIBER:** 0.5g | **ERYTHRITOL:** 4.7g

GRACE'S CHICKEN TENDER SAUCE

MAKES
about 1¼ cups
(2 tablespoons
per serving)

Without a doubt, this is Grace's favorite sauce. In fact, she spent several weeks developing this recipe and getting the proportions just right. We use homemade BBQ sauce (page 114) to make this luscious condiment, so the end result might be a bit different if you use a different kind of BBQ sauce. You can add more mustard if you like and adjust the sweetener to your family's tastes. Our favorite way to use this sauce is for the chicken tenders on page 136, but it's good with any grilled meat or fresh veggies.

1 cup mayonnaise

1 heaping tablespoon low-carb BBQ sauce

2 teaspoons prepared yellow mustard

2 teaspoons lemon juice

3 drops liquid sweetener

Put all of the ingredients in a small bowl and stir to combine. Refrigerate until ready to use. The sauce will keep in the refrigerator for up to a week.

Children who are old enough to use measuring spoons to measure accurately can make this tasty sauce on their own. Let them adjust the BBQ sauce and/or mustard ½ teaspoon at a time if they want to add more or less. The amount of sweetener can also be adjusted to their tastes.

CALORIES: 163 | **FAT:** 19.5g | **PROTEIN:** 0g | **CARBS:** 0.3g | **FIBER:** 0g

PESTO

MAKES
1½ cups
(2 tablespoons
per serving)

Pesto isn't just for pasta! Try it on 90-Second Toast (page 68), eggs, burgers, or grilled meats. It's a great way to add fat and flavor. This recipe calls for pine nuts, as is traditional, but we've also used roasted pecans, macadamia nuts, pistachios, and walnuts; the roasted pecans were our favorite. We grow our own fresh basil, which is fun because the plants seem to thrive on being cut. The more you trim, the more they grow—perfect for making a large batch of pesto.

3 cloves garlic, peeled

⅓ cup pine nuts or roasted pecans

3 cups tightly packed fresh basil leaves, divided

¾ cup grated Parmesan cheese

2 tablespoons lemon juice

½ teaspoon salt

¾ cup extra-light olive oil or avocado oil

1. Put the garlic in a food processor and pulse until chopped. Add the nuts and pulse just until they are in small pieces.

2. Scrape down the sides of the food processor and add 2 cups of the basil, the Parmesan, lemon juice, and salt. Pulse until the basil is just chopped. Pour in the oil and pulse just until combined.

3. Remove the pesto from the food processor. Roughly chop the remaining 1 cup of basil with a knife, then stir the chopped basil into the pesto.

4. Transfer the pesto to small jars and drizzle at least a teaspoon of olive oil over the top of each jar to keep the pesto from browning. It will keep in the refrigerator for up to a week or in the freezer for up to 3 months.

TIP! *Basil tends to attract small green bugs, so make sure to wash it in salty water. We soak it briefly, pick off any vermin, and then allow the basil to dry before tossing the leaves into the food processor.*

Whether you're making one batch or several, this recipe is a great way to spend time with your kids. Have them help harvest the basil if you're growing it. The basil needs to be washed and the leaves picked from the stems. Young fingers can pack the measuring cup with basil leaves and then add them to the food processor. My children also enjoyed learning how to peel garlic. After the pesto is made, have the kids help fill the jars and then top each jar with olive oil to prevent browning.

CALORIES: 168 | **FAT:** 17.3g | **PROTEIN:** 2.5g | **CARBS:** 1.4g | **FIBER:** 0.3g

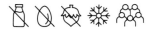

NO-COOK PIZZA SAUCE

MAKES
1 cup (¼ cup per serving)

This simple sauce can be used on pizza or as a dipping sauce for Cheesy Breadsticks (page 56) or Crispy Pizza Chips (page 202). The seasoning in this recipe is minimal to appeal to younger palates. If you like a little more flavor, you can increase the spices, add dried basil or oregano, or even add a few red pepper flakes for a bit of heat.

1 (8-ounce) can tomato sauce

1 heaping tablespoon Italian seasoning

¼ heaping teaspoon onion powder

⅛ teaspoon garlic powder

⅛ teaspoon salt

Put all of the ingredients in a small bowl and stir to combine. Use immediately as a topping for pizza, or let sit for at least 20 minutes before serving as a dip. The sauce will keep in the refrigerator for up to a week.

TIP! *This sauce is freezer-friendly. You can freeze it in ice cube trays before storing the "sauce cubes" in a freezer bag for up to 3 months. Remove as many or as few cubes as you need when making pizza.*

Similar to ketchup or BBQ sauce, you can use this recipe to show kids that making your own pizza sauce not only saves money but also allows you to control the ingredients. You can avoid sweeteners and food starches, which lowers the carb count and also makes the sauce taste much better once taste buds have adapted.

CALORIES: 17 | **FAT:** 0.2g | **PROTEIN:** 0.8g | **CARBS:** 2.7g | **FIBER:** 1.2g

YUM-YUM SAUCE

MAKES
about 1½ cups
(2 tablespoons
per serving)

This mayonnaise-based sauce is ubiquitous at Japanese restaurants and seems to taste good on any meat or veggie it touches. Whether you serve it with shrimp, chicken, pork, or beef, this sauce is subtle and sweet and adds a nice bump of fat to your plate.

---

1 cup mayonnaise

3 tablespoons water

2 tablespoons melted unsalted butter

2 tablespoons granulated sweetener, or equivalent amount of liquid sweetener

2 tablespoons unsweetened rice vinegar, or 1 tablespoon apple cider vinegar

2 teaspoons tomato paste

1 teaspoon garlic powder

1 teaspoon paprika

¼ teaspoon salt

Put all of the ingredients in a small bowl and whisk to combine. Refrigerate for at least 3 hours or overnight to allow the flavors to meld before serving. Refrigerate leftover sauce for up to a week.

Encourage children who can measure with confidence to make this sauce on their own. Because this recipe uses primarily tablespoon and teaspoon amounts, it's a good time to point out the differences in volume to kids who are just learning how to measure.

CALORIES: 153 | **FAT:** 18.1g | **PROTEIN:** 0.1g | **CARBS:** 0.2g | **FIBER:** 0g

SIMPLE CHEESE SAUCE

MAKES
about 2 cups
(¼ cup per
serving)

I think I was in college before I ate broccoli without cheese sauce. It wasn't the broccoli I loved! The secret to creating a delicious and silky-smooth cheese sauce is patience, low heat, and a little more patience. Use a cheese that you really enjoy and you've got a perfect recipe. Make sure to let the cheese come to room temperature and to whisk it in a little at a time after removing the pan from the heat. If the cheese gets too hot, the proteins in the cheese will become stringy and the sauce will be oily. The optional cayenne pepper and garlic powder add just a bit of zing to the sauce. If your family prefers plainer flavors, you can omit those spices.

½ cup (1 stick) salted butter

½ cup heavy cream

Pinch of cayenne pepper (optional)

Pinch of garlic powder (optional)

Salt and ground black pepper

1¼ cups shredded cheddar cheese (about 5 ounces), room temperature

1. Bring the butter and cream to a simmer in a small heavy-bottomed saucepan over medium-low heat. Whisking constantly, simmer until thickened, 4 to 6 minutes.

2. Add the cayenne and garlic powder, if using, and season to taste with salt and pepper. Remove the pan from the heat.

3. Whisk in the cheese a little at a time and continue whisking until the cheese is melted and the sauce is creamy. Allow the sauce to cool a bit before using; it will thicken as it cools.

4. Refrigerate leftover sauce for up to 5 days. To reheat, place the sauce in a small saucepan over low heat. Add a couple of teaspoons of heavy cream and stir constantly until the sauce is smooth and creamy again.

Once your children learn how to make a good cheese sauce, they will be the envy of many adults! The art of the sauce is patience, and this recipe is a great place to begin practicing since the reward is so great. Kids can learn how to adjust the heat to control the temperature of the ingredients. A low simmer helps thicken the butter and cream, but if the mixture is too hot, the cheese will separate. Using low heat and a lot of patience allows the cream mixture to thicken slowly while remaining cool enough to add the cheese.

CALORIES: 199 | **FAT:** 19.4g | **PROTEIN:** 4.4g | **CARBS:** 0.8g | **FIBER:** 0g

CHAPTER 6:
MAINS

This collection of main dishes feels somewhat eclectic. It includes a range of ingredients and flavors meant to provide a variety of eating experiences.

Some of our favorite recipes use Southwestern seasonings such as chili powder and cumin, like the Simple Cheese Quesadillas and the Sheet Pan Fajitas. Our family is also partial to the Asian flavors found in the Cashew Chicken with Broccoli, Chicken Teriyaki Meatballs, Roasted Pork Belly, and Asian Lettuce Cups. There's no doubt that we also have an affinity for Italian food with the inclusion of Deep Dish Supreme Pizza, Open-Faced Calzones, Baked Ziti Keto Style, Mom's Italian Meatballs in Tomato Gravy, and even Pizza Soup in this chapter.

We have given you keto and low-carb versions of classic family favorites to enjoy as well. The homey Hamburger Steaks in Onion Gravy, Chili Cheese Dog Skillet, and Cheesy Corn Dog Nuggets will remind us all of the days when we couldn't wait to be called to the dinner table.

We have also included some new favorite traditions that were created in our kitchen, like the dish Grace dubbed Chicken Mud and the Chicken on a Stick, for which my family has teased me mercilessly but has eaten greedily.

Many of these dishes are great options for tucking into lunch boxes or eating on the go. A number of them can be frozen to reheat and enjoy when no one in the family feels like cooking.

We hope that many of these dishes will grace your own family table!

CASHEW CHICKEN WITH BROCCOLI

MAKES
6 servings

My children love this recipe! They don't care if it's served with or without Fried Cauli-Rice (page 214). They even like the broccoli in it. I suspect it's the wonderful Asian flavors and the crunch of the cashews that they enjoy most. The leftovers are even more delicious and perfect to set aside for lunches.

½ cup chicken broth

¼ cup coconut aminos, or 2 tablespoons lite soy sauce

2 tablespoons sugar-free rice vinegar

1 tablespoon toasted sesame oil

3 drops liquid sweetener (optional)

2 pounds boneless, skinless chicken breasts, cut into 1-inch pieces

2 tablespoons ghee or avocado oil

3 cloves garlic, minced

2 tablespoons grated ginger

1 small onion, chopped

1½ cups broccoli florets, chopped

½ cup roasted unsalted cashew pieces (see Tips)

2 green onion tops, sliced, for garnish (optional)

1. Make the sauce: In a small bowl, mix together the broth, coconut aminos, rice vinegar, sesame oil, and sweetener, if using. Set aside.

2. Brown the chicken in the ghee in a large skillet over high heat, 10 to 12 minutes. Reduce the heat to medium, stir in the garlic, ginger, and onion, and cook until the onion is tender, 7 to 10 minutes.

3. Add the broccoli and pour in the sauce. Stir well. Reduce the heat to low and simmer until the sauce has thickened and the chicken is tender, 15 to 20 minutes. Stir in the cashews and remove the pan from the heat.

4. Just before serving, garnish with the green onions, if desired.

5. Refrigerate leftovers for up to 5 days, or freeze for up to a month.

TIPS! *You can use 1-inch strips of beef, such as sirloin steak, instead of chicken if you prefer.*

The cashews in this dish tend to soften when stored in the sauce. If you're making this dish to have extras for later, set aside the portion you will be storing and add cashews only to the portion you will be serving immediately. Add the remaining cashews to the reheated leftovers just before serving.

 Older kids could learn a lot from browning the chicken over high heat and from thinking about the flavors in the sauce and what they like best. They can also practice their knife skills by chopping the vegetables.

CALORIES: 407 | **FAT:** 19g | **PROTEIN:** 38g | **CARBS:** 6.7g | **FIBER:** 1.1g

DEEP DISH SUPREME PIZZA

MAKES
12 servings

Once I figured out the dough recipe, the hardest part of making this pizza was deciding which pan to use. I've baked it in a 10 by 15-inch baking dish, multiple sizes of cast-iron skillets, and even five personal deep dish pizza pans. All of them work just fine! To determine which size pan to use, consider how thick you want the crust to be and what pans you have and enjoy using. This recipe provides instructions for a 14-inch deep dish pizza pan. If you use a different pan, you will need to adjust the baking time, but that isn't difficult to do. Be sure to use part-skim mozzarella in the crust for best results. My kids' carbivore friends enjoy this crust as much as we do, and they get a kick out of making pizza dough from scratch. For an authentic supreme pizza experience, you can top your pizza with some mushrooms, too; but since many kids won't touch them, I've left them out of this recipe.

CRUST:

½ teaspoon granulated sugar

1 (¼-ounce) packet active dry yeast

1 tablespoon hot (but not boiling) water

1 cup blanched almond flour

⅓ cup oat fiber

¼ cup baking powder

3 cups shredded part-skim mozzarella cheese (about 12 ounces)

1 (8-ounce) package cream cheese, softened

4 large eggs

2 tablespoons olive oil, for the pan

1. Make the crust: Put the sugar, yeast, and hot water in a small bowl. Stir to incorporate and set aside to activate the yeast.

2. In a medium bowl, whisk together the almond flour, oat fiber, and baking powder and set aside.

3. Melt the mozzarella and cream cheese in a 3-quart saucepan over low heat. Stir the flour mixture into the melted cheeses. Remove from the heat.

4. Add the eggs and yeast mixture and use a wooden spoon or your hands to mix the dough until smooth. Cover the dough and set it aside in a warm place to rise for 30 to 35 minutes.

5. Preheat the oven to 375°F. Grease a 14-inch deep dish pizza pan liberally with the olive oil.

6. Transfer the dough to the greased pan. Coat your hands with olive oil and smooth the dough to the edges and at least ¼ inch up the sides of the pan. The dough should not be more than ¼ inch thick across the bottom. Keep your hands covered in oil to prevent the dough from sticking.

Bring all of the children into the kitchen! The yeast needs to be fed, and younger kids will get a kick out of watching it activate. Tweens and teens might, too, but they will never admit it. Family members can prepare the toppings while the dough rises and may even choose to create their own pizzas. This is a great time to let them oil their hands, spread out the dough, and pile on their own toppings. While the pizza bakes, it's a good time to have everyone pitch in to help clean up.

CALORIES: 372 | **FAT:** 29.6g | **PROTEIN:** 19.6g | **CARBS:** 6.1g | **FIBER:** 1.5g

TOPPINGS:

½ cup tomato paste (see Notes)

1 teaspoon Italian seasoning, divided

4 ounces Italian sausage, cooked and crumbled

2 ounces sliced pepperoni

⅓ cup sliced green bell peppers (see Tips)

¼ cup sliced onions (see Tips)

2 cups shredded mozzarella cheese (about 8 ounces)

Chopped fresh basil leaves, for garnish (optional)

7. Dollop small spoonfuls of the tomato paste onto the crust and smooth it out as gently as possible; it doesn't need to be spread evenly. Sprinkle the Italian seasoning evenly over the tomato paste. Top with the sausage, pepperoni, bell peppers, onions, and mozzarella cheese.

8. Bake until bubbly and browned on top, 15 to 20 minutes. Remove from the oven and let sit for at least 10 minutes before serving. Garnish with fresh basil, if desired.

9. Refrigerate leftovers for up to 5 days, or wrap slices in freezer paper and freeze for up to 3 months.

NOTES: *Using tomato paste might seem unorthodox, but it keeps the crust from becoming soggy.*

We like to sauté the onions and bell peppers before using them as toppings, but you don't have to.

135

DRIVE-THRU CHICKEN TENDERS

MAKES
6 servings

This is an update of the pickle-brined tenders from my book *Keto Living Day by Day*. While the brine is the same, I've added some seasonings to the "breading" that make these not only much more like fast-food chicken tenders, but better, because these aren't full of sugars and starches! With only ¼ teaspoon of cayenne pepper, they are not spicy; you can adjust the amount to your family's tastes. You can also skip the brining step, but it makes the chicken much more tender and juicy.

2 pounds boneless, skinless chicken breasts, cut lengthwise into strips about 1½ inches wide

1½ cups dill pickle juice (from a jar of pickles)

1 cup pork rind dust

½ cup grated Parmesan cheese

1 tablespoon unflavored whey protein isolate

1 tablespoon paprika

1 teaspoon garlic powder

¼ teaspoon cayenne pepper

⅛ teaspoon salt

2 large eggs

1 batch Grace's Chicken Tender Sauce (page 120), for serving

1. Place the chicken strips and pickle juice in a 1-gallon freezer bag, seal the bag, and refrigerate for at least 4 hours or overnight. After the chicken has brined, drain the chicken and set it aside. Discard the juice.

2. Preheat the oven to 375°F. Line a large rimmed baking sheet with parchment paper.

3. Make the breading: Place the pork rind dust, Parmesan cheese, whey protein isolate, paprika, garlic powder, cayenne, and salt in a small bowl and mix until well combined. Set aside.

4. In another bowl, beat the eggs until frothy.

5. Dip the brined chicken strips into the beaten eggs, then into the breading mixture, coating all sides. Place the breaded chicken in a single layer on the lined baking sheet.

6. Bake until the tenders are browned and the juices run clear when cut, 18 to 25 minutes. The internal temperature of the chicken should reach 165°F. Serve with the sauce.

7. Refrigerate leftovers for up to 3 days, or freeze for up to a month. Reheat the tenders in an air fryer, or wrap them in aluminum foil and place in a preheated 325°F oven for 15 to 20 minutes.

TIP! *These tenders make great breakfast sandwiches with the Yeasty Low-Carb Rolls on page 62. Use ½ tender per roll.*

For food safety reasons, younger helpers might avoid most of the steps in this recipe except for mixing the breading. Tweens and teens can likely handle most of this recipe on their own, including breading the tenders.

CALORIES: 389 | FAT: 16.5g | PROTEIN: 42.1g | CARBS: 1.1g | FIBER: 0g
(WITHOUT SAUCE) CALORIES: 362 | FAT: 13.2g | PROTEIN: 42.1g | CARBS: 0.7g | FIBER: 0g

HAMBURGER STEAKS IN ONION GRAVY

MAKES
4 servings

Something about a creamy gravy transforms plain ground beef into hamburger steaks worthy of a new title—especially when that gravy is onion gravy.

1 tablespoon ghee

1 small onion, sliced

1 pound 93% lean ground beef (see Tip)

⅓ cup beef broth

⅓ cup heavy cream

1 tablespoon beef bouillon powder (see Note)

⅛ teaspoon salt (see Note)

Dash of freshly ground black pepper

1. Melt the ghee in a large skillet over medium heat. Add the onion and sauté until lightly browned, 8 to 10 minutes.

2. Meanwhile, shape the ground beef into 4 equal-sized patties about ½ inch thick.

3. Remove the onion from the skillet and add the beef patties. Cook until the patties are browned on both sides and the juices run clear, 3 to 4 minutes per side.

4. Add the broth, cream, bouillon powder, salt, and pepper to the pan with the patties. Return the onion to the skillet. Reduce the heat to low and simmer until the gravy has thickened, 15 to 20 minutes.

5. Refrigerate leftovers for up to 4 days, or freeze for up to a month.

TIP! *Using lean ground beef in this recipe renders less fat that won't need to be removed after the patties are cooked.*

NOTE: *The brand of bouillon with the best ingredients I have found is Ketologie. It's a bit pricey, but you can order it from Amazon or the Ketologie website. If you're less careful with ingredients, there's a brand called Better Than Bouillon that makes a hearty beef-flavored base. You will have to adjust the amount of bouillon based on the brand you choose, as the flavor intensity varies. As a general rule, I use about half as much of the Better Than Bouillon brand as I do of the Ketologie brand. You may also need to adjust the amount of salt depending on how salty the brand of bouillon you use is.*

This recipe is just a tad harder than frying hamburgers because of the addition of the gravy, making it an excellent recipe for those who are just gaining confidence in the kitchen. Kids can develop basic cooking skills as they learn to brown onions and simmer the sauce to thicken it into a gravy.

CALORIES: 321 | FAT: 19.8g | PROTEIN: 28.8g | CARBS: 1.8g | FIBER: 0.3g

CHICKEN ON A STICK

MAKES
10 skewers
(1 to 2 per
serving)

"Chicken on a stick? What about the stick gives it great flavor?" David snickered. Grace chimed in on the teasing, asking, "Yeah, Mom, are these special sticks? Why can't you just bake the chicken in the oven on a baking sheet?" Even Jonathan had something to say: "Mom, these sticks add an incredible taste to this chicken. Wow! Who knew?" But this mom had the last laugh when the three of them polished off all of the skewers and asked when I might make Chicken on a Stick again. As is typical, each of us prefers these tenders with a different sauce. Jonathan and David like BBQ Sauce (page 114), while Grace prefers her chicken tender sauce on page 120. My favorite is the Sweet Mustard Sauce (page 116).

---

1 tablespoon paprika

1 teaspoon garlic powder

½ teaspoon onion powder

¼ teaspoon cayenne pepper
(optional)

⅛ teaspoon salt

10 chicken tenderloins (about
1½ pounds)

10 slices bacon

SPECIAL EQUIPMENT:

10 (6- to 7-inch) wooden skewers

TIP! *While the skewers don't add flavor, they do add to the finished texture by helping the tenders and bacon cook more evenly, and they make turning the chicken easier.*

1. Preheat the oven to 375°F. Line a large rimmed baking sheet with parchment paper.

2. Place the spices and salt in a small bowl and mix to combine.

3. Season the chicken, one tenderloin at a time, with the spice mix, coating each side completely. Thread a seasoned tenderloin onto a skewer, starting at the thicker end. The skewer should run through the center of the entire tenderloin. Wrap a slice of bacon around the chicken in a tight spiral, beginning at the thicker end and tucking the end of the bacon into itself. Repeat with the remaining chicken and bacon.

4. Place the skewers on the lined baking sheet. Sprinkle the remaining spice mix over the top.

5. Bake for 20 minutes, then flip the chicken over and bake for another 15 to 20 minutes, until the bacon is thoroughly cooked. Let cool for 5 to 10 minutes before serving.

6. Refrigerate leftover skewers for up to 5 days, or freeze for up to a month. The chicken can be rewarmed in a skillet or wrapped in foil and rewarmed in a preheated 375°F oven. Microwaving can make chicken tough, so use reduced power if reheating these in the microwave.

This recipe involves handling raw chicken and bacon, so it might be a challenge for younger children to do more than mix together the spices. Older kids can likely make the entire recipe with a reminder about handling raw meats safely. Kids also need to be careful if turning the chicken over during baking. Be sure to remove the skewers before serving the chicken to younger kids.

(PER SKEWER) **CALORIES:** 310 | **FAT:** 11.8g | **PROTEIN:** 39.8g | **CARBS:** 0.3g | **FIBER:** 0g

MARINATED BEEF KABOBS

MAKES
9 kabobs
(1 per serving)

This dish is a family favorite when served with Cabbage Noodles (page 220) or Fried Cauli-Rice (page 214). It's easy to prep the ingredients a day in advance, get the kids to help thread the skewers, and then get your spouse to grill. Delegation works! If your minions aren't available to assist, the marinated beef is perfect baked or pan-fried, too.

½ cup avocado oil

½ cup coconut aminos, or ¼ cup lite soy sauce

3 cloves garlic, minced

1 tablespoon minced ginger

1 teaspoon fish sauce (omit if using soy sauce)

3 pounds boneless sirloin steak, cut into 1-inch cubes

1 large onion, cut into 9 wedges

18 grape tomatoes

2 large green bell peppers, sliced into 18 pieces

SPECIAL EQUIPMENT:
9 (11-inch) wooden skewers

1. Put the avocado oil, coconut aminos, garlic, ginger, and fish sauce, if using, in a 1-gallon freezer bag. Add the sirloin, seal the bag, and place in the refrigerator to marinate for at least 8 hours or overnight, turning the bag every few hours.

2. When ready to grill the kabobs, preheat a grill to 350°F.

3. Remove the meat from the marinade and discard the marinade.

4. Thread the marinated meat cubes, onion wedges, tomatoes, and bell pepper pieces onto the skewers, alternating the beef and vegetables and beginning and ending with pieces of meat.

5. Grill the kabobs with the lid closed, turning every 5 to 6 minutes to ensure even doneness, until the veggies are crisp-tender and the internal temperature of the beef reaches 145°F, 12 to 14 minutes. Let rest for 5 to 10 minutes before serving.

6. Refrigerate leftover kabobs for up to 4 days.

OVEN METHOD:
Preheat the oven to 350°F. Place the kabobs on a roasting rack set inside a large rimmed baking sheet and bake until the meat is tender and the veggies are just browned, 23 to 26 minutes.

STOVETOP METHOD:
Sauté the marinated meat, onion, and bell pepper in a large skillet over medium heat until the veggies are crisp-tender and the meat is cooked to the desired doneness, 12 to 16 minutes for medium. Add the tomatoes in the last 2 to 3 minutes of cooking.

Making the marinade is a simple task that is ideal for younger children. Kids with good knife skills can prep the veggies. When everything is ready, get an assembly line going if your kids are old enough to safely handle raw meat and the sharp ends of the skewers. We've found that setting the finished kabobs on a rimmed baking sheet helps catch drips from the marinade and makes it easier to take the kabobs outside to the grill. This is also a great opportunity to teach older children how to use a grill.

CALORIES: 449 | **FAT:** 23g | **PROTEIN:** 34.8g | **CARBS:** 3.1g | **FIBER:** 0.8g

OPEN-FACED CALZONES

MAKES
4 calzones
(1 per serving)

A recipe tester asked, "Isn't an open-faced calzone just a pizza?" Hmm . . . My reaction was, "Of course not; this calzone has ricotta in it!" It also omits the pizza sauce, but it is delicious dipped in my No-Cook Pizza Sauce (page 124). Call them what you want, but these calzones, which you can eat with your hands, are delicious! As they bake, the dough rises and tends to enfold the fillings. You can add other fillings such as mushrooms, olives, and onions, but I'd caution you not to add too many lest they become toppings and turn these calzones into pizzas.

1 cup shredded mozzarella cheese (about 4 ounces)

½ cup ricotta cheese

¼ cup grated Parmesan cheese

1 teaspoon Italian seasoning, plus more for sprinkling if desired

¼ teaspoon garlic powder

1 batch Anything Dough (page 52)

2 ounces sliced pepperoni

Chopped fresh basil leaves, for garnish (optional)

1. Preheat the oven to 350°F. Line a large rimmed baking sheet with parchment paper.

2. Make the filling: Put the cheeses, Italian seasoning, and garlic powder in a medium bowl and stir to combine. Set aside.

3. Divide the dough into 4 equal portions and roll each portion into a ball between your hands. Place each ball on a piece of parchment paper, top with another piece of parchment, and roll out into a circle about 6 inches in diameter.

4. Layer the pepperoni on top of the dough, leaving at least ¾ inch of dough uncovered around the edges. Top the pepperoni with the cheese filling, dividing it evenly among the calzones.

5. Fold the left and right sides of the dough over the filling, leaving the center of the filling uncovered. If desired, sprinkle the calzones with more Italian seasoning.

6. Bake the calzones until the dough is golden brown and the cheeses are just beginning to brown, 26 to 30 minutes. Serve warm, garnished with fresh basil if desired.

7. Refrigerate leftovers for up to 4 days, or freeze for up to a month. Reheat leftovers in the oven or in an air fryer for best results.

Have a calzone party! Let kids roll out the dough, add the fillings, and fold the dough over the fillings. Older kids can also help by preparing the dough in advance.

CALORIES: 489 | **FAT:** 34.5g | **PROTEIN:** 27g | **CARBS:** 6.2g | **FIBER:** 1.8g | **OAT FIBER:** 3g

ORANGE-BRAISED PORK

MAKES
6 servings

This dish is so versatile that you can cook it in an Instant Pot, in a slow cooker, or on the stovetop. All three methods yield tender pork. The thick, rich, slightly spicy sauce with a hint of orange flavor is the star of this dish; it begins with getting a dark sear on the pork and browning the onion. Be sure to simmer down the pan juices for maximum flavor! Serve the pork over Cabbage Noodles (page 220), sautéed bok choy, cauli rice, or sautéed spinach if you like.

2 tablespoons bacon fat, ghee, or coconut oil

2 pounds boneless pork ribs or country-style short ribs (see Tip)

Dash of salt (omit if using tamari)

Dash of ground black pepper

1 medium yellow onion, chopped

4 large cloves garlic, minced

1½ tablespoons minced ginger

⅓ cup sugar-free rice vinegar

2 tablespoons grated orange zest (from about 1 medium orange)

¼ cup fresh orange juice

1 tablespoon Chinese five-spice powder

3 drops food-grade orange oil (optional)

⅔ cup beef broth

⅓ cup coconut aminos or tamari (see Tip)

1½ teaspoons chili garlic sauce

½ teaspoon fish sauce (omit if using tamari)

¼ teaspoon maple extract

INSTANT POT METHOD:

1. Set a 4-quart or larger Instant Pot to the sauté mode. Melt the fat in the pot, then add the ribs, season with the salt and pepper, and sear well on all sides. When the ribs are dark brown, remove them from the pot and set aside on a plate. Leave any drippings in the pot.

2. Put the onion, garlic, and ginger in the Instant Pot and sauté until the onion is tender and browned, 8 to 10 minutes. Add the vinegar, orange zest, orange juice, five-spice powder, and orange oil, if using, and simmer until slightly thickened, 1 to 2 minutes. Cancel the sauté function.

3. Add the remaining ingredients to the Instant Pot and mix well. Return the seared ribs to the pot. Seal the lid and cook on high pressure for 25 minutes, then allow the pressure to release naturally, about 20 minutes. The pork will be fork-tender. Shred the meat and serve with the pan juices. If the juices need thickening, use the sauté function to reduce them for 8 to 10 minutes before serving.

SLOW COOKER METHOD:

1. Melt the fat in a large skillet over medium-high heat. Add the ribs, season with the salt and pepper, and sear well on all sides.

2. Transfer the seared ribs to a 4-quart or larger slow cooker along with the onion. Whisk together the remaining ingredients and pour over the ribs. Cook on low for 6 to 8 hours, until the pork is fork-tender. Shred the meat and serve with the pan juices. If the juices need thickening, transfer them to a 1-quart saucepan and simmer over low heat until reduced, 10 to 12 minutes.

CALORIES: 388 | **FAT:** 25.2g | **PROTEIN:** 30.8g | **CARBS:** 4.5g | **FIBER:** 0.3g

TIPS! *The pork should be a fatty cut. If boneless pork ribs are difficult to source, a pork roast will work. Leaner cuts such as tenderloin or loin will not be as tender or flavorful. If you avoid pork, dark meat chicken such as boneless, skinless thighs also works well in this dish.*

If you use tamari instead of coconut aminos, omit the salt and fish sauce to avoid adding too much salt to the dish.

STOVETOP METHOD:

1. Melt the fat in a 4-quart or larger Dutch oven over medium-high heat. Add the ribs, season with the salt and pepper, and sear well on all sides.

2. Remove the ribs from the pot and set aside on a plate, leaving the drippings in the pot. Add the onion, garlic, and ginger to the pot and sauté until the onion is tender and browned, 8 to 10 minutes.

3. Add the vinegar, orange zest, orange juice, five-spice powder, and orange oil, if using, and simmer until slightly thickened, 1 to 2 minutes. Add the seared ribs and the remaining ingredients. Cover and cook over low heat until the pork is fork-tender, at least 1 hour. Shred the meat in the pot, then simmer uncovered until the juices have reduced to a thick sauce, about 30 minutes.

The amount of involvement appropriate for children may vary depending on the cooking method you choose. This might be a good time to review the cooking methods described on pages 35 to 37. Tweens and older kids can measure the seasonings and learn how to zest citrus (avoid the white pith!).

PIZZA WAFFLES

MAKES
10 mini waffles or
5 regular waffles
(2 mini waffles or
1 regular waffle
per serving)

Foods made mini are just more fun. They also lend themselves to being eaten as finger foods. This waffle batter is prepared in a blender to make it even faster; your batter will be ready by the time the waffle maker is hot. Use kitchen shears to chop the pepperoni. Make a double batch of waffles and use the leftovers for quick meals or snacks later. These waffles make a great bread for grilled sandwiches.

4 large eggs

2 cups shredded mozzarella cheese (about 8 ounces), divided

2 ounces (¼ cup) cream cheese

1 teaspoon Italian seasoning

½ teaspoon garlic powder

⅛ teaspoon salt

3 ounces pepperoni, chopped

No-Cook Pizza Sauce (page 124), for serving (optional)

Chopped fresh basil leaves, for garnish (optional)

SPECIAL EQUIPMENT:
Mini or regular-size waffle maker

1. Preheat a waffle maker according to the manufacturer's instructions.

2. Put the eggs, mozzarella, cream cheese, Italian seasoning, garlic powder, and salt in a blender and blend into a batter. Stir in the pepperoni with a rubber spatula.

3. Pour 2 heaping tablespoons of the batter into the hot waffle maker and cook until browned, about 3 minutes. (If making regular-size waffles, use ¼ cup of batter per waffle.)

4. Use tongs to remove the waffle from the waffle maker and let cool on a cooling rack until ready to serve. Repeat with the remaining batter, making a total of 10 mini waffles or 5 regular waffles. Serve warm, topped with pizza sauce and garnished with fresh basil if desired.

5. Refrigerate leftovers for up to a week. Reheat the waffles in a toaster or skillet.

Have the kiddos measure and toss everything into the blender, or give them the task of chopping the pepperoni. Older children can likely manage the waffle maker on their own; a pair of silicone-tipped tongs is perfect for removing the waffles. If your kids are too young to use a waffle maker, they might help by mixing up some pizza sauce for dipping.

(WAFFLES ONLY) CALORIES: 322 | FAT: 25.1g | PROTEIN: 19.8g | CARBS: 2.2g | FIBER: 0g

BEEF STROGANOFF

MAKES
6 servings

Beef stroganoff is a classic that doesn't need carbs to be comforting. Your family will ask for this tender, beefy meat and gravy dish time after time. Serve it with Cabbage Noodles (page 220), as shown, or with Cheesy Cauli Mash (page 208).

2 tablespoons ghee or bacon fat

2 pounds boneless sirloin steak, cut into 1-inch strips

2 tablespoons unsalted butter

8 ounces button mushrooms, sliced

1 small onion, sliced

1 clove garlic, minced

2 teaspoons Worcestershire sauce

½ teaspoon Dijon mustard (optional)

½ teaspoon salt

⅛ teaspoon cracked black pepper

2 cups beef broth

½ cup heavy cream

1 cup sour cream

Chopped fresh parsley, for garnish (optional)

1. Melt the ghee in a large skillet over high heat. Add the sirloin strips and cook until browned on all sides, 5 to 8 minutes. Remove the meat from the pan, leaving the drippings in the pan, and reduce the heat to medium-low.

2. Add the butter to the pan drippings. Sauté the mushrooms, onion, and garlic until tender, 6 to 8 minutes.

3. Stir in the Worcestershire sauce, mustard (if using), salt, and pepper. Pour in the broth and cream.

4. Return the beef to the pan and bring to a low simmer. Cover and simmer for 30 minutes.

5. Remove the lid and simmer uncovered for another 20 to 25 minutes, until the meat is tender and the gravy has reduced. Remove from the heat, stir in the sour cream, and serve. Garnish with fresh parsley, if desired.

6. Refrigerate leftovers for up to 3 days.

Younger hands likely aren't ready to tackle this recipe, but kids with knife skills, or those practicing their knife skills, can enjoy making this dish with adult supervision. This is also a good time to practice adjusting the heat on the stovetop.

CALORIES: 482 | **FAT:** 30.2g | **PROTEIN:** 42.2g | **CARBS:** 3.2g | **FIBER:** 0.5g

CHICKEN TERIYAKI MEATBALLS

MAKES
16 meatballs
(4 per serving)

This recipe was little more than a hunch when I started to grind the chicken in the food processor. David and Grace were in the kitchen. Out of the corner of my eye, I saw them exchange doubtful glances, which only made me more determined to relish what I knew would be their delight once they tried these meatballs. Even then I knew I should probably double the recipe, but then what if…? I had an additional pound of ground beef on hand just in case I needed a plan B for dinner. Sure enough, the chief complaint on the occasions I've made these meatballs has been that I didn't make enough, even when I doubled the recipe. Your family will like this, too!

SAUCE:

½ cup coconut aminos

¼ cup fish sauce, tamari, or lite soy sauce

¼ cup toasted sesame oil

2 teaspoons sugar-free rice vinegar

2 teaspoons minced ginger

½ teaspoon minced garlic

⅛ teaspoon red pepper flakes (optional)

MEATBALLS:

1 pound ground chicken

⅓ cup pork rind dust

2 tablespoons melted bacon fat or ghee, divided

2 teaspoons minced ginger

½ teaspoon minced garlic

½ teaspoon dried minced onion, or 1 teaspoon minced fresh onion

¼ teaspoon salt

FOR GARNISH:

1 tablespoon toasted sesame seeds

2 green onion tops, chopped

1. Make the sauce: Whisk together all of the ingredients in a small bowl and set aside.

2. Make the meatballs: Put the ground chicken, pork rind dust, 1 tablespoon of the bacon fat, the ginger, garlic, and dried minced onion in a large bowl and use your hands to mix until thoroughly combined. Shape the meat mixture into sixteen 1¼-inch balls.

3. Heat the remaining tablespoon of bacon fat in a large skillet over medium heat. Add the meatballs and pan-fry until browned on all sides, 8 to 10 minutes.

4. When the meatballs are browned, pour the sauce over them and reduce the heat to low. Simmer the meatballs in the sauce, uncovered, until the sauce has reduced by at least one-third, 12 to 15 minutes. Be careful not to burn the sauce.

5. Sprinkle the toasted sesame seeds and green onions over the meatballs just before serving.

6. Refrigerate leftovers for up to 4 days, or freeze for up to a month.

If you grind your own chicken for this recipe, it can be a fun task for kids to tackle. Remind them to remove the skin but to leave any fat on the chicken for a more moist and flavorful meatball. Kids who are too young to handle raw meat can help by mixing up the sauce.

CALORIES: 333 | **FAT:** 23.8g | **PROTEIN:** 28.6g | **CARBS:** 2g | **FIBER:** 0.1g

BALSAMIC BAKED PORK CHOPS

MAKES
4 servings

After I served pork chops for dinner one night, a very young Grace asked, "What meat is this?" When I replied that it was pork chops, she remarked, "Pork chops is hard!" That was over a decade ago, and I'm still a bit paranoid about making sure the pork chops I serve are tender. One way to ensure tender meat is to marinate the pork. This simple balsamic marinade yields tender, flavorful chops, and cooking them couldn't be easier when you let the oven do the work. While the pork chops bake, make some Cheesy Cauli Mash (page 208) or Better Than the Box Mac 'n' Cheese (page 190) for an easy side.

1 pound boneless pork chops, about ½-inch thick

¼ cup olive oil

2 tablespoons balsamic vinegar

1½ teaspoons seasoning salt

1 clove garlic, minced

1. Put the pork chops in a 1-gallon freezer bag and add the remaining ingredients. Seal the bag and toss or massage to blend the ingredients and coat the pork. Place in the refrigerator to marinate for at least 1 hour or overnight, turning the bag halfway through.

2. When ready to bake the pork chops, preheat the oven to 325°F.

3. Remove the pork chops from the marinade and place in a baking dish. Discard the marinade. Bake the chops until tender and lightly browned, 30 to 35 minutes. The internal temperature of the meat should reach 145°F.

4. Refrigerate leftovers for up to 4 days.

 Kids who are old enough to understand how to handle raw meat safely can help make the marinade, put the pork in the marinade, and transfer the marinated pork chops to a baking dish. Use this time to talk with kids about why the marinade is discarded.

CALORIES: 409 | **FAT:** 28.2g | **PROTEIN:** 27.1g | **CARBS:** 0.7g | **FIBER:** 0g

BAKED ZITI KETO STYLE

MAKES
10 servings

Yeah, it's baked ziti, a family favorite! In this version, I've replaced the pasta with shredded cabbage, which is easy to find and inexpensive. Boiling the cabbage in advance really helps mellow the flavor. However, if you're not convinced, you can substitute shirataki noodles made from a combination of konjac flour and oat fiber, which my family much prefers. If you don't like or can't find those, either, you can use your favorite pasta replacement, such as zucchini noodles or noodles made from hearts of palm. Just be sure to cut them into short lengths and squeeze out as much moisture as possible before baking. Vegetable noodles tend to leach a lot of water that can make this dish soupy and less flavorful.

---

1 pound mild Italian sausage, casings removed

1 pound ground beef

1 small onion, diced

3 cloves garlic, minced

1 tablespoon plus 1 teaspoon Italian seasoning, divided

2 teaspoons onion powder

1 teaspoon dried basil

1 teaspoon dried oregano leaves

1 teaspoon salt

1 (28-ounce) can tomato sauce

1 (14.5-ounce) can diced tomatoes, undrained

½ cup beef broth

4 cups thinly sliced cabbage

3 cups shredded mozzarella cheese (about 12 ounces), divided

1 (16-ounce) carton ricotta cheese

½ cup grated Parmesan cheese, plus more for garnish if desired

2 tablespoons chopped fresh parsley

1 large egg

Fresh basil, for garnish (optional)

1. Brown the sausage and ground beef in a large skillet over medium-high heat, 15 to 20 minutes. If desired, drain the fat, making sure to leave at least 2 tablespoons in the pan.

2. Reduce the heat to medium-low. Stir in the onion, garlic, 1 tablespoon of the Italian seasoning, the onion powder, basil, oregano, and salt and cook, stirring occasionally, until the onion is translucent, 8 to 10 minutes.

3. Pour in the tomato sauce, diced tomatoes, and broth. Bring to a simmer and reduce the heat to low. Simmer for 18 to 20 minutes, until the sauce has thickened. Stir occasionally.

4. While the sauce is simmering, bring 3 cups of water to a boil in a saucepan. Add the cabbage and simmer until just tender, 6 to 8 minutes. Remove from the heat and drain well. Squeeze as much moisture as possible from the cabbage using a clean kitchen towel.

5. Put 1½ cups of the mozzarella, the ricotta, Parmesan, parsley, and egg in a bowl. Mix lightly and set aside.

6. Preheat the oven to 350°F.

7. Toss the cabbage with 4 cups of the sauce.

8. Layer half of the cabbage mixture in a 9 by 13-inch baking dish. Add half of the ricotta mixture in dollops on top of the cabbage. Repeat the layers with the remaining cabbage

TIP! *The amount of fat rendered from browning the sausage and ground beef will vary by brand. While you may choose to drain it, make sure to leave at least 2 tablespoons of fat in the pan. You need the fat to hydrate the dried herbs.*

CALORIES: 456 | **FAT:** 29.4g | **PROTEIN:** 32.1g | **CARBS:** 7.9g | **FIBER:** 2.8g

TIP! *For a thicker baked ziti, be sure to do three things. First, drain the noodle substitutes as well as you can and squeeze out the water with a clean kitchen towel. Second, simmer the sauce until it thickens. Lastly, let the dish cool for 15 to 20 minutes before serving it.*

mixture and ricotta mixture. Pour the rest of the sauce over the second ricotta layer and top with the remaining 1½ cups of mozzarella. Sprinkle the remaining 1 teaspoon of Italian seasoning over the top.

9. Bake until the entire dish is bubbly and the cheese is lightly browned, 25 to 30 minutes. Let cool for 15 to 20 minutes. Just before serving, garnish with a sprinkle of fresh basil and/or Parmesan cheese, if desired.

10. Refrigerate leftovers for up to 5 days, or freeze for up to a month.

If using shirataki noodles, let young helpers drain and rinse the noodles. Older children can brown the meats and/or chop the veggies. Kids can also help by measuring out the seasonings.

ROASTED PORK BELLY

MAKES
4 servings

My children will not eat this dish. Now that you know, you may be wondering why I have included it in a book for kids growing up keto. Well, my friend, I have hope for future generations. If we can help them develop a proper palate as children, we can leave a legacy indeed. Sadly, my own children have not yet developed a taste for pork belly, but that isn't entirely tragic since it leaves more for me to enjoy.

1 pound pork belly, cut into 1-inch cubes

2 tablespoons coconut aminos, or 1 tablespoon lite soy sauce

2 tablespoons fresh orange juice

2 tablespoons toasted sesame oil

1 tablespoon minced ginger

1 clove garlic, minced

Toasted sesame seeds, for garnish (optional)

Grated orange zest, for garnish (optional)

1. Place the pork belly in a 1-gallon freezer bag. Add the remaining ingredients, seal the bag, and toss or massage to blend the ingredients. Place in the refrigerator to marinate for at least 6 hours or preferably overnight.

2. When ready to roast the pork belly, preheat the oven to 400°F. Set a baking rack with narrowly spaced grates inside a large rimmed baking sheet or line the baking sheet with parchment paper.

3. Remove the pork belly from the marinade and discard the marinade (see Tip). Place the pork belly on the rack or lined baking sheet. Roast until crisp on the outside, 14 to 18 minutes.

4. Garnish with toasted sesame seeds and/or grated orange zest, if desired, and serve.

5. Refrigerate leftovers for up to 5 days.

TIP! *The marinade can be used as a dipping sauce. Place it in a small saucepan and simmer over low heat for at least 8 minutes before serving.*

Encourage your kids to help mix the marinade. You can explain that marinating meat makes it more tender and flavorful. Before roasting the pork belly, be sure to explain that the marinade must be discarded unless it's cooked since raw meat has been sitting in it.

CALORIES: 578 | **FAT:** 54g | **PROTEIN:** 12.6g | **CARBS:** 1.9g | **FIBER:** 0g

CHILI CHEESE DOG SKILLET

MAKES
8 servings

Leftover chili? Use it up this way! Or maybe you're like me and you intentionally make more chili than you need just so you can make this easy one-skillet meal. This dish is also a great way to use up leftover hot dogs, especially if they've been grilled and already have a deep smoky flavor. If you're in a hurry, you can skip placing the skillet in the oven and just let the cheese melt on top as it sits in the skillet.

16 hot dogs

1 batch Cookout Chili (page 218)

2 cups shredded cheddar cheese (about 8 ounces)

3 tablespoons chopped white onions (optional)

1. Preheat the oven to 375°F.

2. Slice the hot dogs into rounds about ½ inch thick. Pan-fry the hot dogs in a dry 9-inch ovenproof skillet over medium-high heat until just crispy, 5 to 7 minutes.

3. Pour the chili over the fried hot dog rounds and mix to combine. Reduce the heat to low and simmer for 2 to 3 minutes. Remove from the heat and sprinkle the cheese and the onions, if using, over the top.

4. Place the skillet in the oven and bake until the chili is bubbling and the cheese is lightly browned, 12 to 15 minutes.

5. Refrigerate leftovers for up to 4 days, or freeze for up to a month.

Kids with knife skills can help by slicing the hot dogs. Let them experiment by cutting them into rounds, slicing them in half lengthwise and then cutting them into 1-inch-long pieces, or making "worms" by slicing the hot dogs into thin strips. Any of those variations will work. Older kids might also help by searing the hot dogs in the skillet. Someone will also need to take on the task of grating the cheese and chopping the onions.

CALORIES: 511 | FAT: 40.5g | PROTEIN: 32.8g | CARBS: 4.8g | FIBER: 0.4g

MOM'S ITALIAN MEATBALLS IN TOMATO GRAVY

MAKES
8 servings

I'm not sure what we love more about this dish, the tender meatballs or the rich tomato gravy, which is a bit thicker and more heavily seasoned than a simple marinara. Fortunately, we don't have to choose! If you're a batch cooker, it's a good idea to make a double batch of these meatballs: you can eat one batch and freeze the other for later. The meatballs can be frozen raw and cooked when thawed or cooked and then frozen, depending on your needs.

MEATBALLS:

1 pound ground beef

1 pound ground pork

½ cup grated Parmesan cheese

½ cup shredded mozzarella cheese (about 2 ounces)

1 large egg

1 teaspoon Italian seasoning

½ teaspoon garlic powder

½ teaspoon salt

TOMATO GRAVY:

2 (8-ounce) cans tomato sauce

1 cup diced tomatoes

1 cup beef broth

3 cloves garlic, minced

2 tablespoons dried minced onion

1 tablespoon Italian seasoning

2 teaspoons dried basil

2 teaspoons dried oregano leaves

2 teaspoons salt

½ cup grated Parmesan cheese, for serving

1. Preheat the oven to 375°F. Line a large rimmed baking sheet with parchment paper.

2. Make the meatballs: Put all of the ingredients in a large bowl. Mix well with your hands, then shape the mixture into twenty-four 1-inch meatballs.

3. Place the meatballs on the lined baking sheet and bake until browned, 20 to 25 minutes. The internal temperature of the meatballs should reach 160°F.

4. While the meatballs are baking, make the tomato gravy: Put all of the ingredients in a 4-quart saucepan over low heat. Simmer uncovered until the sauce is thickened, 20 to 25 minutes.

5. When the meatballs are done, gently add them to the tomato gravy and continue simmering uncovered over low heat until the meatballs are tender and the sauce is thick, 10 to 15 minutes. Remove from the heat and serve garnished with the Parmesan.

6. Refrigerate leftovers for up to 5 days, or freeze for up to 3 months.

Remind your charges of the safety guidelines for handling raw meat and then let them have a ball rolling the meatballs. Let older children create the tomato gravy and watch over it as it simmers. An adult may need to add the meatballs to the sauce to avoid burns in case the sauce spatters. Sous-chefs might also enjoy grating the Parmesan to serve over the meatballs.

CALORIES: 392 | FAT: 25.5g | PROTEIN: 31.2g | CARBS: 4.2g | FIBER: 0.9g

CHICKEN MUD

MAKES
6 servings

Even before keto, I sometimes used a base of cream cheese and heavy cream to make a sauce for meat. The first time I served it to my then-three-year-old Grace, she looked down at her plate and said, "This looks like mud!" She took a tentative bite— "It's good mud!" We've been enjoying mud for dinner ever since.

1 tablespoon bacon fat or ghee

2 pounds chicken tenderloins

1 cup chicken broth

2 teaspoons balsamic vinegar

3 ounces (6 tablespoons) cream cheese

2 tablespoons unsalted butter

1 teaspoon onion powder

½ teaspoon garlic powder

½ teaspoon salt

½ cup heavy cream

Chopped fresh parsley or dried parsley leaves, for garnish

1. Melt the fat in a large skillet over medium-high heat. Add the chicken and brown on both sides, 3 to 4 minutes per side. When the chicken is thoroughly browned, remove it to a plate and cover with aluminum foil to keep warm.

2. Reduce the heat to medium-low and deglaze the skillet with the broth and vinegar, using a spatula to scrape any tasty bits off the bottom of the pan.

3. Add the cream cheese, butter, onion powder, garlic powder, and salt and stir until the cream cheese is melted. Add the heavy cream, then return the chicken to the pan and simmer uncovered until the chicken is tender and the sauce has thickened, 25 to 30 minutes. Serve garnished with fresh or dried parsley, if desired.

4. Refrigerate leftovers for up to 4 days. The sauce may need to be thinned with a bit of broth when reheated.

TIPS! *Boneless pork chops may be substituted for the chicken.*

Serve this creamy dish over Cabbage Noodles (page 220) or with a side of Cheesy Cauli Mash (page 208).

This dish is something that teens can certainly make unassisted, especially if they are confident using the stovetop. This is a good recipe to let them experiment with different heat levels. High heat browns the chicken and traps the moisture inside. Lower heat lets the chicken simmer and become more tender. Simmering also thickens the sauce. Younger children may not be able to help make this recipe, but they will likely enjoy eating it.

CALORIES: 447 | **FAT:** 26.1g | **PROTEIN:** 44g | **CARBS:** 1.5g | **FIBER:** 0g

ASIAN LETTUCE CUPS

MAKES
4 to 6 servings

Assigning a serving size to this recipe was difficult because it should yield six servings. If you have hungry tweens and teens, however, expect to get only four servings. My kids never tire of this dish and love it made with ground chicken instead of beef. The red chili sauce adds some heat, but you can omit it if your family prefers milder flavors. Serve it with Yum-Yum Sauce (page 126). The leftovers, if you can get them, are even better.

2 pounds ground beef or ground chicken

¼ cup finely chopped onions

1 clove garlic, minced

1 tablespoon minced ginger

¼ teaspoon salt (omit if using soy sauce or tamari)

¼ cup coconut aminos, or 2 tablespoons lite soy sauce

2 teaspoons sugar-free rice vinegar

½ teaspoon red chili sauce (optional)

2 tablespoons toasted sesame oil

1 tablespoon toasted sesame seeds

16 to 18 leaves Bibb lettuce, washed and trimmed

1 green onion top, sliced, for garnish

1. Brown the ground beef in a large skillet over medium-high heat, breaking it up with a wooden spoon or rubber spatula. While the meat is cooking, add the onions, garlic, ginger, and salt, if using, and continue cooking until the meat is fully browned, 15 to 20 minutes.

2. After the meat is browned, add the coconut aminos, vinegar, and chili sauce, if using. Simmer over low heat for 6 to 8 minutes, until most of the liquid has evaporated. Stir in the sesame oil and sesame seeds and remove from the heat.

3. Place the lettuce leaves on a serving plate. Fill each leaf with about ¼ cup of the meat mixture and garnish with the sliced green onions. Alternatively, let each person fill their own leaves as they like.

4. Refrigerate the leftover meat mixture and lettuce leaves in separate containers for up to 5 days. The meat mixture can be frozen for up to a month.

 Let children who are old enough to use the stove try making this simple recipe. Those who aren't can help wash the lettuce and add the seasoned meat to the lettuce cups.

(BASED ON 6 SERVINGS) CALORIES: 435 | FAT: 29g | PROTEIN: 36.5g | CARBS: 2.8g | FIBER: 0.3g

PIZZA SOUP

MAKES
4 servings

This recipe came about when I needed to get lunch on the table quickly, and there weren't many options in the fridge. We nearly always have tomato sauce, broth, pepperoni, and mozzarella on hand, so when I saw that we also had leftover Italian sausage, bell pepper, and mushrooms, pizza soup became a thing!

1 pound mild Italian sausage, casings removed

½ cup sliced button mushrooms

⅓ cup chopped bell peppers, any color

¼ cup chopped onions

1 clove garlic, minced

2 teaspoons dried basil

1 teaspoon dried oregano leaves

¼ teaspoon salt

2 (8-ounce) cans tomato sauce

1 cup beef broth

3 ounces pepperoni, chopped

¼ cup chopped black olives (optional)

1 cup shredded mozzarella cheese (about 4 ounces), for topping (omit for dairy-free)

Fresh or dried basil, for garnish (optional)

1. In a Dutch oven or other heavy-bottomed pot, brown the sausage over high heat, breaking it up with a wooden spoon or rubber spatula, 15 to 20 minutes.

2. Reduce the heat to medium and add the mushrooms, bell peppers, onions, garlic, basil, oregano, and salt. Cook, stirring often, until the vegetables are crisp-tender, 4 to 5 minutes.

3. Pour in the tomato sauce and broth and reduce the heat to low. Simmer uncovered until the soup has reduced and thickened, about 20 minutes.

4. Add the pepperoni and olives, if using, and continue simmering for 10 minutes.

5. Ladle the soup into serving bowls and top each with ¼ cup of the mozzarella cheese, if using. Garnish with a sprinkle of basil, if desired.

6. Refrigerate leftovers for up to 5 days, or freeze for up to a month.

Let kids who are old enough to cook food over higher heat try this recipe on their own—from browning the meat to garnishing the bowls. Younger children might tear the pepperoni rather than chopping it, but kids with good knife skills can prep the veggies.

CALORIES: 400 | FAT: 30.5g | PROTEIN: 23.1g | CARBS: 5.2g | FIBER: 1.5g

BAKED FISH STICKS

MAKES
6 servings

Why yes, my kids did eat frozen breaded fish sticks when they were little. I loved the convenience; they loved the ketchup in which they drowned their fish sticks. When I made this recipe for the first time, the kids were still quite young, and we hadn't been eating keto long. They both came into the kitchen just as I was taking the fish sticks out of the oven, and they were excited when they saw what was on the baking sheet. I held my breath as I fixed their plates and set some low-carb ketchup on the table. My mind raced as I wondered what else I might feed them when they rejected this homemade keto version. But they were delighted! And so was I as they gobbled them up and asked for more. If your kids love ketchup, too, you can serve these with the homemade version on page 118.

2 pounds cod or other white fish fillets

1 cup pork rind dust

½ cup shredded Parmesan cheese

⅓ cup oat fiber (optional; see Tip)

2 large eggs

Finely chopped fresh parsley, for garnish (optional)

Lemon wedges, for serving

1. Preheat the oven to 350°F. Line a large rimmed baking sheet with parchment paper.

2. Cut the fish fillets into pieces about 2 inches wide and 3 inches long. Pat dry to remove the excess moisture.

3. Put the pork rind dust, Parmesan, and oat fiber, if using, in a shallow dish and mix to combine.

4. In a second shallow dish, beat the eggs until frothy.

5. Dip each piece of cod in the beaten eggs, turning to coat. Then coat with the pork rind breading.

6. Place the breaded fish on the lined baking sheet, spacing the pieces at least ¼ inch apart. Bake until the breading is lightly browned and the fish is tender, 18 to 20 minutes. Garnish with fresh parsley, if desired, and serve with lemon wedges.

7. Refrigerate leftovers for up to 3 days.

TIP! *If you omit the oat fiber from the breading, you will need to add 3 tablespoons each of pork rind dust and Parmesan cheese.*

We pulverize our own pork rinds to make dust or panko. Assigning this task to kids allows them to use the blender and is a big help. They can also mix the "breading." Kids who understand food safety protocols for raw eggs and seafood might enjoy getting their hands dirty and dipping and breading the fish. You can also try an assembly line where one person is responsible for the egg dipping and another is responsible for breading the fish. Also, have the kids help prepare any dipping sauces while the fish bakes.

CALORIES: 208 | **FAT:** 7.3g | **PROTEIN:** 32.1g | **CARBS:** 0.9g | **FIBER:** 0g | **OAT FIBER:** 2.7g

SIMPLE CHEESE QUESADILLAS

MAKES
6 servings

Make up a batch of tortillas and you'll have a quick meal whenever anyone complains, "I'm hungry!" or for those times when meal planning just didn't happen. This dish is easy to customize for picky eaters. We have a plain cheese eater, a chicken with extra cheese and spices eater, and two add-all-the-things eaters. This recipe serves us all! Don't forget to serve it with avocado slices or Avocado Salsa (page 188) and some sour cream on the side. A few sprigs of cilantro are a nice touch, too, if you have some on hand.

1 teaspoon chili powder (optional)

1 teaspoon smoked paprika (optional)

½ teaspoon ground cumin (optional)

2 tablespoons unsalted butter, divided

1 batch Tortillas (page 66)

2 cups shredded Monterey Jack cheese (about 8 ounces), divided

Chopped green onion tops, for garnish

1. If using the chili powder, paprika, and cumin, mix them together in a small bowl and set aside.

2. Melt 1 teaspoon of the butter in a skillet over medium-low heat. Place a tortilla in the skillet. Sprinkle ⅓ cup of the cheese over the tortilla, sprinkle with a scant ½ teaspoon of the spice mix, if using, and top with a second tortilla.

3. When the cheese has started to melt, use a wide spatula to flip the quesadilla. Cook until lightly browned on the other side, 3 to 5 minutes.

4. Repeat with the remaining butter, tortillas, cheese, and spice mix.

5. Slice the quesadillas into wedges with a pizza cutter and serve warm, garnished with green onions.

6. Refrigerate leftovers for up to 3 days, or freeze for up to a month.

TIP! *Add grilled chicken strips or browned ground beef in Step 2 for additional protein and flavor. Sautéed bell pepper strips and/or onions are another nice addition.*

Just like making pizzas, letting kids customize their quesadillas with their favorite seasonings or filling ingredients is a great way to get them involved. Younger kids can help in an assembly line of preparing ingredients while older children can man the stove and take turns flipping the quesadillas.

CALORIES: 356 | FAT: 32.2g | PROTEIN: 10.2g | CARBS: 4.2g | FIBER: 3.8g | OAT FIBER: 2.7g

HOMEMADE HOAGIES

MAKES
6 hoagies
(1 per serving)

No, this is not a recipe for a sandwich. This, dear friend, is a *hoagie.* A hoagie has sauce, and this sauce is awesome! You'll catch yourself making extra just because. It's that good, and it turns a simple sandwich into a meal that everyone will enjoy. Feel free to use whatever deli meats or cheeses your family prefers. Fresh, crisp cucumbers are a great substitute for the lettuce. Grace and I also enjoy a few cherry tomatoes on the side.

HOAGIE SAUCE:

⅓ cup mayonnaise

2 teaspoons red wine vinegar

⅛ teaspoon dried basil

⅛ teaspoon dried oregano leaves

⅛ teaspoon Italian seasoning

Dash of salt

Dash of ground black pepper

6 Hoagie Rolls (page 61)

12 slices deli ham

12 slices provolone or mild cheddar cheese

6 pieces romaine lettuce

1. Make the sauce: Put all of the ingredients in a small bowl and stir to combine.

2. Split each roll in half horizontally with a serrated knife. Brush the cut sides with the sauce, reserving any unused sauce for dipping.

3. Place 2 slices of ham, 2 slices of cheese, and a piece of lettuce on each roll and serve immediately.

4. Refrigerate leftover sauce for up to a week; the sandwiches should be consumed within a few hours of assembly and should be kept chilled.

Kids can make these hoagies with friends during sleepovers or make them for their lunches. Preparing the sauce is a great way to practice measuring ingredients. You can explain that using a serrated knife will help cut the bread more evenly.

CALORIES: 388 | **FAT:** 28g | **PROTEIN:** 29.3g | **CARBS:** 2.2g | **FIBER:** 0g | **OAT FIBER:** 1g

WRAPPED PIGGIES

MAKES
8 wraps
(2 per serving)

We wrap these piggies to give them some breathing room because too much bread really is a thing. My family prefers less dough, so making a spiral around the hot dogs keeps the dough from being too much for our tastes as well as from getting soggy. Serve the piggies with BBQ Sauce (page 114), Ranch Dipping Sauce (page 117), or Ketchup (page 118).

½ batch Anything Dough
(page 52)

8 hot dogs, patted dry

1. Preheat the oven to 350°F. Line a large rimmed baking sheet with parchment paper.

2. Divide the dough into 8 equal portions. Using the heel of your hand, apply light pressure to roll each portion into a 6- to 7-inch-long snake.

3. Press the end of the length of dough against one end of a hot dog. Hold the dough in place with one finger and your thumb while wrapping the dough around the hot dog with your other hand.

4. Place the wrapped hot dog on the lined baking sheet with the ends of the dough tucked under the hot dog. Repeat until all 8 hot dogs are wrapped in dough.

5. Bake until the dough is lightly browned and the hot dogs are cooked, 10 to 12 minutes.

6. Refrigerate leftovers for up to 5 days.

Anything Dough is like edible play dough for kids. Not only can they make anything with it, but they can enjoy using it. Let kids get creative with wrapping their hot dogs with strips of dough. They might want to sprinkle sesame seeds or everything bagel seasoning on the outside before baking. With a lot of handling, the dough may become too warm and will not hold its shape. For best results, the wrapped piggies may need to be refrigerated for 30 minutes to 1 hour to chill the dough before baking.

CALORIES: 455 | FAT: 38g | PROTEIN: 24.8g | CARBS: 5.8g | FIBER: 1.8g | OAT FIBER: 3g

SAUTÉED SHRIMP WITH TOMATOES AND PESTO

MAKES
4 servings

Shrimp is expensive where we live, so eating it during the week is a special treat. It's even more of a treat when the recipe is as fast and tasty as this one. Feel free to be generous with the butter and pesto since shrimp is naturally low in fat. You might also sprinkle some freshly grated Parmesan over the shrimp just before serving. We eat this as a meal on its own without sides, but you could serve it with a few slices of Crusty Baguette (page 58) and some Olive Oil Dipping Sauce (page 189).

¼ cup (½ stick) salted butter

2 cloves garlic, minced

4 ounces cherry tomatoes, halved

2 pounds medium raw shrimp, peeled, deveined, and patted dry

¼ cup Pesto (page 122)

2 tablespoons chopped fresh basil

Freshly grated Parmesan cheese, for garnish (optional)

1. In a large skillet over medium-high heat, melt the butter with the garlic.

2. Toss in the tomatoes and sauté until they brighten, 2 to 3 minutes.

3. Add the shrimp and sauté until they turn bright pink and opaque, another 2 to 3 minutes.

4. Remove the pan from the heat and stir in the pesto and basil. Serve immediately, garnished with Parmesan if desired.

5. Refrigerate leftovers for up to 3 days.

TIP! *Use precooked and sliced chicken instead of shrimp for an equally delicious meal.*

TIP! *Cleaning shrimp involves removing the outer shell and tail and then deveining them. You can skip the deveining if you want. The "vein" is really part of the shrimp's intestinal tract, and while it won't hurt you to eat it, removing the intestinal tract and the dark waste that is usually inside it makes eating shrimp more appealing. To remove the vein, make a small cut along the back of the shrimp from the top to the tail. Once the shrimp is cut, the vein is usually easy to remove intact. There are gadgets to help with cleaning shrimp without using a sharp knife. We have a long curved plastic tool with a tip that fits in the end of the shrimp; poke the tip through the shrimp and it pulls away the shell and opens the shrimp so that the vein is easily removed. The shrimp then looks butterflied as it's kept whole but split along the back. After cleaning, rinse the shrimp once more, let them dry, and they are ready to cook.*

This is an excellent recipe for tweens and teens to learn about sautéing foods and to get acquainted with how quickly shrimp cooks. They can take over sous-chef duty or clean the shrimp if purchased whole. Knowing how to clean shrimp is a great life skill!

CALORIES: 315 | **FAT:** 20.4g | **PROTEIN:** 27.6g | **CARBS:** 2.6g | **FIBER:** 0.7g

FRENCH ONION SKILLET CHICKEN

MAKES
6 servings

French onion soup is like a hearty hug from a dear friend—warm, enveloping, and comforting. This keto dish is similar, but instead of a soup, it's a rich chicken entree with all of the best flavors of the traditional soup and none of the carbs from the bread. You can omit the wine, or you can use it as an excuse to enjoy a glass with dinner since the bottle is already open.

1 tablespoon bacon fat or ghee

2 pounds chicken tenderloins

1 clove garlic, minced

¼ teaspoon salt

1 teaspoon fresh thyme leaves, divided

2 large onions, sliced

½ cup (1 stick) unsalted butter

8 ounces button mushrooms, sliced

2 cups beef broth

⅓ cup dry white wine (optional)

⅓ cup heavy cream

2 cups shredded Swiss or Gruyère cheese (about 8 ounces)

TIP! *If you don't have an ovenproof skillet, you can transfer the contents of the skillet at the end of Step 4 to a greased casserole dish. Sprinkle the cheese and thyme over the top and broil as directed in Steps 5 and 6.*

1. Melt the fat in a large ovenproof skillet over medium-high heat. Add the chicken, garlic, salt, and ½ teaspoon of the thyme and cook until the chicken is browned on all sides, 12 to 15 minutes. Remove the chicken to a plate, cover with aluminum foil to keep warm, and set aside. Leave the drippings in the pan.

2. Add the onions and butter to the skillet. Reduce the heat to low and cook, stirring occasionally, until the onions are tender and just browned, 12 to 15 minutes.

3. Add the mushrooms and continue cooking over low heat until the onions are caramelized and the mushrooms are tender, 15 to 18 minutes. Pour in the broth, wine (if using), and cream and scrape the bottom and sides of the skillet to loosen any tasty bits.

4. Return the chicken to the skillet and simmer until the broth has reduced and very little moisture remains, 40 to 45 minutes.

5. Remove from the heat. Sprinkle the cheese over the entire dish, completely covering the top. Then sprinkle the remaining ½ teaspoon of thyme over the cheese.

6. Broil in the oven until the cheese is lightly browned and bubbly, 3 to 4 minutes. Serve immediately.

7. Refrigerate leftovers for up to 4 days.

Older sous-chefs can enjoy learning about caramelizing onions and reducing sauces. You might point out that using high heat to brown the chicken helps sear in the juices and results in more tender and flavorful meat.

CALORIES: 645 | **FAT:** 40.7g | **PROTEIN:** 45.8g | **CARBS:** 5.9g | **FIBER:** 1.1g

CHEESY CORN DOG NUGGETS

MAKES
24 nuggets
(4 per serving)

If you happen to have a corn dog pan, you can make these tasty nuggets into full-sized corn dogs on sticks. Because those gadgets aren't standard kitchen equipment, though, I chose a variation that nearly anyone can make. Whether you like your cornbread savory or a little sweet, you can enjoy this version; simply adjust the amount of sweetener to your liking. Keep in mind that if you add more savory spices and jalapeño (a David favorite), then you might want to omit the sweetener altogether. The corn extract gives the nuggets a more authentic cornbread flavor without the carbs, so I highly recommend including it.

2 tablespoons coconut flour

3 tablespoons oat fiber

3 tablespoons unflavored whey protein isolate or egg white protein powder

Up to 1 tablespoon granulated sweetener (optional)

1 teaspoon baking powder

¼ teaspoon salt

¼ cup (½ stick) unsalted butter, melted

¼ cup water

2 large eggs

¼ teaspoon corn extract (optional)

1 cup shredded cheddar cheese (about 4 ounces)

6 hot dogs, sliced into ¼-inch-thick rounds

SPECIAL EQUIPMENT:

24-well mini muffin tin

1. Preheat the oven to 350°F. Liberally grease a 24-well mini muffin tin.

2. Put the coconut flour, oat fiber, whey protein isolate, sweetener (if using), baking powder, and salt in a small bowl and stir to combine. Add the melted butter, water, eggs, and corn extract, if using, and use a hand mixer to mix into a batter.

3. Pour 1 to 2 teaspoons of the cornbread batter into each well of the greased muffin tin; the wells should be slightly less than half full. Sprinkle the cheese over the batter. Place 5 or 6 slices of hot dog in each well, pushing the hot dogs down into the batter.

4. Bake until the cornbread is lightly browned and firm to the touch, 12 to 15 minutes. Let cool on a cooling rack for at least 10 minutes before serving.

5. Refrigerate leftovers for up to 5 days, or freeze for up to a month.

TIP! *If anyone in your family loves a little heat, add a slice of jalapeño to each muffin well after adding the cheese.*

This is a fun recipe to make with kids, especially if you have more than one helper. The measuring and mixing are really simple. One set of hands can crack the eggs while another measures or mixes the ingredients. Kids can also help slice the hot dogs into rounds. Once the ingredients are prepared and the batter is made, the family can work in an assembly line with one person putting the batter in the tin, another sprinkling in the cheese, and a third person pressing in the hot dogs.

CALORIES: 279 | FAT: 21g | PROTEIN: 18.4g | CARBS: 3.1g | FIBER: 1g | OAT FIBER: 1.5g

SHEET PAN FAJITAS

MAKES
4 servings

Sheet pan meals are amazingly easy to make, and fajitas are no exception. Once everything is sliced, it's as simple as mixing the ingredients, spreading them on a sheet pan (aka rimmed baking sheet), and placing the pan in the oven. When I know time will be tight on weeknights, I prep the ingredients in advance and store them in the fridge. While the oven preheats, I can spread the ingredients on the pan, and dinner is on the table in less than 30 minutes with minimal cleanup. While dinner bakes, I'm free to do other things, like make Avocado Salsa (page 188) and gather the sour cream and shredded cheese toppings.

1 tablespoon chili powder

1 tablespoon paprika

2 teaspoons dried oregano

2 teaspoons ground cumin

1 teaspoon salt

1½ pounds boneless, skinless chicken breasts, sliced into strips

2 cups sliced bell peppers, any color (about 2 large peppers)

1 large onion, quartered and then thinly sliced

2 cloves garlic, minced

¼ cup olive oil, plus more for the pan

2 tablespoons lime juice

Fresh cilantro leaves, for garnish

TIP! *Mix up a double batch of the spice blend to make fajitas even more quickly next time.*

1. Preheat the oven to 400°F. Grease a large rimmed baking sheet generously with olive oil.

2. Mix the spices and salt in a small bowl and set aside.

3. Put the chicken strips, bell peppers, onion, garlic, oil, and lime juice in a large bowl and mix to distribute the oil and lime juice thoroughly. Sprinkle in the spice mix and toss to coat the chicken and vegetables.

4. Spread the chicken and veggies on the greased baking sheet in a single layer. Bake for 20 to 25 minutes, stirring halfway through the baking time, until the chicken is cooked through and tender. If you enjoy a little char on your fajitas, you can place the pan under the broiler for 3 to 5 minutes before serving.

5. Garnish with cilantro and serve.

6. Refrigerate leftovers for up to 5 days, or freeze for up to a month. The leftovers taste even better!

TIP! *Use beef instead of chicken for variety. Sirloin steak strips cook a bit faster than chicken, so I generally don't mix the two meats. The beef is typically cooked and tender after 14 to 17 minutes.*

Older kids can help slice the chicken and veggies. This is a great time to explain that making the pieces somewhat uniform in size is important because it affects the baking time; smaller pieces will cook faster. Also, you might involve kids in tweaking the seasonings. For example, Grace likes less cumin but appreciates ancho chili powder as well as achiote, which give the fajitas a more authentic Southwestern flavor. We enjoy sniffing the spices and experimenting to find our favorite combinations. Younger kids who can't handle knives or may not have a keen sense of smell and taste can enjoy mixing the spices together and sprinkling them over the chicken and vegetables.

CALORIES: 448 | **FAT:** 21.6g | **PROTEIN:** 41.1g | **CARBS:** 5.4g | **FIBER:** 2.3g

CHAPTER 7

SIDES AND SNACKS

On keto, my kids are far less likely to snack than they did when they were eating a lot of ultra-processed and refined carbohydrates. You'll see that we grouped sides and snacks together into one chapter since some of these foods can accompany main dishes or can be enjoyed on their own as a snack. For example, the Nacho Chips can be enjoyed with the Homemade Hoagies (page 174). We've also included some sides that can be added to lunch boxes or eaten on the go, like the Pepperoni Cheese Chips.

Some of these sides can be turned into a complete meal just by adding a simple protein like a hamburger patty, sliced hot dogs, or shredded rotisserie chicken. The Cheddar Broccoli Soup and Better Than the Box Mac 'n' Cheese are just two examples. The Three Amigos Dip can also be a complete meal or served as a side with Sheet Pan Fajitas (page 184).

Grace likes the Orange Blossom Trail Mix because she can eat it on the go. Have I mentioned that she isn't a morning person? The light orange flavor is a really nice way to start the day. She can enjoy it by the handful or put it in a bowl with a simple mix of heavy cream and almond milk and eat it like a traditional breakfast cereal.

Many of these sides are great for parties, too. Whether a group of kids are gathering at your house or you're sending your children off with food to share, the Crispy Pizza Chips, French Onion Dip, or Marinated Roasted Cheese will give them a little fat or protein to round out the carbs they're likely to be served. Any host will welcome these dishes to the buffet table.

As you're creating your own favorite sides, just remember that veggies should always be a vehicle for fat. We've set an example by adding olive oil to the Avocado Salsa; loading up the zucchini skins with fat and protein in the form of bacon, cheese, and sour cream; and making the Cheesy Cauli Mash extra fatty,

AVOCADO SALSA

MAKES
6 servings

Unlike a traditional salsa, this one isn't spicy, and it's lower in carbs because tomatoes play a lesser role. Grace and I really enjoy it over salmon. It's good with Mexican-inspired dishes like Sheet Pan Fajitas (page 184) as well. This salsa can be served right away or made in advance and refrigerated until you are ready to eat it.

1 medium Hass avocado, chopped

1 medium tomato, seeded and chopped

⅓ cup chopped red bell peppers

2 tablespoons chopped fresh cilantro

1 tablespoon finely chopped red onions

1 tablespoon avocado oil or olive oil

1 tablespoon lime juice

⅛ teaspoon salt

Put all of the ingredients in a small mixing bowl and stir to coat the chopped ingredients with the oil and lime juice. Refrigerate for up to 4 days.

Any child who can handle a knife can make this simple salsa. Those too young to safely handle knives might enjoy washing the cilantro and picking off the leaves. I like to use kitchen shears to cut the cilantro; younger kids could practice using scissors as they help. This is also a great time to show them how to cut an avocado.

CALORIES: 65 | **FAT:** 5.8g | **PROTEIN:** 0.7g | **CARBS:** 3.7g | **FIBER:** 2g

OLIVE OIL DIPPING SAUCE

MAKES
2 servings

I created this recipe in a flash when someone asked for an olive oil–based dipping sauce for the baguettes on page 58. Grace enjoys it so much that she tends to double it to have one batch for herself. In addition to bread, you can dip cheese in this sauce. Yes, cheese! Cucumbers and tomatoes are also yummy when used as dippers.

½ teaspoon Italian seasoning

¼ teaspoon dried basil

¼ teaspoon dried minced garlic

¼ teaspoon dried minced onion

¼ teaspoon dried oregano leaves

⅛ teaspoon salt

Dash of red pepper flakes

1½ tablespoons olive oil

Sprinkle the seasonings onto a small bread plate. Drizzle the olive oil over the seasonings and serve.

If kids can measure, this is an ideal recipe for them to try making solo. They will enjoy mixing the spices and then pouring the oil over them. Task them with finding small plates or tiny bowls to serve the dip. They might also enjoy arranging the bread or other dippers on a serving plate.

CALORIES: 95 | **FAT:** 10.1g | **PROTEIN:** 0.3g | **CARBS:** 0.8g | **FIBER:** 0.1g

BETTER THAN THE BOX
MAC 'N' CHEESE

MAKES
4 servings

While I love an old-fashioned baked macaroni and cheese, a quick stovetop mac 'n' cheese with only five ingredients has its place in any kitchen that feeds kids, even those who are only young at heart. This recipe uses oat fiber–based shirataki noodles, which, in my opinion, have a better texture than the konjac-based versions. If you can't find them or don't like them, sliced cabbage has a neutral taste and also works well in this recipe.

14 ounces shirataki fettuccine or steamed sliced cabbage

6 tablespoons (¾ stick) unsalted butter

⅔ cup heavy cream

⅓ cup Anthony's powdered cheese (see Note)

1 cup shredded mild cheddar cheese (about 4 ounces), room temperature

1. Cut the fettuccine into bite-sized pieces and cook according to the package directions. Drain and pat dry with a clean kitchen towel to remove the excess moisture. Set aside.

2. Melt the butter in a 1½-quart saucepan over low heat. Whisk in the cream and simmer until thickened, about 10 minutes.

3. Whisk in the powdered cheese. When smooth, stir in the noodles and turn off the heat. Sprinkle in the cheddar cheese and stir until melted. Serve immediately.

4. Refrigerate leftovers for up to 4 days.

NOTE: *While I don't typically recommend particular brands, many commercial cheese powders contain food starches or sugars. At the time of this writing, Anthony's is the only brand I feel comfortable recommending.*

My daughter has become an expert at making this dish, which shows that older kids can make it easily. Younger children might enjoy draining the noodles. You can also let them use kitchen shears to trim the fettuccine into smaller pieces. This is another recipe that reminds them to let the cheese come to room temperature and remove the pan from the heat before adding the cheese to keep it from separating.

CALORIES: 419 | **FAT:** 40.8g | **PROTEIN:** 9.1g | **CARBS:** 3.8g | **FIBER:** 1g

CAULI RISOTTO

MAKES
4 servings

When I created this recipe, I was trying to make low-carb grits but ended up with something more like risotto. The corn extract is optional, but my family thinks it's what makes this dish crave-worthy. (You'll also use it when making the corn dogs on page 182.) If you use frozen riced cauliflower, this is a super quick side for weeknight meals.

¾ cup heavy cream

2 tablespoons unsalted butter

12 ounces fresh or frozen riced cauliflower (see Note)

⅛ teaspoon salt

¼ teaspoon corn extract (optional)

¾ cup shredded mild cheddar cheese

¼ cup cooked and crumbled bacon, for topping (optional)

1. In a large saucepan over medium heat, bring the cream and butter to a simmer. Reduce the heat to low and simmer until thickened, 5 to 8 minutes.

2. Stir in the riced cauliflower and increase the heat to medium-low. Simmer until the cauliflower is tender and the cream mixture has thickened further, another 6 to 8 minutes.

3. Remove from the heat and stir in the salt and corn extract, if using. Sprinkle the cheese over the risotto and stir to combine. Top with the bacon, if using.

4. Refrigerate leftovers for up to 5 days, or freeze for up to a month.

NOTE: *If using frozen riced cauliflower, thaw it first and then squeeze out as much of the excess moisture as you can with a clean kitchen towel.*

TIP! *Include the bacon and add some diced or shredded roasted chicken to make this easy side a complete meal.*

Let older children learn about controlling the temperature on the stovetop as they first simmer the cream and butter over medium heat and then reduce the heat to simmer out the last of the liquid. It's important to keep an eye on the final simmer so that the risotto becomes thick but doesn't scorch.

CHEDDAR BROCCOLI SOUP

MAKES
6 servings

While this soup is simple to make, it's important to note a few key steps to ensure success. First, don't skip browning the onion, which adds a depth of flavor that you won't want to miss. I also prefer to cook the broccoli until it's very tender, then purée some of the soup and mix it back in. This way, there are some small pieces of broccoli and onion to provide texture, but the rest of the soup is thick and hearty. Lastly, be sure to let the cheese come to room temperature and remove the pot from the heat before adding the cheese to the soup. If the soup is too hot, the proteins in the cheese will separate from the fat, creating a stringy, gloopy mess that no one is going to want to eat. To be safe, you may want to turn off the heat, set a timer for five minutes, and then add the cheese.

½ medium onion, chopped

1 clove garlic, minced

2 tablespoons unsalted butter

½ teaspoon dry mustard

½ teaspoon smoked paprika

⅛ teaspoon cayenne pepper (optional)

⅛ teaspoon salt

Dash of ground black pepper

2 cups chicken broth

1½ cups heavy cream

3 cups chopped fresh broccoli (small stems and florets)

2½ cups shredded mild cheddar cheese (about 12 ounces), room temperature

1. Sauté the onion and garlic in the butter in a 4-quart saucepan over medium heat. When the onion is just starting to brown, stir in the mustard, paprika, cayenne (if using), salt, and black pepper.

2. Pour in the broth and cream and bring to a simmer. Reduce the heat and simmer for 20 to 25 minutes, until the liquid is reduced and slightly thickened. Add the broccoli and simmer for an additional 10 to 15 minutes, until the broccoli is tender.

3. Remove 2 cups of the soup and purée in a blender. Return the puree to the saucepan and stir to blend it into the rest of the soup. Remove the pan from the heat and stir in the cheese a little bit at a time, stirring continuously as the cheese melts. Serve immediately.

4. Refrigerate leftovers for up to 3 days. Warm leftover soup in a 1-quart saucepan over low heat. If using the microwave, use reduced power so that the cheese does not separate.

NOTE: *This soup is categorized as a side dish because it doesn't contain enough protein to be a complete meal. To make it a meal, add at least 3 ounces of cooked protein per serving. Chicken and ground beef are good choices.*

Older children might enjoy making this recipe from start to finish. Please caution them to use care when transferring the hot soup to the blender and then pouring it back into the pot. They may also need to be reminded to remove the pan from the heat before adding the cheese.

CALORIES: 457 | **FAT:** 41.5g | **PROTEIN:** 16.5g | **CARBS:** 5.4g | **FIBER:** 1.3g

MARINATED ROASTED CHEESE

MAKES
4 servings

This dish was inspired by a recipe for tofu. My family generally avoids soy, but we really like firm cheeses such as paneer, halloumi, and queso fresco. Queso fresco is usually the least expensive of the three and is easy to find in most grocery stores, which is why I chose to use it in this recipe. The cheese can be marinated for longer than four hours, so you can roast it whenever you're ready. The bonus is that you only have to pop it in the oven—there's no fussing over the stove.

10 ounces queso fresco, cut into ½-inch cubes

¼ cup coconut aminos, or 2 tablespoons lite soy sauce

2 tablespoons toasted sesame oil

2 teaspoons minced ginger

½ teaspoon minced garlic

1. Place all of the ingredients in a quart-sized resealable plastic bag, seal the bag, and shake to coat the cheese cubes with the marinade. Refrigerate for at least 4 hours, turning the bag occasionally.

2. When ready to roast the cheese, preheat the oven to 400°F. Line a large rimmed baking sheet with parchment paper.

3. Remove the cheese from the marinade and reserve the marinade for use as a dipping sauce, if desired. Place the cheese cubes on the lined baking sheet in a single layer.

4. Roast until the cheese is browned, 8 to 12 minutes. Remove from the oven and let cool for 5 to 10 minutes before serving.

5. Refrigerate leftovers for up to 4 days.

Younger kids tend to love marinades, and this is one they can easily mix. They can also drop the cheese cubes into the marinade. After the bag is sealed, let them shake or massage it to distribute the ingredients.

CALORIES: 303 | FAT: 23.9g | PROTEIN: 12.8g | CARBS: 3.5g | FIBER: 0g

LOADED ZUCCHINI SKINS

MAKES
4 servings

If you've ever sat around a shared platter of roasted potato skins, then you'll appreciate this recipe. It's perfect for game days and sleepovers because you're essentially roasting the zucchini planks and then topping them as you would potato skins. You can let kids choose their own toppings if you have picky eaters, such as someone who dislikes green onions or doesn't eat dairy.

2 medium zucchini

½ cup shredded mild cheddar cheese (about 2 ounces)

¼ cup chopped cooked bacon

1 green onion top, chopped

4 tablespoons sour cream, for serving

1. Use a vegetable peeler or sharp knife to cut the zucchini lengthwise into ½-inch-thick planks. Press the planks between paper towels to remove the excess moisture.

2. Preheat the oven to 400°F.

3. Place the zucchini planks on a wire baking rack and set the rack inside a large rimmed baking sheet. Roast until tender and browned, 30 to 35 minutes.

4. Remove from the oven and transfer the zucchini to a serving plate. Sprinkle the cheese, bacon, and green onion over the roasted zucchini. Serve with the sour cream.

5. Refrigerate leftovers for up to 4 days.

TIPS! *If you have time, you can sweat the zucchini planks to make them more tender and less soggy when baked. Place the zucchini on the wire rack and sprinkle with salt. Let the zucchini sweat for 20 to 30 minutes before using a paper towel to press out as much moisture as possible.*

If you don't have a wire baking rack, line a rimmed baking sheet with parchment paper. The zucchini will be softer, but equally delicious when topped.

It takes a bit of knife skill to cut the zucchini in even planks, but after the zucchini is roasted, you can encourage kids to add the cheese, bacon, and green onion.

CALORIES: 120 | **FAT:** 8.8g | **PROTEIN:** 6.2g | **CARBS:** 3.4g | **FIBER:** 1.1g

FRENCH ONION DIP

MAKES
about 1¼ cups
(2 tablespoons
per serving)

As a kid, I used to eat French onion dip every chance I got. Every chip that I'd pop into my mouth was weighed down with dip. It was clearly the dip I loved most. One day, I realized that making my own French onion dip should be pretty simple. I set about trying to recreate the beefy, oniony flavor of the classic dip I adored, which set me on a path to investigate nearly every brand of powdered bouillon on the market. (See the note below for more on bouillon.) This recipe also uses dried minced onion to mimic commercial dips.

As for the chips? Replace potato chips with pork rinds, pepperoni chips, or sliced raw veggies like cucumber, radish, broccoli, or cauliflower.

1 cup sour cream

2 tablespoons dried minced onion

2 teaspoons beef bouillon powder (see Note)

1 teaspoon onion powder

Mix all of the ingredients together in a small bowl. Cover and refrigerate for at least 30 minutes to soften the onion before serving. Refrigerate for up to a week.

NOTE: *The brand of bouillon with the best ingredients I have found is Ketologie. It's a bit pricey, but you can order it from Amazon or the company's website. If you're less careful with ingredients, there's a brand called Better Than Bouillon that makes a hearty beef-flavored base. You will have to adjust the amount of bouillon based on the brand you choose, as the flavor intensity varies. As a general rule, I use 1½ tablespoons of the Ketologie brand but only 2 teaspoons of the Better Than Bouillon brand in this recipe. Start with 2 teaspoons and then add ½ teaspoon at a time until the dip is seasoned as you like it.*

This recipe requires only measuring and mixing, so it's perfect for involving younger children; slightly older ones can probably tackle it alone. Remind them that the dried onion needs time to rehydrate in the fridge, and that's why the dip gets better over time.

CALORIES: 47 | **FAT:** 4.5g | **PROTEIN:** 0.7g | **CARBS:** 1.3g | **FIBER:** 0g

CRISPY PIZZA CHIPS

MAKES
16 chips
(4 servings)

Pizza chips are great for travel, including lunch boxes. I tend to make them most often when the kids have friends over. This is one of those snacks that doesn't feel "different." It's just a tasty chip that tastes a bit like pizza, especially if you dip it in No-Cook Pizza Sauce (page 124). You can either bake the chips in the oven or make them in the microwave; you'll find directions for both methods below.

2 cups shredded part-skim mozzarella cheese (about 8 ounces)

½ cup finely shredded Parmesan cheese

1½ teaspoons dried Italian seasoning

¼ teaspoon dried oregano leaves

¼ teaspoon onion powder

¼ teaspoon paprika (optional)

⅛ teaspoon garlic powder

9 slices pepperoni (about ½ ounce), chopped

OVEN METHOD:

1. Preheat the oven to 375°F. Line an 11 by 17-inch rimmed baking sheet with parchment paper.

2. In a large bowl, use a spatula or wooden spoon to toss the cheeses, seasonings, and pepperoni. Spread the mixture on the parchment paper in a 10 by 12-inch rectangle that is about ⅛ inch thick.

3. Bake until melted and browned, 15 to 18 minutes. The rectangle will be firm but malleable. Use a pizza cutter or sharp knife to cut it into sixteen 1½-inch triangles by making alternating diagonal cuts.

4. Turn the chips over so that the browned sides are facedown, then return them to the oven for 6 to 8 more minutes, until browned on top. Remove from the oven and let cool to crisp, or turn off the oven and allow the chips to cool in the oven with the oven door ajar.

5. Refrigerate leftovers for up to 5 days, or freeze for up to a month.

Kids can be involved in making most of this recipe, including mixing and spreading the cheese mixture over the baking sheet. Take care to avoid burns when cutting the rectangle into chips.

CALORIES: 233 | **FAT:** 15.9g | **PROTEIN:** 18.1g | **CARBS:** 3.1g | **FIBER:** 0.2g

TIPS! *Use a clean set of kitchen shears to cut the chips into triangles or any shape you prefer.*

If the chips are not crispy enough, or if they lose their crispiness after being refrigerated, microwave them in small batches for 10 seconds at a time.

MICROWAVE METHOD:

1. Line a large flat microwave-safe dish with parchment paper.

2. In a large bowl, use a spatula or wooden spoon to toss the cheeses, seasonings, and pepperoni. Drop tablespoons of the mixture onto the parchment paper in small piles, leaving at least 1 inch of space between piles. A standard dinner plate will hold about 4 piles. Cover with a second piece of parchment paper to avoid spatters.

3. Microwave for 55 to 60 seconds. Let cool for at least 1 minute before removing the chips from the microwave. Repeat with the remaining mixture.

4. Refrigerate leftovers for up to 5 days, or freeze for up to a month.

ORANGE BLOSSOM TRAIL MIX

MAKES
8 servings
(about ½ cup
per serving)

It's 8 a.m. somewhere when we have a batch of this trail mix around! I intentionally used the lowest-carb ingredients I could in order to make the serving size reasonable enough to enjoy. If your kids won't eat pork rinds, don't let them help you make this recipe. I promise they will never know that there are pork rinds in it if you don't tell them. Also, remember to use the large, fluffy pork rinds and avoid the smaller, harder pork cracklin's that have a much stronger taste.

1½ cups bite-sized pork rind pieces

1 cup chopped raw almonds

½ cup raw cashew pieces or sliced macadamia nuts

½ cup raw pecan pieces

¼ cup raw pumpkin seeds

1 large egg white

2 tablespoons fresh orange juice

¼ teaspoon vanilla extract

3 drops liquid sweetener

1 teaspoon salt

⅓ cup powdered sweetener

1 tablespoon grated orange zest

1 teaspoon ground cardamom (optional)

1. Preheat the oven to 200°F. Line a large rimmed baking sheet with parchment paper or aluminum foil that has been lightly greased.

2. In a large bowl, toss the pork rinds, nuts, and pumpkin seeds. In a separate small bowl, whisk the egg white until frothy. Add the orange juice, vanilla extract, liquid sweetener, and salt to the egg white and continue whisking until blended and frothy.

3. Pour the egg white mixture over the nut mixture and toss to thoroughly coat each piece.

4. Sprinkle the powdered sweetener, orange zest, and cardamom, if using, over the trail mix, stirring so that each piece is seasoned.

5. Spread the trail mix in a single layer on the prepared baking sheet. Bake for 25 to 30 minutes before using a spatula to stir the pieces. Continue baking in 25- to 30-minute increments until the trail mix is lightly browned and crisp, 2 to 2½ hours.

6. When the trail mix is crisp, turn off the oven, open the oven door slightly, turn on the oven light, and leave the mixture to cool for at least 1½ hours or overnight. The trail mix will become crisper as it sits in the oven.

7. Remove from the oven and let cool to room temperature before serving. Store in an airtight container at room temperature for up to 2 weeks.

If you buy the nuts already chopped, kids of all ages can help measure and mix the ingredients. While you might not want very young children touching the raw egg white mixture, most kids will be able to mix up the nuts and spread them over the prepared baking sheet. Older children can also stir the trail mix during the baking time. Be sure to reserve the job of packaging up the trail mix for the person who is most trustworthy to package more than they eat!

CALORIES: 225 | FAT: 19.7g | PROTEIN: 10.5g | CARBS: 5g | FIBER: 2.8g | ERYTHRITOL: 8.9g

NACHO CHIPS

MAKES
4 servings

These chips are perfect for packing in lunches, taking on picnics, or snacking on at soccer practice. We've made them with pork rinds, cheese chips, and even pepperoni chips—my favorite! If you keep the nacho cheese seasoning mixed up, children can easily make these anytime they are feeling a little snacky. My kids prefer this seasoning with cheese chips instead of pork rinds, and it's easy to sprinkle the seasoning into a single-serve bag of cheese chips while on the go.

4 cups fluffy pork rinds (about 1½ ounces)

2 tablespoons Nacho Cheese Seasoning (page 112)

Put the pork rinds in a large resealable plastic bag. Sprinkle the seasoning over the pork rinds, seal the bag, and toss to coat. Store the chips in an airtight container at room temperature for up to 5 days.

TIPS! *Microwave the pork rinds on reduced power for 15 to 20 seconds to help the seasoning stick to them.*

If using cheese chips in place of pork rinds, you might want to reduce the amount of nacho cheese seasoning.

Let the kids make up a batch or two of the Nacho Cheese Seasoning so that they can create this tasty snack anytime they want. Because this is as simple as sprinkle and shake, younger kids can use this recipe as an opportunity to (gently) shake away the wiggles.

CALORIES: 84 | **FAT:** 4.8g | **PROTEIN:** 8g | **CARBS:** 1.8g | **FIBER:** 0g

CHEESY CAULI MASH

MAKES
6 servings

We love cauli mash! Even David, who doesn't love to cook, can make it without more than a glance at the recipe. Steaming the cauliflower in the microwave is not only fast but helps reduce some of the moisture. That's the trick to thick, creamy cauli mash—squeeze as much moisture as you can from the cooked cauliflower before putting it in the blender.

4 cups chopped cauliflower (stems and florets)

½ cup (1 stick) unsalted butter, softened

½ cup heavy cream, plus more if needed

2 ounces (¼ cup) cream cheese

½ cup sharp cheddar cheese, shredded (about 2 ounces)

¼ teaspoon salt

Dash of garlic powder

1. Put the cauliflower in a microwave-safe dish (do not add water or other liquid) and microwave for 6 to 7 minutes, until soft. Use a clean kitchen towel or paper towel to squeeze the excess moisture from the steamed cauliflower.

2. Transfer the cauliflower to a blender. Add the butter, heavy cream, cream cheese, cheddar, salt, and garlic powder. Blend until the mixture is puréed and creamy, adding more cream if the mash is too thick. Serve immediately.

3. Refrigerate leftovers for up to 5 days.

TIPS! *Bring all of the dairy ingredients to room temperature before beginning this recipe so the cauliflower stays warm when the dairy ingredients are added to the blender. You can heat the finished cauli mash in the microwave if it is too cool after blending.*

If you're being mindful about dairy, you can add a bit of broth instead of cream if the mash is too thick.

Let younger children add ingredients to the blender and enjoy pressing the buttons. Older kids can chop and steam the cauliflower, but do caution them about avoiding burns when removing the moisture from the steamed cauliflower.

CALORIES: 292 | **FAT:** 29g | **PROTEIN:** 4.7g | **CARBS:** 4.8g | **FIBER:** 1.8g

THREE AMIGOS DIP

MAKES
8 servings

Three best friends come together in this hardy dip to do what friends do—make life better! Cheese, beef, and chiles are the primary ingredients. My family enjoys this dip alongside Sheet Pan Fajitas (page 184). David and I prefer it made with chorizo, a spicy sausage. If you opt for chorizo, note that some brands are spicier than others; you might want to leave out the seasonings until you taste-test the cooked sausage and then season the dip to your liking.

1 pound ground beef (80/20) or Mexican-style (fresh) chorizo

1 (4-ounce) can diced green chiles, drained

¼ cup chopped onions

1 teaspoon ground cumin

½ teaspoon chili powder

¼ teaspoon dried oregano leaves

2½ cups shredded Monterey Jack cheese (about 10 ounces)

FOR GARNISH:

1 small Roma tomato, chopped

Chopped fresh cilantro leaves

1. Brown the ground beef in an 8- to 10-inch ovenproof skillet over medium-high heat, 15 to 20 minutes. Drain some of the fat, if desired, making sure to leave at least a tablespoon or two in the pan.

2. Add the green chiles, onions, and seasonings and reduce the heat to low. Sauté until the onions are tender, 6 to 8 minutes. Remove the pan from the heat and sprinkle the cheese over the top.

3. Place an oven rack so that the skillet will be 7 to 8 inches from the heating element. Preheat the oven to broil.

4. Place the skillet under the broiler until the cheese is bubbling and lightly browned, 4 to 6 minutes. Remove from the oven, garnish with the tomato and cilantro, and serve immediately.

5. Refrigerate leftovers for up to 5 days.

Kids who are old enough to chop onions and brown meats can make this recipe on their own. It's a great option for them to make and serve to friends. Be sure to talk to them about how to drain the fat and dispose of it properly.

CALORIES: 224 | **FAT:** 16.2g | **PROTEIN:** 17.8g | **CARBS:** 1.4g | **FIBER:** 0.6g

GREEN BEAN FRIES

MAKES
6 servings

Why, these aren't french fries, but they make a nice alternative to fries. We like them very well done, but you may want to remove them from the oven before they get too dark. The high heat makes the green beans taste a bit sweeter than usual, and the Parmesan cheese adds a nice salty crunch to complement that sweetness. These fries can be dipped in homemade ketchup (page 118).

1 pound fresh green beans, trimmed

1 tablespoon bacon fat, melted

1 teaspoon salt

½ teaspoon coarsely ground black pepper

¼ cup shredded Parmesan cheese

1. Preheat the oven to 400°F. Line a large rimmed baking sheet with parchment paper.

2. Put the green beans in a large bowl. Pour the melted bacon fat over the beans and sprinkle with the salt and pepper. Use tongs or a spatula to toss the beans, coating them in the fat and seasonings.

3. Spread the green beans in a single layer on the lined baking sheet. Roast until they begin to develop dark brown patches, 12 to 14 minutes.

4. Remove from the oven and transfer to a serving plate. Sprinkle with the Parmesan cheese and serve warm.

5. Refrigerate leftovers for up to 3 days.

Let the kids help from beginning to end when you make this easy recipe. They can reduce the amount of black pepper if they aren't big fans. Younger kids can sprinkle the Parmesan on the green beans right before they are served.

CALORIES: 65 | FAT: 3.8g | PROTEIN: 2.7g | CARBS: 4.2g | FIBER: 2g

FRIED CAULI-RICE

MAKES
6 servings

This is one of the few veggie sides that both of my offspring enjoy, which is why I make it pretty frequently. Even when I don't have celery on hand, they still gobble it up, so if your kids object to celery, just leave it out. The flavor is mild, and it's really good with any grilled meat. The kids like to eat it with rotisserie chicken. It pairs nicely with the Asian Lettuce Cups (page 166) as well.

2 tablespoons unsalted butter, ghee, or coconut oil

1 green onion, chopped

1 stalk celery, chopped

¼ teaspoon garlic powder

½ teaspoon onion powder

¼ teaspoon salt (omit if using tamari)

¼ cup coconut aminos, or 2 tablespoons lite soy sauce

12 ounces fresh or frozen riced cauliflower (see Note)

3 large eggs, beaten

1 tablespoon toasted sesame oil or unsalted butter

1 green onion top, sliced, for garnish (optional)

1. Melt the butter in a large skillet over medium heat. Add the chopped green onion, celery, garlic powder, onion powder, and salt, if using, and cook until the vegetables are crisp-tender, 3 to 5 minutes.

2. Add the coconut aminos and simmer until the sauce is reduced, 8 to 10 minutes. Add the riced cauliflower and sauté until just tender, 2 to 3 minutes.

3. Add the eggs to the skillet and cook, stirring, to scramble the eggs into the other ingredients. Remove from the heat, drizzle the sesame oil over the skillet, garnish with the green onion top, if desired, and serve.

4. Refrigerate leftovers for up to 5 days, or freeze for up to a month.

NOTE: *If using frozen riced cauliflower, thaw it first and then remove as much moisture as possible with a clean kitchen towel before adding it to the skillet.*

Kids who can confidently use the stove will likely be able to make this recipe on their own, assuming that they are also comfortable using a knife to chop the onion and celery. They may need help initially with knowing how long to simmer the dish to thicken the sauce. They will likely enjoy cracking in the eggs and scrambling them at the end of the cooking time.

CALORIES: 105 | **FAT:** 7.4g | **PROTEIN:** 4.5g | **CARBS:** 4.6g | **FIBER:** 1.5g

PEPPERONI CHEESE CHIPS

MAKES
2 servings

Simple foods can taste fantastic! This "recipe" is a perfect example. We've eaten these chips with dips, like the No-Cook Pizza Sauce (page 124) or the French Onion Dip (page 200), and with salads and soups, but most often we just enjoy them plain. They should stay crisp in an airtight container in the refrigerator, but if they don't, you can zap them in the microwave for five to ten seconds and they should crisp back up as they cool. The cook time may vary depending on the type of cheese you use. The chips are done when the cheese is browned. They will crisp up as they cool. If the cheese stays runny or fails to crisp, then microwave the chips longer.

1 cup shredded mozzarella or mild cheddar cheese (about 4 ounces)

16 slices pepperoni

1. Preheat the oven to 375°F. Line an 11 by 17-inch rimmed baking sheet with parchment paper.

2. Scatter the cheese evenly across the pan in a 12 by 10-inch rectangle. Arrange the pepperoni on top of the cheese, spaced about ½ inch apart, in 4 rows, leaving at least 1 inch of space between rows.

3. Bake until the cheese is melted and lightly browned, 7 to 10 minutes. Use a pizza cutter or sharp knife to cut the rectangle into 16 squares with a slice of pepperoni in the center of each.

TIP! *These chips can be made without the pepperoni for those who don't care for pepperoni.*

Definitely get the kids involved in this recipe! Small fingers can help place the cheese and pepperoni on the parchment paper. Kids ages eight and up can likely make these alone, although they may need to be taught how to remove the chips from the oven without burning themselves.

CALORIES: 247 | FAT: 18.6g | PROTEIN: 16.5g | CARBS: 1.6g | FIBER: 0g

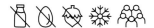

COOKOUT CHILI

MAKES
4 cups
(about ⅔ cup
per serving)

I've always loved a good chili dog or chili on a hamburger, and since commercial versions are generally loaded with sugars and starch, chili is something I've truly missed. When a follower sent me her family recipe, I decided to try to make it low-carb—which meant I spent nothing shy of five days learning everything I could about the finely ground beef sauce commonly used on hot dogs and hamburgers. Notes in hand, I started to the kitchen, not with a recipe but with lists of all of the ingredients I'd read about as I pored over the internet. A little of this, a little of that, a sniff, a sprinkle, and then a taste. In that first bite, I was transported to Martin's Grill in Albemarle, North Carolina, a tiny family-owned burger joint that had the best footlong hot dogs I ever ate. I hadn't thought about that chili in decades and wasn't even thinking about that restaurant until that taste. Taste buds have a powerful memory.

If you're not familiar with using chili as a topping for hamburgers or hot dogs, then you're in for a treat. In the South, an order of "all the way" will get you a hot dog or hamburger with chili, coleslaw, and raw onions. Add cheese and you've got one of the best meals you will ever eat. Just hold the bun!

The sweetener in this recipe is optional. It's such a small amount that it doesn't really add a sweet taste but rather blunts the acidity of the tomatoes. If you're used to a sweeter chili, you can add a bit more sweetener to your taste.

---

1 pound ground beef (80/20)

⅓ cup chopped onions

1 cup beef broth

3 tablespoons tomato paste

1 tablespoon plus ¼ teaspoon prepared yellow mustard

½ teaspoon apple cider vinegar

½ teaspoon Worcestershire sauce

2 heaping teaspoons chili powder

¾ teaspoon salt

¼ teaspoon garlic powder

1 drop liquid sweetener, or 2 teaspoons granulated sweetener (optional)

1. Brown the ground beef in a medium skillet over medium-high heat, using a spatula to break up the meat into fine pieces. When it is just browned, drain most of the fat, leaving at least 2 tablespoons of fat in the pan. Stir in the onions and cook until just tender, 6 to 8 minutes.

2. Reduce the heat to medium-low and stir in the broth, tomato paste, mustard, vinegar, Worcestershire sauce, chili powder, salt, garlic powder, and sweetener, if using. Simmer until the meat is tender and the sauce has thickened, 10 to 12 minutes. Serve immediately over hot dogs or burgers.

3. Refrigerate leftovers for up to 5 days, or freeze for up to a month.

TIP! *Make a double batch and freeze portions in pint jars, or use the second batch to make a Chili Cheese Dog Skillet (page 160).*

Let younger kids help measure the seasonings for this recipe. Older kids will need to brown the beef, chop the onion, and drain the fat. An adult may also have to keep an eye on the skillet while the chili is simmering so that it doesn't burn.

CALORIES: 206 | **FAT:** 12.3g | **PROTEIN:** 20.3g | **CARBS:** 2.2g | **FIBER:** 0.5g

CABBAGE NOODLES

MAKES
6 servings

Of all the veggie noodles that are popular on ketogenic diets, cabbage noodles are my favorite. Carb for carb, they are an even better option than zucchini noodles or cauliflower rice. What's more, they don't get watery or overly soft. The texture stays al dente, and the flavor is fairly neutral. My family is especially fond of cabbage noodles served under a pile of Orange-Braised Pork (page 146), Beef Stroganoff (page 150), or Chicken Mud (page 164) or covered in creamy Alfredo sauce. These simple noodles also pair well with Asian dishes.

1 quart water

½ head green cabbage

2 tablespoons unsalted butter or ghee

1 tablespoon salt

1. Bring the water to a boil in a large pot. While the water is heating, slice the cabbage into ½- to 1-inch-wide strips.

2. Add the cabbage to the boiling water and boil until tender, 7 to 10 minutes. Drain well. Stir in the butter and salt until the butter melts and thoroughly coats the cabbage. Serve immediately.

3. Refrigerate leftovers for up to 4 days. Reheat in the microwave or on the stovetop with an additional tablespoon of butter or ghee.

Older children who want to practice knife skills can help out by slicing the cabbage. This recipe also provides an opportunity for them to see how quickly the texture of a veggie can change when it's steamed. An adult may need to drain the noodles or provide guidance for avoiding burns when draining them.

CALORIES: 53 | FAT: 3.9g | PROTEIN: 1g | CARBS: 4.3g | FIBER: 2g

CHAPTER 8:
DESSERTS AND TREATS

Many of the recipes in this chapter are low-carb or keto versions of kid favorites, including holiday favorites. In short, these recipes are meant to help all kids feel as Jonathan did when he said, "Mom, I'm not missing a thing!" He can mainly thank Grace for that, as she inspired some of my older recipes, such as the Chocolate Mini Cakes, Chocolate Buttercream Frosting, Sullivano Chocolate Sandwich Cookies, and Ice Cream Sandwiches, as well as the Chocolate Chip Scones that he adores.

These recipes give kids options to share with their peers and to feel included in special occasions. Once you find a sweetener that your family enjoys (see pages 40 and 41 for more on low-carb sweeteners), these desserts are generally well accepted. In fact, not many families make homemade treats anymore, so my children's friends are often impressed that this mom can whip up a batch of marshmallows, simmer caramel sauce, or create nearly any flavor of ice cream in our own kitchen. A friend of Jonathan's once whispered to him, "Your mom's making brownies, and she's not using a box. I didn't know you could do that!" When his mother picked him up, I felt a bit guilty when he explained to her that she too could make brownies without a box.

Because these are treats and some of them take a bit longer to prepare, I don't make them frequently. When I do, it's typically for a special occasion or because the kids have requested them. To help with portion control, some of these recipes make small batches, like the mini cakes, minute brownies, Chocolate Peanut Clusters, and Keto Chocolate Turtles. Recipes that yield larger quantities can often be portioned into single servings and frozen. We tend to do this with the pound cake and cheesecake—but we don't often have leftovers!

Because it takes a bit more time to make treats from scratch instead of using convenience products, I try to trim my time commitment by making up dry mixes in advance. For example, when I'm making a batch of scones, it's just as easy to measure two or three batches of the dry ingredients. I can bake one batch and put the others in freezer bags for later. I store them in the fridge or freezer to help keep them fresh. My favorite dry mixes to make in advance are for the mini cakes and the chocolate waffles. Once the mix is packaged and labeled, the kids can finish the recipe quickly by adding the wet ingredients. That's even better than a box mix because I know the ingredients are good for them.

OPTION

CHOCOLATE MINI CAKES

MAKES

2 mini cakes
(1 per serving)

Over the years, I've made several versions of mug cakes, so when I was developing this version, the kids were not overly excited to taste-test it. And then they did. Whenever they ask, "Can you make this again?" I know it's good. This cake is moist and chocolatey with a perfect texture. We enjoy it plain, with a dollop of whipped cream, or as a classic layer cake with chocolate frosting, as pictured.

¼ cup plus 1 tablespoon blanched almond flour

2 tablespoons granulated sweetener

1½ tablespoons unsweetened cocoa powder

¼ teaspoon baking powder

Dash of salt

2 tablespoons unsalted butter or coconut oil, divided

1 large egg

⅛ teaspoon vanilla extract (optional)

¾ cup Chocolate Buttercream Frosting (page 226; optional)

TIP! *Making four cakes is as easy as making two! We often make these in tandem with two bowls and two batches of ingredients.*

You can also measure the dry ingredients and freeze the mix for later. Just add the butter, egg, and vanilla and you can have mini cakes in a minute.

1. Put the almond flour, sweetener, cocoa powder, baking powder, and salt in a small bowl and whisk to combine. Set aside.

2. Put 1 tablespoon of butter in each of two 8-ounce ramekins. Microwave on reduced power in 15-second increments until the butter has just melted. Tilt the ramekins to coat the bottoms and sides with the melted butter, then pour the excess butter into the bowl with the dry ingredients.

3. Add the egg and vanilla extract to the bowl with the dry ingredients and mix well with a rubber spatula until the batter is smooth. Divide the batter evenly between the greased ramekins and smooth the tops.

4. Microwave both ramekins together for 1 minute. The cakes may look a bit wet in the center, but they will continue cooking as they cool. If the cakes seem too wet, microwave for an additional 20 seconds, until just set.

5. Use a hand towel or an oven mitt to remove the cakes from the microwave. Let cool in the ramekins for 5 minutes, then run a knife around the edge of each ramekin to loosen the cakes and invert the cakes onto a plate or cooling rack.

6. To make a frosted layer cake, place one cake on a plate and frost the top with a layer of buttercream. Stack a second cake on top and frost the top and sides.

Younger kids will enjoy mixing the batter even if they are too young to measure the ingredients. Kids who are old enough to measure ingredients with accuracy can likely make these simple cakes all by themselves. Encourage children to use care when removing the hot ramekins from the microwave.

CALORIES: 220 | **FAT:** 23.5g | **PROTEIN:** 7.7g | **CARBS:** 4.8g | **FIBER:** 3.2g | **ERYTHRITOL:** 14.2g

CHOCOLATE BUTTERCREAM FROSTING

MAKES
1½ cups (¼ cup per serving)

Chocolate lovers, this recipe is for you! In fact, some people might prefer to reduce the amount of unsweetened chocolate just a bit. But if you believe that too much chocolate really isn't a thing, then you will find this rich buttercream super satisfying. Purists may scoff at the use of cream cheese; however, low-carb buttercream often needs more body, and adding just two ounces of cream cheese ensures that this buttercream will hold up to piping without tasting of cream cheese. We use this frosting primarily to frost mini layer cakes. To make a cake like the one pictured, you will need about half a batch.

1½ ounces unsweetened chocolate (100% cacao)

2 teaspoons refined coconut oil

5 tablespoons unsalted butter, softened

2 ounces (½ cup) cream cheese, softened

½ cup powdered sweetener

1 tablespoon unsweetened cocoa powder

½ teaspoon vanilla extract

⅓ cup heavy cream

1. Melt the chocolate and coconut oil in a double boiler, or place in a microwave-safe bowl and heat in 15-second intervals in the microwave. Stir frequently so that the chocolate does not burn. Set aside to cool.

2. In a separate bowl, whip the butter and cream cheese using a hand mixer until smooth. Add the sweetener and cocoa powder and continue whipping until well combined.

3. Pour in the melted chocolate mixture and the vanilla extract and whip until smooth. Then add the cream and whip again until smooth. If the frosting is too thick, add more cream, 1 tablespoon at a time, until it reaches your desired consistency.

4. Refrigerate leftover frosting for up to a week.

While the task of melting the coconut oil and chocolate is probably best left to older children, younger kids might enjoy operating the mixer, especially if you use a stand mixer. Kids who enjoy more independence in the kitchen can likely make this frosting on their own and enjoy a delicious sense of accomplishment.

CALORIES: 211 | **FAT:** 22.8g | **PROTEIN:** 2g | **CARBS:** 3.3g | **FIBER:** 1.3g | **ERYTHRITOL:** 18.9g

ENGLISH POSSET

MAKES
6 servings

There is so much to love about this recipe. First, it uses ingredients you probably keep stocked. Second, it works because of the chemical reaction with the heavy cream, so it's like a science experiment you can eat! Third, the posset has a creamy puddinglike texture that thickens as it sits uncovered, so you can control the consistency by adjusting the amount of time you leave the posset uncovered.

2 cups heavy cream

⅓ cup granulated sweetener

Dash of salt

¼ cup lemon juice

A handful of fresh berries, for garnish (optional)

6 fresh mint sprigs, for garnish (optional)

1. Put the cream, sweetener, and salt in a 1½-quart saucepan over low heat. Bring to a simmer, then continue to simmer until the cream begins to thicken, 6 to 8 minutes.

2. Remove from the heat and stir in the lemon juice. Set aside to cool for 20 to 30 minutes. A skin may form on the top, but you can stir it in to make it disappear.

3. Stir the mixture, then divide it evenly among six 8-inch ramekins. Refrigerate uncovered for at least 3 hours before serving. After 3 hours, cover and continue to refrigerate until ready to serve. Garnish each portion with a few berries and a mint sprig, if desired.

4. Refrigerate leftover posset for up to a week.

TIP! *Change up the flavor by using lime juice instead of lemon juice.*

Definitely get the kids involved in making this recipe! Kids who are too young to simmer the cream mixture can stir in the lemon juice. Have them label each ramekin and check the consistency over time when the posset is left uncovered. They should find that the longer the ramekin is left uncovered, the thicker the posset gets. In this way, they can discover their own "perfect" texture and determine how long to let the posset sit uncovered.

CALORIES: 272 | FAT: 28.6g | PROTEIN: 2.3g | CARBS: 2.2g | FIBER: 0g | ERYTHRITOL: 12.3g

DOUBLE-STUFFED CHOCOLATE WAFFLE DESSERT

MAKES
3 stacks
(6 servings)

Admittedly, these waffles are best when cool. If you try them warm, you may be disappointed in their soft texture. Let them cool and then layer them with filling, however, and your kids will love you forever. We like the rich flavor of dark cocoa powder in these waffles, but regular cocoa powder works just as well.

CREAM FILLING:

1 (8-ounce) package cream cheese, softened

½ cup sour cream

⅓ cup powdered sweetener

¼ cup heavy cream

1 teaspoon vanilla extract

WAFFLES:

¾ cup blanched almond flour

¼ cup granulated sweetener

3 tablespoons unsweetened dark cocoa powder, or ¼ cup unsweetened cocoa powder

1 teaspoon baking powder

Dash of salt

½ cup heavy cream

3 large eggs, beaten

1 teaspoon vanilla extract

Fresh berries, for serving

SPECIAL EQUIPMENT:

Mini waffle maker

1. Prepare the filling: Put all of the filling ingredients in a medium bowl and mix with a hand mixer until smooth and creamy. Set aside.

2. Make the waffles: Preheat a mini waffle maker. Put the almond flour, sweetener, cocoa powder, baking powder, and salt in another medium bowl and whisk to combine. Add the cream, eggs, and vanilla extract and mix with a rubber spatula to form a batter.

3. Put about 2 tablespoons of the batter in the waffle maker and cook following the manufacturer's directions. Remove the waffle to a cooling rack and repeat with the remaining batter, making a total of nine 4-inch waffles.

4. When the waffles have cooled, assemble the stacks: Place a waffle on a serving plate, then a layer of a generous 3 tablespoons of filling, a second waffle, another 3-tablespoon layer of filling, and a third waffle. Top the stack with a dollop of filling. Repeat with the remaining waffles and filling, creating a total of 3 stacks.

5. Cut each stack in half and serve with fresh berries, if desired.

6. The waffles can be made in advance and refrigerated until ready to use. Refrigerate leftover waffles and filling in separate containers for up to a week. Assemble just before eating.

These chocolate waffles are as fun to make as they are to eat! While one child makes waffles, another can whip up the filling. Then let them assemble the stacks. Kids can also get creative with garnishes. A sprinkle of chocolate chips, some berries, or a few shavings of chocolate can help them to finish this dessert with a flourish!

CALORIES: 403 | **FAT:** 37.1g | **PROTEIN:** 10.5g | **CARBS:** 6.2g | **FIBER:** 2.5g | **ERYTHRITOL:** 23.6g

MARSHMALLOWS

MAKES
24 marshmallows

I never thought I'd be that mom making homemade marshmallows, and I never thought I could enjoy a sugar-free marshmallow. But here I am, living the dream. While the thought of making marshmallows might be a bit daunting, the process is easier than you probably think, especially if you have a stand mixer, a timer, and a day that isn't too humid. Although a stand mixer works best for this recipe, you can use a hand mixer.

Be sure to read through the entire recipe before you begin. I also suggest laying out all of the ingredients in advance. Once you've made these marshmallows a time or two, you can toss them together in no time. It's a good thing, too, because you're likely to be making double batches.

1⅓ cups cold water, divided

5 tablespoons unflavored gelatin

⅔ cup xylitol

½ cup allulose

¼ teaspoon salt

2½ teaspoons vanilla extract

4 drops liquid sweetener (optional)

NOTE: *You can use all xylitol or all allulose, but after a lot of trial and error, we found that this combination yields the best texture. You can also use erythritol or an erythritol blend; however, when cooled, marshmallows made with erythritol are likely to become gritty or grainy.*

1. Line a 9 by 13-inch baking dish with parchment paper, leaving some overhanging for easy removal of the marshmallows.

2. Pour ⅔ cup of the water into the bowl of a stand mixer (or a mixing bowl if using a hand mixer). Sprinkle the gelatin over the water and stir gently. Set aside.

3. Bring the remaining ⅔ cup of water, the xylitol, allulose, and salt to a boil in a 1-quart saucepan over medium-low heat. As soon as the mixture begins to boil, set a timer for 3 minutes.

4. After 3 minutes, remove the pan from the heat. Work quickly by turning the mixer on low speed and then slowly streaming the hot mixture into the gelatin. Stop to quickly scrape any gelatin from the sides of the bowl.

5. Increase the mixer speed to medium and set a timer for 3 minutes. Add the vanilla extract and liquid sweetener, if using, just before the timer goes off.

6. After 3 minutes, increase the mixer speed to high and continue whipping until the marshmallow mixture has doubled in volume, 9 to 10 minutes.

7. Quickly pour the mixture into the lined baking pan and smooth it from edge to edge. (It will begin to thicken as soon as you stop mixing, so work fast!) Set aside to cool at room temperature for at least 2 hours. Use the parchment paper to lift the marshmallows out of the pan and place on a cutting board. Cut into 24 squares using a lightly greased knife.

8. Refrigerate leftover marshmallows, using sheets of parchment paper to separate the layers, for up to 2 weeks. If your house isn't humid, they can also be stored on the countertop.

CALORIES: 9 | **FAT:** 0g | **PROTEIN:** 2.3g | **CARBS:** 0g | **FIBER:** 0g

TIP! *During the initial mixing stage, I cover my stand mixer with a kitchen towel to avoid having splatters cover the surrounding area.*

VARIATIONS:

MARSHMALLOW FLUFF. Reduce the final mixing time to 4 to 5 minutes, stopping just before the marshmallow mixture has doubled in volume. Use the fluff over ice cream or mini cakes, or enjoy with a dollop of peanut butter.

MARSHMALLOW KEBABS. A fun use for these marshmallows is to cut them into smaller squares and then stack them on small skewers with fresh berries.

Watching the mixture get fluffier and transform into marshmallows is fun regardless of age! Younger kids can help operate the mixer, but even older children will need to take care with the boiling syrup that gets poured into the mix. Kids who are able can assist by setting and monitoring the timer—timing is a very important part of the success of this recipe.

OPTION

PEANUT BUTTER CHOCOLATE MINUTE BROWNIES

MAKES
2 brownies
(1 per serving)

My daughter, who typically doesn't enjoy peanut butter and chocolate together, enjoys this brownielike mug cake. So does my son, who has been known to consume both brownies at once. Do yourself a favor and plan to make two batches of these. Any leftover brownies will be delicious when eaten later. For the peanut butter, you can use either creamy or crunchy. While I enjoy the texture of crunchy peanut butter, both Grace and Jonathan prefer creamy.

2 tablespoons unsalted butter or coconut oil, plus more for greasing

2 tablespoons salted peanut butter

3 tablespoons granulated sweetener

1½ tablespoons unsweetened cocoa powder

¼ teaspoon baking powder

Dash of salt

1 large egg

⅛ teaspoon vanilla extract (optional)

1. Grease two 8-ounce ramekins with butter. Set aside.

2. In a small microwave-safe mixing bowl, melt the butter and peanut butter on 70% power in the microwave for 20 to 25 seconds. Use a rubber spatula to stir until melted and smooth. Add the remaining ingredients and continue to mix until a thick, well-blended batter forms.

3. Divide the batter evenly between the greased ramekins. Smooth the tops. Microwave both ramekins together for 1 minute. Let sit for a minute or two before removing from the microwave using an oven mitt or a kitchen towel; the ramekins will be hot. Let cool for at least 5 minutes before eating.

4. Refrigerate leftover brownies for up to 5 days, or freeze for up to 3 months.

TIP! *Be sure that the egg is well beaten into the batter. If not, it will cook on its own.*

Any minute muffin or egg cake is usually simple enough for older children to make on their own. This is no exception. Younger children can help with mixing the batter. Caution children that the ramekins will be hot when finished. This is also a great recipe to practice math skills by doubling the recipe.

CALORIES: 244 | FAT: 22.7g | PROTEIN: 8g | CARBS: 5.4g | FIBER: 2.8g | ERYTHRITOL: 21.3g

VANILLA POUND CAKE

MAKES
12 servings

Pound cake was Jonathan's first favorite dessert. He celebrated his fourth birthday sitting on top of the table in his pajama pants, shirtless, eating pound cake warm from the oven. He had confidently sliced himself a large chunk of cake and was eating it without a plate or napkin. At the time, I cringed, but he was happy and could have cared less that the scene wasn't Pinterest worthy. That was my award-wining high-carb version. To remain a Southern cook, I simply had to devise a low-carb pound cake that the family could enjoy. This is a simple vanilla cake, and it isn't a perfect approximation, but it can pass at the church buffet table any day of the week. Keep in mind that the yield is smaller than a traditional pound cake. It bakes perfectly in a 4-cup Bundt pan but can also be made in a 4 by 8-inch loaf pan.

1 cup blanched almond flour

⅓ cup coconut flour

¼ cup oat fiber, or 2 additional tablespoons coconut flour (see Note, page 52)

2 tablespoons unflavored whey protein isolate or egg white protein powder

1 teaspoon baking powder

½ teaspoon salt

½ cup (1 stick) unsalted butter, softened, plus more for greasing

½ cup granulated sweetener

5 large eggs

½ cup heavy cream

2 teaspoons vanilla extract

3 to 4 drops liquid sweetener (optional)

SPECIAL EQUIPMENT:

4-cup Bundt pan

1. Preheat the oven to 350°F. Grease a 4-cup Bundt pan with butter.

2. In a large bowl, whisk together the flours, oat fiber, whey protein isolate, baking powder, and salt. Set aside.

3. In a separate bowl, use a hand mixer or stand mixer to cream the butter and granulated sweetener.

4. In another bowl, using clean mixer blades, beat the eggs until frothy.

5. Add the beaten eggs to the butter mixture and beat until smooth. Stir in the cream and vanilla extract by hand using a rubber spatula.

6. Add the dry ingredients to the wet ingredients and mix by hand, being careful not to overmix. Stir in the liquid sweetener, if using.

7. Pour the batter into the greased pan and bake until the center springs back to the touch and a toothpick inserted in the center comes out clean, 35 to 45 minutes. Let cool completely before slicing and serving.

8. Refrigerate leftover cake for up to a week, or freeze for up to 3 months.

Budding bakers can easily tackle this foundational recipe. With a little experience knowing how the finished cake might look, they can try baking as cupcakes or in shaped baking pans. Younger children can help with the measuring and mixing.

CALORIES: 218 | FAT: 19.1g | PROTEIN: 6.5g | CARBS: 4.7g | FIBER: 3.6g | ERYTHRITOL: 9.2g | OAT FIBER: 1g

CHOCOLATE CHIP COOKIES

MAKES
12 cookies

These cookies were among the first low-carb baked goods that Jonathan really enjoyed. He's a discerning fella who prefers them made with xylitol because it allows baked goods to brown better than other sweeteners and gives these cookies a more traditional look. Like most low-carb cookies, these tend to be soft. It's difficult to get a truly crisp keto cookie.

1¼ cups blanched almond flour

⅓ cup granulated sweetener

¼ teaspoon baking soda

¼ teaspoon cream of tartar

6 tablespoons cold salted butter, sliced into ½-inch pieces

1 large egg

1 teaspoon vanilla extract

2 ounces low-carb milk chocolate, chopped

2 tablespoons chopped raw pecans (optional)

TIPS! *If you don't have time to chill the dough, you can bake it in an 8-inch square baking pan lined with parchment paper for 15 to 20 minutes.*

1. Put the almond flour, sweetener, baking soda, and cream of tartar in a food processor and mix until combined. Add the butter and process until you have coarse crumbs. Add the egg and vanilla and process until a dough comes together.

2. Use a rubber spatula to stir the chocolate and pecans, if using, into the dough. Shape the dough into a log 2½ to 3 inches in diameter. Wrap the dough in parchment paper or plastic wrap and refrigerate for at least 3 hours.

3. When ready to bake the cookies, preheat the oven to 350°F. Line a cookie sheet with parchment paper.

4. Remove the chilled dough from the fridge and cut the log into 12 equal slices. Place on the lined cookie sheet, spacing the cookies at least ¼ inch apart.

5. Bake until golden brown, 10 to 15 minutes. The cookies will be very soft straight from the oven. Allow to cool on the cookie sheet for at least 15 minutes before transferring to a cooling rack to cool completely. For crisper cookies, place the cookies on the cooling rack back in the oven and let cool for several hours with the oven door ajar.

6. Refrigerate leftover cookies for up to 10 days, or freeze for up to 3 months.

Kids who enjoy using appliances might enjoy mixing up this simple dough in a food processor. Once the dough is chilled, let them slice the dough with a butter knife if you are concerned that a sharp knife isn't safe. For very young children, an adult can slice the cookies and let the children place them on the cookie sheet.

CALORIES: 129 | **FAT:** 12.8g | **PROTEIN:** 3.1g | **CARBS:** 2.8g | **FIBER:** 1.7g | **ERYTHRITOL:** 6.1g

PUMPKIN SPICE CAKE

MAKES
one 8-inch square cake (12 servings)

We love this simple, humble, unassuming spice cake. It's baked in an 8-inch square pan, and it's a bit thinner than a traditional spice cake, but it packs great flavor and texture. When it's warm, slather it with softened butter. When cold, add a dollop of freshly whipped cream and a sprinkle of cinnamon. If you use coconut flour, the texture will be less fluffy and more coarse, but it's still delicious!

⅔ cup blanched almond flour

½ cup granulated sweetener

⅓ cup oat fiber, or 3 tablespoons coconut flour (see Note, page 52)

2 teaspoons psyllium husk powder

2 teaspoons pumpkin pie spice

2 teaspoons baking powder

½ teaspoon salt

¼ teaspoon ground cinnamon

¼ cup pumpkin puree

2 tablespoons unsalted butter, melted, plus more for greasing

2 tablespoons unsweetened almond milk

2 large eggs

1 teaspoon vanilla extract

½ teaspoon maple extract (optional)

4 drops liquid sweetener (optional)

1. Preheat the oven to 350°F. Grease an 8-inch square baking pan with butter.

2. In a medium mixing bowl, whisk together the dry ingredients. Add the pumpkin puree, melted butter, and almond milk and mix with a rubber spatula to form a thick batter. Stir in the eggs, extracts, and liquid sweetener, if using .

3. Pour the batter into the greased pan and smooth it from edge to edge. Bake until the top feels firm to a light touch or a toothpick inserted in the center comes out clean, 35 to 40 minutes.

4. Let cool in the pan for 5 to 10 minutes before slicing and serving.

5. Refrigerate leftover cake for up to a week, or freeze single servings for up to 3 months.

TIP! *You can omit the pumpkin puree and add your desired spices, such as ginger, cloves, or apple pie spice, or increase the cinnamon.*

Kids who have never baked a thing can easily start here. Let younger kids help mix and measure. The basic recipe is a good starting point to experiment with various flavors, and older kids can have fun adjusting the spices to their preferred tastes.

CALORIES: 66 | **FAT:** 5.7g | **PROTEIN:** 2.2g | **CARBS:** 1.7g | **FIBER:** 1.1g | **ERYTHRITOL:** 9.2g | **OAT FIBER:** 1.3g

CHOCOLATE CHIP SCONES

MAKES
8 scones (1 per serving)

I was introduced to scones during my junior year of college, when I was studying abroad in England. Perhaps it was my Southern accent, but my flat-mates kept correcting my pronunciation. "It's *scone!* With a long *o*, like *'it's gone'*—SCONE!" To this country girl, it sure seemed like a sweet biscuit with chocolate chips. I didn't think life could get much better until I enjoyed afternoon tea with scones and clotted cream. I'd give up citizenship for that stuff alone, but heaped on a sweet scone? Take my passport, y'all!

Years later, I enjoyed creating scones for my young children and teaching them how to say *scone* properly. After we went keto, Jonathan requested a batch. It didn't seem fair to make them for him without giving Grace an option to enjoy, so I began experimenting with my old recipe. When Jonathan, the pickiest eater of the family, mistook Grace's low-carb batch for his own, I knew the low-carb version was a success. These days I make only one version, but I still make two batches.

These scones will spread if the dough is too warm. For best results, freeze or refrigerate the shaped scones for an hour before baking.

---

1 cup blanched almond flour

½ cup plus 2 tablespoons granulated sweetener, divided

⅓ cup oat fiber, or 2 tablespoons coconut flour, plus ¼ cup oat flour for shaping and cutting

3 tablespoons unflavored or vanilla-flavored whey protein isolate

1 teaspoon baking powder

¼ teaspoon salt

½ cup (1 stick) cold unsalted butter, cut into ½-inch slices

1 large egg

1 teaspoon vanilla extract

¼ cup low-carb chocolate chips

NOTE: *The texture of these scones improves as they cool, and the outsides become a bit more crisp. The difficulty is waiting that long to try them!*

1. Preheat the oven to 325°F and line a large cookie sheet with parchment paper.

2. Put the almond flour, ½ cup of the sweetener, the oat fiber, whey protein isolate, baking powder, and salt in the bowl of a stand mixer or food processor and mix until combined. Add the butter one slice at a time while the mixer is running. Leave the mixer on low speed until the mixture resembles small pebbles.

3. Add the egg and vanilla extract and mix just until a dough forms. Use a rubber spatula to stir in the chocolate chips.

4. Lay a second piece of parchment paper on a countertop or other work surface. Sprinkle 2 tablespoons of oat fiber over the parchment.

5. Put the dough on the floured parchment paper and use your hands to shape it into a 6- to 7-inch circle, about ¾ inch thick. If the dough is sticky, sprinkle the remaining 2 tablespoons of oat fiber over the dough (or use it to coat your fingers) so that you can shape the dough more easily.

6. Use a sharp knife or pizza cutter dusted with oat fiber to cut the dough into 8 even wedges. Use an offset spatula to lift the wedges onto the lined cookie sheet, spacing them at least ½ inch apart.

CALORIES: 250 | **FAT:** 23.2g | **PROTEIN:** 9.5g | **CARBS:** 3.8g | **FIBER:** 2.4g | **ERYTHRITOL:** 14.2g | **OAT FIBER:** 2g

TIPS! *You can combine the dry ingredients in advance and store the mix in the freezer. When it's time to make scones, add the cold butter and remaining ingredients and have a batch ready even before the oven is preheated.*

For best results, be sure to keep the ingredients and the dough cold to help prevent spreading while baking. In fact, you might freeze the unbaked scones on a cookie sheet prior to baking.

7. Bake until just beginning to brown, 25 to 30 minutes. Remove from the oven and sprinkle with the remaining 2 tablespoons of sweetener. Let cool on the pan for 5 to 10 minutes. Transfer the scones to a cooling rack and let cool for at least 20 minutes for a more authentic scone texture (see Note, opposite).

8. Store leftover scones at room temperature for up to 3 days, in the refrigerator for up to a week, or in the freezer for up to 3 months.

VARIATION:

BLUEBERRY SCONES. Use ¼ cup of fresh blueberries instead of chocolate chips.

This is a great recipe for kids since it involves a few different steps. You can include kids who can measure with or without supervision and those who can use or learn to use a food processor or stand mixer. Younger hands can help pat the dough into a circle on a piece of parchment paper, and then an older child can use a pizza cutter or sharp knife to cut the scones. A steady hand is needed to lift the slices onto the parchment paper, but even the littles should be able to sprinkle the granulated sweetener over the tops.

CREAMY DAIRY-FREE VANILLA ICE CREAM

MAKES

3 cups (½ cup per serving)

Most dairy-free ice cream tastes like ice milk because it isn't creamy at all, so I set my mind to making this version as creamy as I could. The eggs and oil really help. Before you wrinkle your nose at the notion of oil in ice cream, just try it! Be sure to use a mild-tasting oil such as avocado oil, Manzanilla olive oil, walnut oil, or hazelnut oil.

1¼ cups unsweetened almond milk

1 cup unsweetened coconut milk

6 large egg yolks

⅓ cup allulose or xylitol

⅓ cup mild-flavored oil

2 teaspoons vanilla extract

⅛ teaspoon salt

SPECIAL EQUIPMENT:

Ice cream maker

1. In a heavy 1-quart saucepan over low heat, warm the almond and coconut milks, stirring with a whisk. Add the egg yolks and continue whisking until the custard begins to thicken.

2. Add the sweetener and whisk until completely dissolved. Continue heating, whisking constantly, until the custard thickens further, about 10 minutes. When it coats the back of a wooden spoon and/or reaches 140°F on a candy thermometer, remove the pan from the heat. Do not allow the custard to warm to over 140°F or the eggs will begin to cook.

3. Carefully pour the custard into a blender. Add the oil, vanilla extract, and salt and blend for at least 1 minute to combine. Place the blender cup in the refrigerator and let cool, about 45 minutes.

4. Pour the cooled ice cream mixture into an ice cream maker and churn following the manufacturer's directions until the ice cream is frozen or reaches your desired consistency.

5. Freeze leftover ice cream for up to a month.

TIP! *This is a very basic recipe that can be used to make a variety of flavors. Use your imagination for mix-ins or toppings.*

If your child is dairy-free, this ice cream will be a treat to make. Use caution when heating the egg mixture not only to avoid burns, but also to keep the eggs from cooking. Letting kids learn how to use a thermometer will be helpful in making this recipe. Younger kids can press the buttons on the blender and help pour the mixture into the ice cream maker before pressing those buttons as well. Let children scoop the churned ice cream into containers for freezing.

CALORIES: 174 | **FAT:** 17.7g | **PROTEIN:** 3g | **CARBS:** 1g | **FIBER:** 0g

CREAMY VANILLA ICE CREAM

MAKES
1 quart (½ cup per serving)

My family loves ice cream of all flavors, so it was difficult to limit this book to three ice cream recipes. We decided to include basic vanilla and chocolate since those are classic kid favorites. Promise us that you'll be creative and try a few new flavors as you become more comfortable in the kitchen. Hint: The cookie dough from the Chocolate Chip Cookies (page 238) and leftover cheesecake pieces (page 256 or 268) are great places to start when looking for mix-ins. In lieu of heating the ice cream mixture, it can be whipped up in a blender if you use pasteurized eggs.

2¼ cups heavy cream

6 large egg yolks

⅓ cup allulose or xylitol

2 teaspoons vanilla extract

⅛ teaspoon salt

SPECIAL EQUIPMENT:

Ice cream maker

1. In a heavy 2-quart saucepan over low heat, warm the cream, stirring often with a whisk. Add the egg yolks and continue whisking until the custard begins to thicken, 8 to 10 minutes.

2. Add the sweetener and whisk until completely dissolved. Continue heating, whisking constantly, until the custard is thick enough to coat the back of a wooden spoon or reaches 140°F on a candy thermometer, about 10 minutes. Do not allow it to warm to over 140°F or the eggs will begin to cook.

3. Remove the pan from the heat and stir in the vanilla extract and salt. Place in the refrigerator to cool, about 45 minutes.

4. Pour the cooled ice cream mixture into an ice cream maker and churn following the manufacturer's directions until the ice cream is frozen or reaches your desired consistency.

5. Freeze leftover ice cream for up to a month.

NOTE: *For a lighter ice cream with fewer carbs, you can substitute 1 cup of unsweetened almond milk for 1 cup of the heavy cream.*

Learning to make a homemade frozen custard (that is, an egg yolk–based ice cream like this one) is as important as learning to ride a bike or change a tire. You simply need this skill before reaching adulthood. Let younger kids measure in the ingredients. Children can also separate the eggs or use a handy egg separator tool to do so. It's not a problem if a bit of the egg white gets into the yolk in this recipe. Help children to keep an eye on the custard mixture so that it doesn't get too hot. This is also a great time to let them use a kitchen thermometer as well as the ice cream maker.

CALORIES: 268 | **FAT:** 27.5g | **PROTEIN:** 3.9g | **CARBS:** 1.9g | **FIBER:** 0g

MASON JAR CHOCOLATE ICE CREAM

MAKES
2 servings

Kids fidgety? Keep them busy by having them help make this sugar-free chocolate ice cream—no ice cream maker required. We've enjoyed setting up an assembly line of jars and ingredients and letting each person make their own custom flavor. Also, while the recipe calls for vigorously shaking the jar, we've also found that using the whip attachment on an immersion blender works really well. Blend the mixture until the volume nearly doubles and sticks to the whip attachment just as heavy cream would.

½ cup heavy cream

1 large egg (see Tips)

2 tablespoons allulose or xylitol

2 teaspoons unsweetened cocoa powder

1 teaspoon vanilla extract

⅛ teaspoon salt

1. Put all of the ingredients in a pint-sized mason jar or similar-sized glass jar. Seal the lid and shake vigorously for at least 5 minutes. The volume of the ice cream mixture will expand to fill the jar.

2. After 5 minutes, place the jar in the freezer. Freeze for at least 3 hours or until set.

3. Freeze leftover ice cream for up to a month.

VARIATIONS:

VANILLA ICE CREAM. Simply omit the cocoa powder.

COCONUT ALMOND ICE CREAM. Add ¼ teaspoon almond extract, ¼ teaspoon coconut extract, 2 tablespoons unsweetened coconut flakes, and 1 tablespoon slivered almonds before shaking the ice cream mixture.

MOCHA ALMOND ICE CREAM. Add ½ teaspoon almond extract, ½ teaspoon instant espresso powder, 1 tablespoon slivered almonds, and 1 tablespoon chopped low-carb chocolate chips before shaking the ice cream mixture.

TIPS! *If you're concerned about consuming raw egg, you can heat the cream, egg, and sweetener, stirring continuously, until the mixture reaches a temperature of 140°F on a candy thermometer. Then combine all of the ingredients in the jar and shake vigorously. You can also buy pasteurized eggs.*

For a creamier consistency, use xylitol or an erythritol blend. Erythritol makes ice cream very hard. If you do use erythritol, let the ice cream sit out at room temperature for 5 to 7 minutes before serving.

This simple recipe depends on vigorously shaking the ice cream mixture. Kids can roll the jar back and forth to each other or set a timer and shake to their hearts' content. They can even mix up their own jars and have a dance party while they shake the jars! They will stay busy, and the whole family can enjoy the results.

CALORIES: 245 | **FAT:** 24.4g | **PROTEIN:** 5.2g | **CARBS:** 3g | **FIBER:** 0.7g

CARAMEL SAUCE

MAKES
about 1 cup
(2 tablespoons
per serving)

There are two key hurdles to making a keto caramel sauce: choosing the right sweeteners and determining how long to simmer the sauce to thicken it to your preference. I've experimented with three sweeteners: erythritol, xylitol, and allulose. You need a sweetener that will caramelize. Xylitol is the best at caramelizing, followed by allulose and then erythritol, which doesn't brown quite as well. The cons with xylitol are that it is toxic to pets, has a slightly higher glycemic index, and, in large quantities, can cause upset stomach. Allulose caramelizes nicely and is safe for pets; however, it yields a very soft, less chewy texture. It can also have a laxative effect if you consume too much of it. Erythritol doesn't caramelize as well, can have a slight cooling effect when used by itself rather than in combination with other sweeteners, and becomes grainy when chilled. I tested this sauce at least a dozen ways, and my family's favorite was this combination of allulose and xylitol. Using both sweeteners yields the best flavor and texture. You can use ½ cup of any of these three sweeteners, but your results will vary depending on the sweetener(s) you use.

Enjoy a dollop of this sauce over homemade ice cream, use it to make Keto Chocolate Turtles (page 262), or eat it straight from a spoon!

½ cup heavy cream

¼ cup (½ stick) unsalted butter

¼ cup allulose

¼ cup xylitol

⅛ teaspoon salt

½ teaspoon vanilla extract

½ teaspoon maple extract (optional)

1. Heat the cream and butter in a 1-quart saucepan over medium heat until the butter has melted.

2. Stir in the sweeteners and salt, reduce the heat to low, and bring the mixture to a simmer. When it reaches a simmer, set a timer for 15 minutes. Simmer, stirring occasionally with a wooden spoon and watching carefully to make sure it doesn't burn, until the sauce develops a deep amber color and leaves a thick coating on the back of the spoon, at least 15 minutes or up to 22 minutes, depending on how thick you want the sauce to be (see Notes, opposite).

3. Remove the pan from the heat. Add the vanilla extract and maple extract, if using. Let the sauce cool before pouring into a glass jar.

4. Store at room temperature for up to 3 days or in the refrigerator for up to 2 weeks. This sauce also freezes well.

Kids may need some supervision the first time they attempt to make caramel. Encourage them to use a kitchen timer and to keep a careful eye on the stovetop. They will also need to be able to frequently stir the hot caramel without getting burned.

CALORIES: 101 | **FAT:** 11g | **PROTEIN:** 0.5g | **CARBS:** 0.4g | **FIBER:** 0g

NOTES: *If you want a smooth, pourable sauce, simmer it for 12 to 15 minutes. If you want a much thicker, richer caramel that has a slight chew when refrigerated, simmer it for 20 to 22 minutes. (This thicker version is what you want if you are making the Keto Chocolate Turtles on page 262.) Use the color of the sauce to guide you. The darker the caramel, the thicker it will be when cool.*

Be sure to set the timer after the butter has melted and the mixture has started to simmer, not before. Remember that the sauce will thicken as it cools. It may take some delicious trial and error to find exactly how much time to simmer it to your desired thickness. Lastly, be sure to simmer it over low heat. The sauce can burn if you don't keep an eye on it.

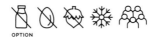

DARK CHOCOLATE SYRUP

MAKES
about 1½ cups
(2 tablespoons
per serving)

Eating differently from the mainstream can be hard; we know this firsthand from living keto. My children have friends who aren't keto but also eat differently from the mainstream. Some are dairy-free, others are vegetarian, and a few are vegan. That's why it was important to us to include this recipe in the book. Not only is it vegan-friendly, but it's also dairy-free if you use coconut oil rather than butter. For us it's about inclusiveness. There's room at our table for all eaters, and all of the varieties can be delicious. This syrup can be used to make chocolate "milk" with nondairy milk options. It can also be drizzled over mug cakes or over Creamy Dairy-Free Vanilla Ice Cream (page 244) for a dairy-free sundae.

1 cup water

⅔ cup unsweetened cocoa powder

½ cup allulose (see Tips)

¼ cup xylitol

2 tablespoons unsalted butter or refined coconut oil

¼ teaspoon salt

1 teaspoon vanilla extract

1. In a 1-quart saucepan over low heat, whisk together the water, cocoa powder, and sweeteners. When dissolved, add the butter and salt. Stir until the butter has melted and the mixture comes to a simmer.

2. Simmer for 2 to 3 minutes, then remove from the heat and stir in the vanilla extract. Pour the syrup into a small container for serving. It will thicken as it cools.

3. Refrigerate leftover syrup for up to a week, or freeze for longer.

TIPS! *This combination of allulose and xylitol yields the best texture, but you can use all of one or the other sweetener. Using allulose and xylitol helps the syrup stay smooth regardless of temperature. If you use erythritol instead, the syrup will crystallize when cool.*

To warm syrup that has been refrigerated, microwave it on reduced power in 20-second increments or set it in a pan of hot water for 10 to 15 minutes.

Let kids who can comfortably simmer on a cooktop make this recipe completely on their own. There's something satisfying about taking ingredients and coming up with a delicious sauce that can be used in a variety of ways. This is also a great recipe for kids to make with, or for, friends.

CALORIES: 28 | **FAT:** 2.6g | **PROTEIN:** 0.9g | **CARBS:** 2.4g | **FIBER:** 1.8g

MILK CHOCOLATE SYRUP

MAKES
about 2 cups
(2 tablespoons
per serving)

Milk chocolate is a family favorite, and this syrup is often requested by my family. This recipe yields a huge batch. If we aren't using it for a large dessert or a party, then we freeze the leftover syrup in 4-ounce glass jars, which are perfect for impromptu desserts. It's delicious served over Classic Cheesecake (page 256) or Creamy Vanilla Ice Cream (page 246).

1 cup water

¾ cup unsweetened cocoa powder

2 tablespoons unsalted butter

½ cup allulose (see Tips, page 252)

½ cup xylitol

⅛ teaspoon salt

½ cup heavy cream

1½ teaspoons vanilla extract

1. In a 1-quart saucepan over low heat, whisk together the water and cocoa powder. Add the butter, sweeteners, and salt and whisk until the butter has melted and the sweeteners have dissolved.

2. Pour in the cream and simmer, stirring frequently, until the syrup has thickened, 4 to 5 minutes. Remove from the heat and stir in the vanilla extract. Pour the syrup into a small container for serving. It will thicken as it cools.

3. Refrigerate leftover syrup for up to a week, or freeze for longer.

TIP! *To warm syrup that has been refrigerated, microwave it on reduced power in 20-second increments or set it in a pan of hot water for 10 to 15 minutes.*

Kids who are comfortable controlling heat on a stovetop can whip up this syrup quickly. They will need to pay careful attention to the syrup and whisk frequently.

CALORIES: 47 | **FAT:** 4.7g | **PROTEIN:** 1g | **CARBS:** 2.2g | **FIBER:** 1.4g

CLASSIC CHEESECAKE

MAKES
one 8-inch cake
(12 servings)

Everyone needs to know how to make a classic cheesecake. Not only is it easy and delicious, but a plain cheesecake can serve as a blank canvas for berries, caramel sauce, or chocolate syrup, which is how we prefer ours. Plus, adding a sauce is a great way to hide a not-so-perfectly-smooth top. A traditional cheesecake recipe is easy to adapt to low-carb or keto just by swapping out the sweeteners, so if you already have one that is a family favorite, you might want to experiment. If you don't, this basic recipe is a great place to start.

CRUST:

1½ cups blanched almond flour

3 tablespoons granulated sweetener

Dash of salt

3 tablespoons unsalted butter, melted

FILLING:

3 (8-ounce) packages cream cheese, softened

½ cup granulated sweetener

⅓ cup sour cream, room temperature

2 teaspoons vanilla extract

1 teaspoon lemon juice

3 large eggs, room temperature

FOR TOPPING (OPTIONAL):

⅓ cup Dark Chocolate Syrup (page 252)

Fresh raspberries or other berries of choice

SPECIAL EQUIPMENT:

8-inch springform pan

1. Preheat the oven to 350°F. Line an 8-inch springform pan with parchment paper.

2. Make the crust: Put the almond flour, sweetener, salt, and melted butter in a bowl and use a spatula to mix to a fine crumb. Press the mixture into the bottom of the lined springform pan. Par-bake the crust until just browned, 6 to 8 minutes. Remove from the oven and set aside to cool.

3. While the crust is cooling, make the filling: Whip the cream cheese in the bowl of a stand mixer or in a mixing bowl with a hand mixer until fluffy. Add the sweetener and beat until dissolved.

4. Beat in the sour cream, vanilla extract, and lemon juice until smooth. Add the eggs, one at a time, and mix just until incorporated, using a rubber spatula to scrape down the sides of the bowl as needed. Do not overmix.

5. Reduce the oven temperature to 325°F. Pour the filling into the par-baked crust.

6. Bake the cheesecake until just set, 60 to 70 minutes. It may still jiggle just a bit in the center. Turn off the oven and let the cake cool in the oven with the door ajar for at least 30 minutes.

7. Remove from the oven, run a knife around the edge of the pan, and let the cake cool to room temperature, about 1 hour.

8. When completely cool, cover and refrigerate the cheesecake for at least 8 hours before slicing and serving. Remove the outer ring from the springform pan and top the cake with the chocolate syrup and/or berries, if desired.

9. Refrigerate leftover cheesecake for up to 5 days, or freeze for up to 2 months.

CALORIES: 342 | **FAT:** 32.6g | **PROTEIN:** 8.3g | **CARBS:** 5g | **FIBER:** 1.2g | **ERYTHRITOL:** 11.8g

TIP! *While we don't strive for perfection here, a few simple tips will help yield better results. First, to avoid cracks in the top of the cheesecake, let it cool gradually. Running a knife around the edge of the pan as soon as the cake comes out of the oven will help prevent cracking as the cake cools and contracts. Second, for the best texture, avoid overmixing the eggs. You can also bake the cheesecake in a water bath, but we generally skip that extra step. Lastly, be sure to let the cake cure in the refrigerator for at least 8 hours (overnight is better) for the best flavor and texture.*

Kids and adults can learn that good things come to those who wait! Making a cheesecake can be a lesson in patience. You need to wait until the ingredients are at room temperature and then wait for the cheesecake to cool in stages. Last, wait for the cheesecake to be chilled a full eight hours or overnight. The reward is a creamy, perfect cheesecake. Younger kids can enjoy making the crust and pressing it into the springform pan. Kids can also help by cracking the eggs (in a separate bowl) and by mixing the batter.

SULLIVANO CHOCOLATE SANDWICH COOKIES

MAKES
24 sandwich cookies (1 per serving)

My daughter called from school to ask, "Can you make low-carb Milano cookies?" I could hear in her voice that she felt deprived (she lives on campus), so I asked whether her friends had been enjoying some. They had. Within days, I was in the kitchen with a rough plan for how to make Sullivanos, my low-carb version of the crisp vanilla cookies with a dark chocolate filling. Let's be honest: This recipe is not quick, and it's not as easy as most of the recipes in this book. Taking the time to pipe out the wafers is, well, time-consuming. I found a shortcut by using an éclair pan or a muffin top pan to make the wafers rather than piping them by hand, so feel free to use either of those if you have it. If not, well . . . a mama's heart doesn't mind a piping bag when one is needed.

WAFERS:

½ cup heavy cream

1½ teaspoons white vinegar

¾ cup blanched almond flour

¼ cup unflavored whey protein isolate

1 tablespoon oat fiber

1 teaspoon baking powder

⅛ teaspoon salt

¼ cup granulated sweetener

2 tablespoons unsalted butter, melted but not hot

1½ teaspoons vanilla extract

CHOCOLATE FILLING:

8 ounces low-carb chocolate chips

2 tablespoons refined coconut oil or cocoa butter

1. Place one oven rack in the upper third position and one rack in the lower third position, then preheat the oven to 300°F. Line 2 cookie sheets with parchment paper.

2. Make the wafers: Put the cream and vinegar in a small bowl and mix to combine; set aside.

3. In a medium bowl, whisk together the almond flour, whey protein isolate, oat fiber, baking powder, and salt.

4. In a separate bowl, mix together the sweetener, melted butter, and vanilla extract. Mix the wet mixture into the dry ingredients, then add the cream and vinegar mixture and stir until combined.

5. Transfer the batter to a pastry bag or a plastic bag with a corner snipped off. Pipe the batter onto the lined cookie sheets in strips about 1½ inches wide and ¼ inch thick. The wafers will spread as they cook, so be careful not to create strips that are too big or place them too close together.

6. Bake both pans of wafers until the edges are just starting to brown, 10 to 15 minutes. Turn off the oven, leave the door ajar with the oven light on, and let the wafers sit for at least 2 hours or up to overnight. It will take several hours for them to crisp up.

Admittedly, my kids would rather eat than make these. When they have helped, they are handy with the piping bag to create the cookies. Younger kids can help with creating the batter as well. The chocolate filling is easy enough for older children to make and the entire family can enjoy brushing the cookies with the melted chocolate to create the sandwiches.

CALORIES: 112 | **FAT:** 10.8g | **PROTEIN:** 3.9g | **CARBS:** 3.6g | **FIBER:** 1.6g | **ERYTHRITOL:** 3.8g | **OAT FIBER:** 0.3g

TIPS! *Using cocoa butter yields a chocolate that is more stable at room temperature and that yields a "snap" when eaten, especially when chilled.*

For round sandwich cookies, you can bake the wafers in a muffin top pan.

7. After the wafers have become crisp, make the filling: Melt the chocolate chips and coconut oil in a small microwave-safe bowl for 30 seconds. Stir until combined and fully melted; you may need to microwave the mixture in additional 15-second intervals, but be sure to stir between intervals to avoid burning the chocolate.

8. Brush the melted chocolate mixture onto the bottoms (flat side) of 24 of the wafers, then top with the remaining wafers, to make 24 sandwich cookies. Refrigerate for 20 to 30 minutes, until the chocolate filling is set, before serving.

9. Refrigerate leftover cookies for up to a week—preferably in a paper bag labeled "liver" so that no one discovers them and devours them all. You can also freeze them for up to 3 months.

COCOA ROASTED ALMONDS

MAKES
2 cups (¼ cup per serving)

Make these chocolate-flavored almonds in advance for any time you or the kids are on the go. They tuck nicely into lunches or overnight bags and can easily be shared with friends. I appreciate that it's a treat that also has some fat and protein. The nuts are crunchy and lightly sweet; sprinkle them with a bit of flaked sea salt after baking if you'd like.

⅓ cup powdered sweetener

2 tablespoons unsweetened cocoa powder

¼ teaspoon salt

⅛ teaspoon ground cinnamon

1 large egg white

2 cups raw almonds

Flaked sea salt, for garnish (optional)

1. Preheat the oven to 250°F. Line a large rimmed baking sheet with parchment paper.

2. In a small bowl, whisk together the sweetener, cocoa powder, salt, and cinnamon and set aside.

3. In a large bowl, whisk the egg white until frothy. Add the almonds and use a rubber spatula to coat the nuts with the egg white.

4. Sprinkle the almonds with the cocoa powder mixture a little at a time, stirring to evenly coat the nuts. Spread the nuts in a single layer on the lined baking sheet.

5. Bake for 15 to 20 minutes, then stir the almonds. Continue baking until they are lightly roasted and crisp on both sides, another 15 to 20 minutes. Sprinkle with flaked salt, if desired. Allow to cool for at least 1 hour before serving.

6. Store leftover almonds at room temperature for up to 3 days or in the refrigerator for up to 2 weeks.

Younger kids will enjoy mixing up the dry seasoning and tossing the nuts to coat them. Caution older children about the potential for burns when using the oven and when stirring the roasted nuts. Children might also choose to gift these almonds to caregivers or other adults and can enjoy packaging the almonds and decorating the packages.

CALORIES: 146 | FAT: 12.4g | PROTEIN: 5.9g | CARBS: 5.7g | FIBER: 3.3g | ERYTHRITOL: 9.2g

KETO CHOCOLATE TURTLES

MAKES
24 turtles

This is one of those building block recipes that uses other recipes as a foundation for creating something new. You already have a recipe to make caramel sauce, and caramel is a key ingredient in candy turtles. So grab some pecans and go make some candy! These turtles are fun to make and to eat.

⅔ cup roasted pecan halves and pieces, frozen

1½ ounces cocoa butter or refined coconut oil (see Tips)

7 ounces low-carb chocolate

¼ cup Caramel Sauce (page 250) (see Tips)

SPECIAL EQUIPMENT:

24-well mini muffin tin

1. Line a 24-well mini muffin tin with parchment paper liners.

2. Place just enough pecans in each well to cover the bottom of the liner, 3 to 5 pieces.

3. In a 1-quart saucepan, melt the cocoa butter over low heat. Once melted, turn off the heat and stir in the chocolate until melted.

4. Drizzle about ⅛ teaspoon of the chocolate mixture over the pecans in each well to help hold them together. Spoon about ¼ teaspoon of caramel sauce over the top of the pecans and chocolate in each well. Drizzle another ½ teaspoon of the chocolate mixture over the top of each turtle.

5. Let cool to room temperature or refrigerate until hardened, at least 45 minutes, before serving.

6. Store leftovers at room temperature or in the refrigerator (see Tips) for up to 2 weeks, or freeze for up to 3 months.

TIPS! *Turtles made with cocoa butter will remain solid at room temperature and don't need to be refrigerated unless room temperature is above 78°F. Turtles made with coconut oil do need to be refrigerated since they are more likely to melt at room temperature.*

For best results, make the caramel sauce far enough in advance that it is at least room temperature, if not chilled, when you begin this recipe. You want a thicker caramel for these turtles, so make sure to simmer it for at least 20 minutes.

These turtles are easier to prepare when you have an assembly line of workers. Younger children can fill the mini muffin tin with liners while older kids or parents prepare the chocolate mixture. After the tin is lined, someone can place the pecans in each well. Melting chocolate is not difficult, but the mixture will become warm in the microwave, and care should be taken so that younger children do not burn themselves. When the chocolate has cooled slightly, two helpers can continue the assembly line by adding caramel and chocolate to each well.

CALORIES: 105 | **FAT:** 11.1g | **PROTEIN:** 1.6g | **CARBS:** 3.4g | **FIBER:** 1.7g

PUMPKIN SPICE ROLL

MAKES
12 servings

Yes, this dessert looks intimidating, but don't let it be. Take a deep breath and repeat after me: "Even if my pumpkin roll falls apart and doesn't look perfect, it will taste perfect." See? All better. Worst case, you can toss it all into a serving bowl and layer it up like a trifle! But I promise that if I can make this, you can make it. Just go slowly while rolling the cake, and don't let it dry out before filling. Then relax while it chills before serving. This recipe uses six egg whites; you can use the leftover yolks to make ice cream (see pages 244 to 249).

CAKE:

Unsalted butter, for greasing

¼ cup blanched almond flour

¼ cup granulated sweetener

2 tablespoons oat fiber

2 tablespoons unflavored whey protein isolate

2 teaspoons pumpkin pie spice

¼ teaspoon ground cinnamon

6 large egg whites

1 teaspoon cream of tartar

1 teaspoon vanilla extract

½ teaspoon maple extract

FILLING:

1 cup powdered sweetener, plus more for serving

1 (8-ounce) package cream cheese, softened

¼ cup (½ stick) unsalted butter, softened

1 teaspoon vanilla extract

½ teaspoon maple extract

½ teaspoon pumpkin pie spice

⅛ teaspoon salt

1. Preheat the oven to 350°F. Line a 15 by 10 by ¾-inch jelly roll pan with parchment paper and lightly grease the parchment with butter.

2. Make the cake: In a mixing bowl, whisk together the almond flour, granulated sweetener, oat fiber, whey protein isolate, pumpkin pie spice, and cinnamon; set aside.

3. In a separate bowl, use a hand mixer to whip the egg whites. When they begin to form soft peaks, sprinkle in the cream of tartar and continue beating to stiff peaks. Use a spatula to gently fold in the dry ingredients and the extracts.

4. Gently spread the batter in the prepared pan and smooth it from edge to edge. Bake until just set, 12 to 14 minutes. Let cool in the pan for 5 to 7 minutes before inverting the cake onto a clean piece of parchment paper and peeling away the bottom piece of parchment. Let cool completely.

5. While the cake is cooling, prepare the filling: Put the powdered sweetener, cream cheese, and butter in a bowl and use the hand mixer to mix until smooth and creamy. Add the extracts, pumpkin pie spice, and salt and whip until fluffy.

6. When the cake is cool, spread the filling evenly over the cake, covering it from edge to edge. Beginning at a long edge, use the parchment paper to help you roll the cake over the filling.

7. Wrap the cake roll in parchment paper and place in the refrigerator to chill for at least 1 hour. Just before serving, dust the roll with powdered sweetener, then use a serrated knife to cut it into 1¼-inch slices.

8. Refrigerate leftover cake roll for up to 5 days.

CALORIES: 131 | **FAT:** 11.6g | **PROTEIN:** 5.6g | **CARBS:** 1.6g | **FIBER:** 0.3g | **ERYTHRITOL:** 22g | **OAT FIBER:** 0.3g

If your kids enjoy cooking and aren't afraid to tackle just a smidgen of a challenge, let them join you in making this recipe. Kids can whip the egg whites or smooth the batter across the jelly roll pan before baking the cake. They can also help measure and whip the filling. Rolling the cake over the filling is really easier than they (or you) might think. Encourage them to take their time, approach the task with humor, and not worry too much if it isn't perfect. They might find creative ways to cover up any imperfections with powdered sweetener or whipped cream.

ICE CREAM SANDWICHES

MAKES
16 sandwiches

What's summer without an ice cream sandwich? Heck, what's fall, winter, or spring? We bet you'll like this recipe at any time of year. The filling we've used technically isn't ice cream, but feel free to use your favorite flavor of ice cream instead. We developed this filling because it's faster and easier than making a batch of ice cream. It's also easier to shape in the form you want.

COOKIES:

1 cup blanched almond flour

⅓ cup granulated sweetener

¼ cup oat fiber, or 2 tablespoons coconut flour

¼ cup dark cocoa powder

¼ teaspoon salt

3 tablespoons unsalted butter

3 tablespoons refined coconut oil

1 large egg

1 teaspoon vanilla extract

FILLING:

½ cup heavy whipping cream

¼ cup powdered sweetener

⅓ cup sour cream

1½ teaspoons vanilla extract

1. Preheat the oven to 350°F. Line a large rimmed baking sheet with parchment paper.

2. Make the cookies: Put all of the ingredients in a food processor or stand mixer and mix until a thick dough forms.

3. Scoop up about 1½ teaspoons of the dough and form into a ball about ¾ inch in diameter. Repeat with the remaining dough, making a total of 32 balls. Place the dough balls on the lined baking sheet and, using the bottom of a drinking glass, flatten each ball into a cookie that is 2½ to 3 inches in diameter. Place a smaller piece of parchment paper between the dough and the glass to keep it from sticking.

4. Bake until just done but still soft, 6 to 8 minutes. Do not overbake. Let cool on the pan for at least 15 minutes before transferring to a wire rack to cool completely.

5. While the cookies are cooling, make the filling: In a bowl, whip the cream to stiff peaks. Then beat in the sweetener, sour cream, and vanilla extract.

6. When the cookies are cool, spread about 2 tablespoons of filling on one cookie. Gently top with a second cookie. Repeat with the filling and cookies to make 16 sandwiches.

7. Place the sandwiches in a single layer on a cookie sheet. Freeze until set, about 2 hours.

8. Store the ice cream sandwiches in a freezer-safe container for up to a month. Before serving, remove from the freezer and set on the counter for 3 to 5 minutes to thaw slightly.

CALORIES: 127 | **FAT:** 12.6g | **PROTEIN:** 2.5g | **CARBS:** 2.2g | **FIBER:** 1g | **ERYTHRITOL:** 9.2g | **OAT FIBER:** 0.5g

TIPS! *These cookies are even better the next day, so it's a good idea to make them ahead. You can even make several batches and store them in the freezer.*

For true ice cream sandwiches, use the Creamy Vanilla Ice Cream (page 246) instead of this filling. For dairy-free sandwiches, use the Creamy Dairy-Free Vanilla Ice Cream (page 244) for the filling, omit the butter from the cookies, and use 6 tablespoons of coconut oil instead of 3 tablespoons.

If you're struggling to keep the top cookie from crushing the cream filling, top 16 cookies with filling, freeze, and then top each with a second cookie to make sandwiches.

Bring the kids in to help make the cookies. They can measure ingredients, press buttons on the food processor, and form the dough balls. Kids will also enjoy whipping the cream and taste-testing the filling. Older kids can help create the sandwiches, but younger ones might struggle to handle them carefully enough to keep the cream from squishing out. Kids of all ages will want to devour them!

PEANUT BUTTER CHEESECAKE BROWNIES

MAKES
24 brownies
(1 per serving)

These delicious brownies look far fancier than they are difficult to make. Yes, you will dirty a few dishes, but once you take the first bite, you'll forget all about the suffering. There really is no wrong way to swirl the cream cheese filling into the brownie batter. Don't be afraid to make long, deep passes with a butter knife. You can also make these as plain brownies without the peanut butter cheesecake swirl; just be sure to reduce the baking time. The brownies are done when the center doesn't yield to light pressure.

BROWNIE BATTER:

4 ounces unsweetened chocolate (100% cacao), chopped

¾ cup (1½ sticks) unsalted butter

1 cup granulated sweetener

4 large eggs

1 cup blanched almond flour

2 teaspoons vanilla extract

¼ teaspoon salt

PEANUT BUTTER CHEESECAKE FILLING:

1 (8-ounce) package cream cheese, softened

½ cup salted creamy peanut butter

⅓ cup powdered sweetener

1 large egg

1 tablespoon vanilla extract

1. Preheat the oven to 350°F. Line a 9 by 13-inch baking pan with parchment paper, leaving some paper hanging over the sides for easy removal of the brownies.

2. Make the brownie batter: Use the microwave or a 1-quart saucepan to melt the chocolate and butter over low heat. Once melted, add the granulated sweetener and stir until dissolved. Mix in the eggs, almond flour, vanilla extract, and salt by hand. When thoroughly combined, pour the batter into the lined pan.

3. Make the cheesecake filling: Put the cream cheese, peanut butter, powdered sweetener, egg, and vanilla extract in the bowl of a stand mixer or in a mixing bowl if using a hand mixer and mix until smooth and creamy.

4. Drop spoonfuls of the cheesecake filling over the brownie batter. Use a butter knife to swirl the filling into the batter.

5. Bake until set, 32 to 35 minutes. Do not overbake or the brownies will be dry. Let cool completely in the pan before slicing and serving.

6. Refrigerate leftover brownies for up to a week, or freeze for up to 3 months.

Younger kids will enjoy measuring and mixing the ingredients for these brownies. There are plenty of tasks to divide among young helpers, such as making the batter, mixing the cream cheese filling, and swirling it together. Take care when melting the chocolate so that no one gets burned.

CALORIES: 179 | **FAT:** 17.3g | **PROTEIN:** 4.8g | **CARBS:** 3.3g | **FIBER:** 1.9g | **ERYTHRITOL:** 13g

CHOCOLATE PEANUT CLUSTERS

MAKES
12 clusters
(1 per serving)

When I first prepared this recipe, my family's chief complaint was that I made only a dozen candies. My rationale for making a small batch was fear that these candies would be far too tempting. I was right. Jonathan has eaten one and a half batches in one sitting! The good news is that this recipe can easily be doubled or tripled. You can substitute coconut oil for the cocoa butter, but coconut oil melts at lower temperatures, so the clusters will need to be refrigerated. You can also use a low-carb chocolate instead of unsweetened chocolate if you prefer; just omit the sweetener.

½ ounce cocoa butter or refined coconut oil (see Tips)

1 ounce unsweetened chocolate, chopped

6 drops liquid sweetener, or to taste

½ cup roasted salted peanuts

1. In a microwave-safe bowl, melt the cocoa butter in 15- to 20-second increments in the microwave. When melted, add the chocolate and stir to combine. If the chocolate doesn't melt completely, heat the mixture in 10-second bursts and stir until just melted and combined.

2. Add the sweetener and stir in the peanuts. When the peanuts are coated with chocolate, drop the mixture into 12 equal-sized piles on a piece of parchment paper.

3. Let cool at room temperature or refrigerate until hardened, at least 45 minutes, before serving.

4. Store leftovers at room temperature or in the refrigerator (see Tips) for up to 2 weeks, or freeze for up to 2 months.

TIPS! *Heat the cocoa butter until melted and then stir in the chocolate. If the chocolate mixture is too hot, it will be too thin and runny and will spread when dropped on the parchment paper.*

Clusters made with cocoa butter will remain solid at room temperature and don't need to be refrigerated unless the temperature is above 78˚F. Clusters made with coconut oil do need to be refrigerated since they are more likely to melt at room temperature.

This recipe is so simple that kids really should be involved. The mixture should not get too hot for little ones to participate; the heat from the cocoa butter will just melt the chocolate. Also, remind them that coconut oil melts at a much lower temperature than cocoa butter. Encourage children to use a tablespoon to scoop the candy mixture into 12 equal-sized clusters.

CALORIES: 58 | FAT: 5.5g | PROTEIN: 1.7g | CARBS: 2.1g | FIBER: 0.8g

CHAPTER 9:
BEVERAGES

My children mostly drink water, but there are times when they enjoy a flavored beverage. Sometimes they want the option when they are with their friends, during holidays or celebrations, or as seasonal treats. And I think they should have options. Even though they enjoy them infrequently, it's important to them, and to me, that they do not feel deprived. The serving sizes for the recipes in this chapter are intentionally small to keep the carbs low.

We have included recipes for a few of our favorite summer drink-ades along with comforting classics like hot chocolate, chocolate milk, and strawberry milk—a fun way to relive your own childhood by sharing this favorite with your kids.

When it comes to lemonade and limeade, we like them strong! Grace and I measure in the citrus juice and then dribble in a few more drops for good measure. When we pour it over crushed ice, the ice melts and brings the citrus flavor down to a more reasonable level, so you can start strong and finish smooth.

If your tastes are on the milder side, you may want to use these recipes as concentrates, adding a little more water or using a lot of ice. I tend to mix them up in pitchers so the kids can enjoy them. Grace sometimes adds a little unsweetened iced tea to her lemonade to enjoy an Arnold Palmer with a sprig of mint from the yard.

LEMONADE

MAKES
4 servings

Our favorite lemonade should come with a warning label. It's both tart and sweet, which is how lemonade should be. The drink is meant to stay flavorful, even as the ice melts. You can reduce the sweetener and/or lemon juice if you prefer a less tart or less sweet lemonade.

2 cups warm water

¾ cup granulated sweetener

⅔ cup lemon juice

4 cups ice

Lemon slices, for garnish

TIP! *You can put the ice in the pitcher and then refrigerate before serving; serve over additional ice.*

1. Pour the water into a quart-sized pitcher. Add the sweetener and stir until dissolved. Add the lemon juice and continue stirring until mixed.

2. Put 1 cup of ice in each of 4 tall glasses. Pour the lemonade over the ice, dividing it evenly, and stir. Garnish with lemon slices just before serving.

3. Refrigerate leftover lemonade for up to 4 days.

Tweens and teens can, and should, make this recipe for themselves to develop an appreciation for what they can do on their own. Even younger kids can help by pouring in the measured ingredients and stirring to dissolve the sweetener. This is a great opportunity to explain that using warm water dissolves the sweetener or other dry ingredients more easily.

CALORIES: 9 | **FAT:** 0g | **PROTEIN:** 0g | **CARBS:** 2.2g | **FIBER:** 0.1g | **ERYTHRITOL:** 36g

VARIATIONS:

FIZZY LEMONADE. Use seltzer water instead of plain water for a refreshing fizzy drink.

STRAWBERRY LEMONADE. To give your lemonade a strawberry twist, reduce the sweetener to ½ cup and add 2 tablespoons of unsweetened freeze-dried strawberry powder (see Notes, page 86) along with the sweetener in Step 1. We use freeze-dried strawberries to make strawberry lemonade because they're available year-round, and because the powder adds an intense flavor without those pesky seeds getting stuck in your teeth.

LIMEADE

MAKES
4 servings

Limes seem somehow more sophisticated to me than lemons—maybe because we never really had them in the house when I was growing up. I buy them now, especially when I want the kids to be able to enjoy a limeade treat!

2 cups warm water

½ cup granulated sweetener

½ cup lime juice

4 cups ice

Lime slices, for garnish

TIP! *You can put the ice in the pitcher and then refrigerate before serving; serve over additional ice.*

1. Pour the water into a quart-sized pitcher. Add the sweetener and stir until dissolved. Add the lime juice and continue stirring until mixed.

2. Put 1 cup of ice in each of 4 tall glasses. Pour the limeade mixture over the ice, dividing it evenly. Stir the limeade just before serving.

3. Refrigerate leftover limeade for up to 4 days.

Let the kids experiment by using more or less lime juice or sweetener or using seltzer water. You can also let them have fun creating garnishes.

CALORIES: 8 | FAT: 0g | PROTEIN: 0g | CARBS: 2.1g | FIBER: 0.1g | ERYTHRITOL: 26.3g

STRAWBERRY LIMEADE. For a fun twist, make your limeade a little sweeter and a little pinker by adding 2 tablespoons of strawberry powder (see Notes, page 86) along with the sweetener in Step 1. The end result rivals any commercial cherry limeade, especially if you use fizzy water instead of still water. We make strawberry limeade mainly in the spring and fall, but I could imagine using this recipe as the basis for a holiday punch by making the concentrate and adding sparkling or seltzer water to the punch bowl.

HOT CHOCOLATE DRINK MIX

MAKES
about 10 tablespoons (1½ tablespoons per serving)

This mix came about when my kids were asking me to make hot chocolate every other day. I figured if I could make a big batch of the mix, I'd save a little time and potentially convince them to make their drinks themselves. It worked! This is also a great mix to send with your children when they have social activities that include hot cocoa. They can have cocoa just by adding hot water, although we prefer to add a blend of heavy cream and hot water.

⅓ cup unsweetened cocoa powder

¼ cup granulated sweetener

⅛ teaspoon salt

Place all of the ingredients in a glass jar and mix or shake to combine. Store in the pantry for up to 3 months.

TIP! *This drink mix makes a fun gift for keto or low-carb friends. You can print the Creamy Hot Chocolate recipe (opposite) on a little card and attach it to the jar.*

Let kids measure the ingredients and then let them scoop the powdered mix into pretty jars. They might have fun labeling or decorating the storage container.

CALORIES: 13 | **FAT:** 0.7g | **PROTEIN:** 0.7g | **CARBS:** 3g | **FIBER:** 2.2g | **ERYTHRITOL:** 13.2g

CREAMY HOT CHOCOLATE

MAKES
1 serving

If you're going to make hot chocolate, make it ultra-creamy by adding some heavy cream to your mug. Grace and Jonathan often start by pouring cream into a mug and then using the 8-ounce setting on our single-serving coffee maker to get hot water. The cream cools the hot water just enough to make the hot chocolate the perfect temperature. Mom or Dad might add instant coffee to enjoy a mocha with the kiddos; see the variation below. For a dairy-free version, use coconut cream or a nut milk.

1½ tablespoons Hot Chocolate Drink Mix (opposite)

1 cup hot water

¼ cup heavy cream

⅛ teaspoon vanilla extract (optional)

Granulated sweetener (optional)

1. Put the drink mix in a mug and pour in the hot water. Stir until the cocoa powder has completely dissolved.

2. Add the cream, vanilla extract (if using), and sweetener to taste, if desired, and stir to combine.

VARIATION:

CREAMY HOT MOCHA. Add 1 heaping teaspoon of instant coffee powder.

TIP! *To use hot water from a coffee maker, simply put all of the ingredients except the water in a large coffee mug. Put the mug under the dispenser and dispense the hot water, then stir to dissolve the mix and enjoy. The water and cream can also be warmed in the microwave in 30-second bursts until the mixture reaches the desired drinking temperature, which is about 90 seconds at our house. Then add the remaining ingredients and enjoy!*

This recipe is super easy for tweens and older children as long as they know how to handle hot water carefully.

STRAWBERRY MILK

MAKES
1 serving

My kids had never tried commercial strawberry milk, so they thought I was a complete wizard when I made up this recipe and asked them to taste it. Their carbivore friends enjoy this drink, too. Grace pours it over ¼ cup or so of crushed ice to keep it chilled.

1 tablespoon unsweetened freeze-dried strawberry powder (see Notes, page 86)

1 tablespoon granulated sweetener, or 3 drops liquid sweetener

¾ cup water

⅓ cup heavy cream

Sliced fresh strawberries, for garnish (optional)

Place all of the ingredients in a tall glass and mix together until the strawberries and sweetener have dissolved. Garnish with strawberry slices, if desired.

VARIATION:

BLUEBERRY OR RASPBERRY MILK. Use unsweetened freeze-dried blueberry or raspberry powder in place of the strawberry powder.

 Chances are your children's friends haven't heard of strawberry milk, so this is your chance to win best parent! Introduce your kids to strawberry milk and then let them enjoy making this simple drink by themselves, including the garnish.

CALORIES: 275 | FAT: 28.6g | PROTEIN: 2.7g | CARBS: 5.5g | FIBER: 0.8g | ERYTHRITOL: 13.1g

CHOCOLATE MILK

MAKES
1 serving

Who doesn't love chocolate milk? It was always my choice over white milk back when milk was served with the mid-morning snack at school. I can still feel the cardboard carton under my fingers, and I remember my frustration when the paper drinking spout ripped and wasn't smooth. Of course, I drank the milk anyway!

Store-bought chocolate milk was such a favorite in our house that I knew I had to give the kids, and David, a low-carb option. I was a bit nervous when they tried it for the first time, but they all found it to be a reasonable substitute for the sugar-filled kind. My husband likes a little less cocoa powder in it, so feel free to adjust the amount according to your taste preference.

2 tablespoons granulated sweetener, or 3 drops liquid sweetener

1 tablespoon unsweetened cocoa powder

¾ cup water

⅓ cup heavy cream

Put the sweetener and cocoa powder in a tall glass, add the water, and stir to combine using a long spoon. Pour in the cream and stir again until well mixed.

This is a great opportunity to explain that the cocoa powder will dissolve much more easily in the water than the heavy cream because of the fat content in the cream. Once the cocoa powder and water are mixed, the cream blends in easily. If you have a doubter, as I do, you can show them the difference.

CALORIES: 280 | FAT: 29g | PROTEIN: 2.8g | CARBS: 4.8g | FIBER: 2g | ERYTHRITOL: 26.3g

ACKNOWLEDGMENTS

I am so grateful that Grace and Jonathan joined me to create this book. Their insight as kids who are truly growing up keto was invaluable. They endured taste tests, lots of food photo days, and lots of talking about their experiences. None of us could have finished the project with David—their dad, my husband, and the backbone that pulls us all together even as he's washing the gabillionth dish. These three are my muses every single day.

As we pulled together the content, the folks at Victory Belt once again made the magic happen. The designers put together a cover that we all could love and surprised me by incorporating pansies, a favorite flower for the three of us. We're also grateful for the time they spent poring over family photos to select the images for this book. Pam Mourouzis is also the most easygoing and thoughtful editor with whom I've ever worked. I look forward to her edits because she always makes my writing better. I'm also grateful to Erich Krauss and Lance Freimuth for their confidence in letting me try one more project.

A special thank you to my friend Mary, who has become one of the family. Mary worked tirelessly on marathon food photo days. She is always willing to cook, clean, or hold a reflector. She will even attempt baking, a task she doesn't love, when needed! Mary tests the recipes as she helps prepare them for photos, so you all should be grateful for her as well.

I'm especially grateful to the moderators of my closed Facebook group. Not only do they also test recipes, but they spend time answering questions and supporting members, which allows me more time to create. They are an amazing part of my team, and they do it graciously every day. They have no idea what they mean to me.

And lastly, to my readers, thank you so much for your support. We too often are connected through our shared stories of struggle with weight and health and of feeling unworthy, unsuccessful, and hopeless. Thank you for buying my books, trusting my recipes, and joining my community. Your success is an inspiration to others who share the same struggles and who don't know how to make it better. Thank you for joining me on this journey, and thank you for inspiring others on this journey. Thank you also for making a difference in the lives of your family members. You're creating a legacy for future generations.

For more information about the recipe icons, see page 48.

RECIPE	PAGE	🍼	🚫🥚	❄️🍓	❄️	🛍️	👨‍👩‍👧
Anything Dough	52		✓				
Easy Cheesy Biscuits	54				✓	✓	✓
Cheesy Breadsticks	56						✓
Crusty Baguettes	58			✓	✓	✓	✓
Rolls Without Rolls	60			✓	✓	✓	✓
Yeasty Low-Carb Rolls	62				✓	✓	✓
Sesame Bagels	64		✓		✓	✓	✓
Tortillas	66	✓	✓	✓	✓	✓	✓
90-Second Toast	68	O			✓	✓	✓
Egg Wraps	72			✓	✓		
Sausage and Cheese Pinwheels	74		✓		✓	✓	✓
Cinnamon Walnut Cream Cheese Spread	76		✓				✓
Classic French Toast	78				✓		✓
Creamy Bacon Gravy	80		✓	✓			✓
Easy Boiled Eggs with Butter	82			✓			
Eggs in a Basket	84			✓			✓
Grace's Good Morning Strawberry Protein Smoothie	86		O	✓			✓
Chocolate Hazelnut Muffins	88				✓	✓	✓
Peanut Butter Waffles	90				✓	✓	✓
Sausage-Crusted Meat Lover's Quiche	92			O	✓	✓	✓
Grace's Good Morning Chocolate Peanut Butter Smoothie	94		O				✓
Savory Breakfast Crepes	96						✓
J's Eggs and Bacon	98	✓		✓			
Mom's Eggs	99			✓			
Veggie Bacon Cream Cheese Spread	100		✓	✓			✓
Cinnamon Maple Crepes	102				✓		✓
Sheet Pan Blueberry Pancakes	104				✓	✓	✓
Bacon, Egg, and Cheese Breakfast Tacos	106			✓		✓	
Creamy Baked Eggs	108			✓			✓
Taco Seasoning	112	✓	✓	✓			
BBQ Sauce	114	O	✓	✓	✓	✓	✓
Sweet Mustard Sauce	116	✓		✓			✓
Ranch Dipping Sauce	117			✓			✓
Ketchup	118	✓	✓	✓	✓	✓	✓
Grace's Chicken Tender Sauce	120	✓		✓			✓
Pesto	122		✓		✓		✓

RECIPE	PAGE	🥛	⊘	⊘	❄️	🛍️	👥
No-Cook Pizza Sauce	124	✓	✓	✓	✓		✓
Yum-Yum Sauce	126			✓			✓
Simple Cheese Sauce	128		✓	✓			
Cashew Chicken with Broccoli	132	✓	✓		✓		✓
Deep Dish Supreme Pizza	134				✓		✓
Drive-Thru Chicken Tenders	136			✓	✓	✓	✓
Hamburger Steaks in Onion Gravy	138		✓	✓			✓
Chicken on a Stick	140	✓	✓	✓	✓	✓	✓
Marinated Beef Kabobs	142	✓	✓	✓			✓
Open-Faced Calzones	144		✓	✓	✓	✓	✓
Orange-Braised Pork	146	✓	✓	✓	✓		✓
Pizza Waffles	148			✓		✓	✓
Beef Stroganoff	150		✓	✓			✓
Chicken Teriyaki Meatballs	152	✓	✓	✓	✓	✓	✓
Balsamic Baked Pork Chops	154	✓	✓	✓			✓
Baked Ziti Keto Style	156			✓	✓	✓	✓
Roasted Pork Belly	158	✓	✓	✓			✓
Chili Cheese Dog Skillet	160		✓	✓	✓	✓	✓
Mom's Italian Meatballs in Tomato Gravy	162		✓	✓	✓	✓	✓
Chicken Mud	164		✓	✓			
Asian Lettuce Cups	166	✓	✓	✓	✓	✓	✓
Pizza Soup	168	O	✓	✓	✓	✓	✓
Baked Fish Sticks	170			✓			
Simple Cheese Quesadillas	172		✓	✓	✓	✓	
Homemade Hoagies	174			✓		✓	✓
Wrapped Piggies	176		✓			✓	✓
Sautéed Shrimp with Tomatoes and Pesto	178		✓				✓
French Onion Skillet Chicken	180		✓	✓			✓
Cheesy Corn Dog Nuggets	182		O	✓	✓	✓	✓
Sheet Pan Fajitas	184	✓	✓	✓	✓	✓	✓
Avocado Salsa	188	✓	✓	✓			✓
Olive Oil Dipping Sauce	189	✓	✓	✓			✓
Better Than the Box Mac 'n' Cheese	190		✓	✓		✓	✓
Cauli Risotto	192		✓	✓	✓		✓
Cheddar Broccoli Soup	194		✓	✓		✓	✓
Marinated Roasted Cheese	196		✓	✓		✓	✓
Loaded Zucchini Skins	198		✓	✓			✓
French Onion Dip	200		✓	✓			✓
Crispy Pizza Chips	202		✓	✓	✓	✓	✓

RECIPE	PAGE	🥛	🚫	🥥	❄️	🛍	👪
Orange Blossom Trail Mix	204	✓			✓	✓	✓
Nacho Chips	206		✓	✓			
Cheesy Cauli Mash	208		✓	✓			
Three Amigos Dip	210		✓	✓	✓		✓
Green Bean Fries	212		✓	✓			
Fried Cauli-Rice	214	O		✓	✓		✓
Pepperoni Cheese Chips	216		✓	✓		✓	✓
Cookout Chili	218	✓	✓	✓	✓		✓
Cabbage Noodles	220	O	✓	✓			
Chocolate Mini Cakes	224	O			✓	✓	✓
Chocolate Buttercream Frosting	226		✓	✓			✓
English Posset	228		✓	✓			✓
Double-Stuffed Chocolate Waffle Dessert	230						✓
Marshmallows	232	✓	✓	✓		✓	✓
Peanut Butter Chocolate Minute Brownies	234	O			✓	✓	✓
Vanilla Pound Cake	236				✓	✓	✓
Chocolate Chip Cookies	238				✓	✓	✓
Pumpkin Spice Cake	240				✓	✓	✓
Chocolate Chip Scones	242				✓	✓	✓
Creamy Dairy-Free Vanilla Ice Cream	244	✓			✓		✓
Creamy Vanilla Ice Cream	246			✓	✓		✓
Mason Jar Chocolate Ice Cream	248			✓	✓		✓
Caramel Sauce	250		✓	✓	✓		✓
Dark Chocolate Syrup	252	O	✓	✓	✓		✓
Milk Chocolate Syrup	254		✓	✓	✓		✓
Classic Cheesecake	256				✓		✓
Sullivano Chocolate Sandwich Cookies	258		✓		✓		✓
Cocoa Roasted Almonds	260	✓				✓	✓
Keto Chocolate Turtles	262		✓		✓		✓
Pumpkin Spice Roll	264						✓
Ice Cream Sandwiches	266				✓		✓
Peanut Butter Cheesecake Brownies	268				✓		✓
Chocolate Peanut Clusters	270	✓	✓		✓		✓
Lemonade	274	✓	✓	✓			✓
Limeade	276	✓	✓	✓			✓
Hot Chocolate Drink Mix	278	✓	✓	✓		✓	✓
Creamy Hot Chocolate	279	O	✓	✓			✓
Strawberry Milk	280		✓	✓			✓
Chocolate Milk	282		✓	✓			✓

RECIPE INDEX

BREADS

52

Anything Dough

54

Easy Cheesy Biscuits

56

Cheesy Breadsticks

58

Crusty Baguettes

60

Rolls Without Rolls

62

Yeasty Low-Carb Rolls

64

Sesame Bagels

66

Tortillas

68

90-Second Toast

CHAPTER 4

BREAKFAST

Egg Wraps

72

Sausage and Cheese Pinwheels

74

Cinnamon Walnut Cream Cheese Spread

76

Classic French Toast

78

Creamy Bacon Gravy

80

Easy Boiled Eggs with Butter

82

Eggs in a Basket

84

Grace's Good Morning Strawberry Protein Smoothie

86

Chocolate Hazelnut Muffins

88

Peanut Butter Waffles

90

Sausage-Crusted Meat Lover's Quiche

92

Grace's Good Morning Chocolate Peanut Butter Smoothie

94

Savory Breakfast Crepes

96

Scrambled Eggs Two Ways

98

Veggie Bacon Cream Cheese Spread

100

Cinnamon Maple Crepes

102

Sheet Pan Blueberry Pancakes

104

Bacon, Egg, and Cheese Breakfast Tacos

106

Creamy Baked Eggs

108

SAVORY SAUCES AND SEASONINGS

112

Taco Seasoning

114

BBQ Sauce

116

Sweet Mustard Sauce

117

Ranch Dipping Sauce

118

Ketchup

120

Grace's Chicken Tender Sauce

122

Pesto

124

No-Cook Pizza Sauce

126

Yum-Yum Sauce

128

Simple Cheese Sauce

MAINS

132

Cashew Chicken with Broccoli

134

Deep Dish Supreme Pizza

136

Drive-Thru Chicken Tenders

138

Hamburger Steaks in Onion Gravy

140

Chicken on a Stick

142

Marinated Beef Kabobs

144

Open-Faced Calzones

146

Orange-Braised Pork

148

Pizza Waffles

150

Beef Stroganoff

152

Chicken Teriyaki Meatballs

154

Balsamic Baked Pork Chops

156

Baked Ziti Keto Style

158

Roasted Pork Belly

160

Chili Cheese Dog Skillet

162

Mom's Italian Meatballs in Tomato Gravy

164

Chicken Mud

166

Asian Lettuce Cups

168

Pizza Soup

170

Baked Fish Sticks

172

Simple Cheese Quesadillas

174

Homemade Hoagies

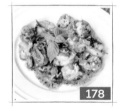

176

Wrapped Piggies

178

Sautéed Shrimp with Tomatoes and Pesto

180

French Onion Skillet Chicken

182

Cheesy Corn Dog Nuggets

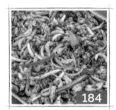

184

Sheet Pan Fajitas

SIDES AND SNACKS

188
Avocado Salsa

189
Olive Oil Dipping Sauce

190
Better Than the Box Mac 'n' Cheese

192
Cauli Risotto

194
Cheddar Broccoli Soup

196
Marinated Roasted Cheese

198
Loaded Zucchini Skins

200
French Onion Dip

202
Crispy Pizza Chips

204
Orange Blossom Trail Mix

206
Nacho Chips

208
Cheesy Cauli Mash

210
Three Amigos Dip

212
Green Bean Fries

214
Fried Cauli-Rice

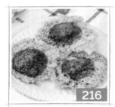
216
Pepperoni Cheese Chips

218
Cookout Chili

220
Cabbage Noodles

DESSERTS AND TREATS

224
Chocolate Mini Cakes

226
Chocolate Buttercream Frosting

228
English Posset

230
Double-Stuffed Chocolate Waffle Dessert

232
Marshmallows

234
Peanut Butter Chocolate Minute Brownies

236
Vanilla Pound Cake

238
Chocolate Chip Cookies

240
Pumpkin Spice Cake

242
Chocolate Chip Scones

244
Creamy Dairy-Free Vanilla Ice Cream

246
Creamy Vanilla Ice Cream

248
Mason Jar Chocolate Ice Cream

250
Caramel Sauce

252
Dark Chocolate Syrup

254
Milk Chocolate Syrup

256
Classic Cheesecake

258
Sullivano Chocolate Sandwich Cookies

260
Cocoa Roasted Almonds

262
Keto Chocolate Turtles

264
Pumpkin Spice Roll

266
Ice Cream Sandwiches

268
Peanut Butter Cheesecake Brownies

270
Chocolate Peanut Clusters

BEVERAGES

Lemonade

Limeade

Hot Chocolate
Drink Mix

Creamy Hot
Chocolate

Strawberry Milk

Chocolate Milk

GENERAL INDEX

W

X

Y

Z